FROM HARLEM
TO HOLLYWOOD

D0068693

CRITICAL STUDIES IN
BLACK LIFE AND CULTURE
(VOL. 26)

GARLAND REFERENCE LIBRARY
OF SOCIAL SCIENCE
(VOL. 826)

CRITICAL STUDIES IN BLACK LIFE AND CULTURE
C. James Trotman, Advisory Editor

FROM HARLEM
TO HOLLYWOOD
The Struggle for Racial and Cultural Democracy
1920–1943

Bruce M. Tyler

GARLAND PUBLISHING, INC. • NEW YORK & LONDON
1992

Library of Congress Cataloging-in-Publication Data

Tyler, Bruce Michael, 1948–
    From Harlem to Hollywood : the struggle for racial and cultural
democracy, 1920–1943 / Bruce M. Tyler.
        p.   cm. — (Critical studies in Black life and culture ; vol.
26)   (Garland reference library of social science ; vol. 826)
    ISBN 0–8153–0814–0
    1. Afro-American arts. 2. Harlem Renaissance. 3. Afro-Americans—
Social conditions—To 1964. I. Title. II. Series: Critical
studies in Black life and culture ; v. 26.   III. Series: Garland
reference library of social science ; v. 826.
NX512.3.A35T95 1992
700'.89'96—dc20   91–42174
                                                                  CIP

Printed on acid-free, 250-year-life paper
Manufactured in the United States of America

This is for a cute and smart
little girl named Aziza.

CONTENTS

ACKNOWLEDGMENTS

I researched and wrote *From Harlem to Hollywood: The Struggle for Racial and Cultural Democracy, 1920–1943* in about two and a half years. I did not even plan to write this book. I started out writing an article that grew into a book. It became clear to me after I finished the book that it had been developing subconsciously for many years.

At Compton Community College in Compton, California, I was a student in Dr. Michael Widener's course on black literature and read some Harlem Renaissance writers. I also came under the influence of Dr. Albert Mortenson, whom I immediately admired so much as a person, eloquent lecturer, and historian that I decided then and there to major in American history. At California State University, Long Beach, I became a student of Dr. David A. Williams (a long-time friend of Mortenson who advised me to introduce myself to Williams as soon as I was enrolled and he would take me under his wing, and he did as a loving father would a son), who decisively turned my interest to black California history. I took another black literature course taught by a black Jamaican who lectured from Robert A. Bone's book, *The Negro Novel in America*. He covered the Harlem Renaissance section of the book, which fascinated me. These people and influence remain with me to this day.

I enrolled in a doctoral program in history at the University of California, Los Angeles, and studied under Dr. Stanley Coben who introduced me to Harold Cruse's *The Crisis of the Negro Intellectual*. Cruse wrote passionately about the Harlem Renaissance. Coben was very impressed by the book and his enthusiasm rubbed off on me. Also, I studied with Dr. Richard Weiss who chaired my doctoral committee and became my "intellectual father," and I studied with Dr. Thomas Hines who, brilliant in many areas, had a passion for popular culture that deeply influenced me. Thus the stage was set for merging my growing research and knowledge about the Harlem Renaissance, black Los Angeles, and popular culture. The result is this book.

Ljilja Kuftimec of Interlibrary Loan at the University of Louisville diligently and with good cheer located all of the research material I needed. Herman Landau of Louisville read, edited, and encouraged me in preparing the manuscript. Paula Ladenburg of Garland Publishing read and edited the manuscript again. Chuck Bartelt reviewed and checked the computer disks. Phyllis Korper oversaw the whole project and finally brought this book to press. Jesse Hiraoka, editor of *The Journal of Ethnic Studies*, and a mentor, granted permission to reprint the Harlem Jive and White Repression chapter. I deeply appreciate and thank all of these people, and others, especially one anonymous reader who made a withering critique of the early manuscript which improved it immeasurably, and early readers who corrected needless errors of fact and judgment. In the end, I accept any errors and shortcomings which remain. Whatever judgment is made about this book, I must say it is my child. I am its father and I am proud of it.

INTRODUCTION

The Harlem Renaissance began at the turn of the century. It blossomed in the 1920s but appeared to decline by 1930, a victim of the Great Depression and internal bickering among its supporters and detractors. The Harlem Renaissance has been recognized as a nationally important movement. David L. Lewis in his seminal book *When Harlem Was in Vogue* (1981) recognized the importance of black veterans of World War I as a vital source of the "New Negro" movement for racial and cultural democracy. What is more, he included the emergence of jazz as part of the renaissance. J.A. Rogers had recognized jazz in his article, "Jazz at Home," published in *The New Negro* (1925) edited by Alain Locke, as part of the music of the emerging Harlem Renaissance.

Robert A. Bone in *The Negro Novel in America* (1958) discussed the literature of the Harlem Renaissance writers and judged it basically as joy filled. In *Marcus Garvey and the Vision of Africa* (1974) John Henrik Clarke, with the assistance of Amy Jacques Garvey, revealed the central role of Garvey and his followers in the Harlem Renaissance. Their perception opened new ground by expanding the scope of social forces operating during the renaissance. Nathan Irvin Huggins's *Harlem Renaissance* (1971) critically analyzed the internal workings of the New Negro movement and its artists. Houston A. Baker Jr. in *Modernism and the Harlem Renaissance* (1987) argues persuasively that Booker T. Washington was the "first modern" and rejected the charges by David Lewis and Nathan Huggins and some participants that the renaissance failed to sustain itself and a thrust for civil rights. Rayford W. Logan's "The Historical Setting of the New Negro" (pp. 18-25), in Rayford W. Logan et al., eds., *The New Negro Thirty Years Afterward* (1955), cites unimpeachable evidence that Washington published material on the "New Negro" at the turn of the century. Yet he and his followers have been excluded as precursors and participants in the Harlem Renaissance. Harold Cruse in *The Crisis of the Negro Intellectual: From Its Origins to the*

Present (1967) proved that, through economic activity, followers of Booker T. Washington created black Harlem. On the other hand, blacks failed to create, sustain, and gain ownership of Harlem's vital cultural institutions. As a result, the Harlem Renaissance failed, in his view, and never recovered.

None of these writers, save Baker whose concern is more theoretical with precious little historical evidence to demonstrate the breadth and depth of the renaissance and Cruse whose seminal study fully grasped the crisis but failed to note the different route and reappearance of the renaissance in other areas of culture and institutions, has looked at how far and wide the Harlem Renaissance spread or the depth of its infusion into the broader culture of blacks and whites after 1934. The Harlem Renaissance as a nationally, even internationally, significant movement simply could not have died or faded away by the early 1930s.

The Harlem Renaissance was part of a larger movement for social, ethnic, religious, and cultural pluralism and democracy which intensified as a result of the upheaval wrought by the dislocations of World War I. The 1920s resulted in a massive assault against Victorian culture and norms in the United States. Many jazz clubs opened; there was public dancing, smoking, drinking bootleg liquor, pre-marital sex; more women lived alone, wore their hair shorter, and raised their dress hemlines; and other social and cultural patterns emerged contrary to the conservative mores of years gone by. The Harlem Renaissance was an integral part of this movement to challenge and dismantle Victorian culture and pseudo-scientific racism. Old and new agents of the Harlem Renaissance continued to promote its culture and values after some of the movement's literary writers and artists declined and dispersed.

A movement emerged in the Los Angeles black community and its Central Avenue business, social, and entertainment district to duplicate Harlem Renaissance culture, especially in jazz, dance, entertainment, dress, and grooming styles. Black cultural and community leaders in Los Angeles, from Central Avenue and the black film colony in Hollywood in the 1920s and 1930s and during World War II, continued the Harlem Renaissance ideology and struggle for racial and cultural pluralism.

Mayor Fiorello H. La Guardia of New York City, Walter White of the National Association for the Advancement of Colored People (NAACP), and Wendell Willkie attempted to lure the

Hollywood film industry back to New York to increase the entertainment business of New York and to modify its anti-black stereotypes. They failed, but Harlem's top black entertainers made a steady trek to Hollywood and some took with them the ideology of the Harlem Renaissance. The impact was a noticeable improvement for blacks. Film historians have not recognized the impact of Harlem Renaissance culture and ideology on Hollywood. Historians of the Harlem Renaissance and of blacks in Hollywood films have neatly compartmentalized their subjects. As a result, few have recognized the continuation of the Harlem Renaissance in other settings and in different cultural institutions. Harlem Renaissance culture and agents directly challenged Hollywood's negative images of blacks and compelled Hollywood moguls to modify their practices.

The Harlem Renaissance early on included both black and white patrons, supporters, and detractors. It was not an all-black affair. There were people like Carl Van Vechten (white), who played a role in the emergence of modern black culture. Blacks and whites borrowed from each other's cultures. Increasingly, black and white artists shared the same art and culture. Harlem Renaissance culture became diffused throughout the nation by the 1920s. It continued to spread in the 1930s and blossomed again during World War II.

During World War II, jazz or swing music spread to the armed forces of the United States. This culture was called G.I. Jive. It challenged traditional martial music associated with John Philip Sousa. Black and white musicians and promoters of G.I. Jive or jazz fought a hard struggle for cultural recognition and respectability during the war. It became the preferred music of many, and probably of most, American citizens. Harlem entertainers played a key role in this movement.

The United Service Organizations (USO) sponsored Hollywood and Broadway culture and entertainment in its programs for the armed forces of the United States. Blacks had already established themselves, even if in stereotyped roles, in both cultural institutions. A faction of blacks and whites in the USO clubs attacked segregation and discrimination. They promoted racial and cultural democracy by joining forces to defend their art and culture.

Blacks brought the culture of Harlem into the G.I. Jive

movement. Many whites defended jazz and jive in the USO, in various canteens patterned after USO clubs, and in the armed forces. These whites aided their black allies against widespread Jim Crow practices. The diffusion of Harlem Renaissance culture in jazz and swing bands, both white and black, helped dismantle Victorian culture and encouraged cultural and racial democracy despite a well-established pattern of segregated entertainment. Blacks and whites who brought jazz into the armed forces won a major victory for their art and cultural democracy.

Finally, the enemies of racial and cultural democracy provoked race riots everywhere during World War II. Blacks played a role in racial confrontations during the war as well. Black leaders promoted the Double V: it meant racial democracy and pluralism at home and abroad as part of the war goals. Increasingly, blacks insisted on their rights, recognition of their culture, and respect for their ethnic identity. They confronted whites more and more on these issues. Racist whites in and out of government responded with repression.

Ultimately, because of the Great Depression, the 1935 and 1943 race riots, and the exploitation of blacks, Harlem declined as a viable cultural capital. It was unable to maintain its cultural institutions and thrust with sufficient strength to attract a broad cross section of people and races. As a result, it failed to become an independent and viable economic and cultural capital dominated by blacks and their white allies (or exploiters) with the capacity to challenge Broadway and Hollywood for white and black patrons.

From Harlem to Hollywood

From *California Eagle,* July 14, 1938, p. B4, col. 5.

THE ART IDEOLOGY OF THE HARLEM RENAISSANCE

Black Americans have long been plagued by negative images projected by racists who used stereotypes to maintain white supremacy and racial segregation. From the turn of the century, with the emergence of new, mass media techniques, blacks have struggled against negative racial images projected by motion pictures, the stage, literature, and radio. Blacks finally launched an offensive against stereotypes by promoting the emerging "Harlem Renaissance" which had become evident at the turn of the century. It was a massive effort to project positive black images to break down the racial stereotypes perceived as barriers to freedom and opportunity.

The movement gained impetus after Charles S. Johnson, a black social worker, intellectual, and promoter of black art, spoke at the National Conference of Social Work in Washington, D.C., on May 23, 1923. In his talk, "Public Opinion and the Negro," he argued that racist art and literature undergirded the Jim Crow system of racial segregation and discrimination. Johnson contended that public opinion was formed by three factors:

1. The facts on which opinion rests;
2. The theories about the facts; and
3. The actions of people based on the theories or facts or their distortion.

He charged that "jokes about Negroes, news stories, anecdotes, gossip, the stage, the motion pictures, the Octavus Roy Cohen, Hugh Wiley, and Irvin S. Cobb types of humorous fiction, repeated with unvarying outline, have helped to build up and crystallize a fictitious being unlike any Negro."[1]

The first step for blacks and their white allies was developing an art theory to guide the emergence of what became known as the Harlem Renaissance. The supporters believed in cultural pluralism, yet many of them rejected censorship as a method of attacking stereotypes. W.E.B. Du Bois advocated art as propaganda to attack stereotypes and to promote civil rights for blacks. Most white and black artists, writers, editors, and publishers, however, rejected art propaganda. This led to bitter debates within the group that dissipated its strength.

Eventually, three distinct positions emerged from these debates. The first was that blacks had a unique racial gift and character. Many blacks such as W.E.B. Du Bois, Jessie Fauset, Claude McKay, Charles S. Johnson, Alain Locke, Marcus Garvey, and others held this view. This group split between supporters and critics of black urban hepster culture, ghetto licentiousness, and anti-black stereotypes as injurious to racial progress. This school had two branches: Du Bois, Fauset, Johnson, and Locke strongly supported rural folk, sophisticated primitivism, and "polite" or urban black Victorians as artistic models. Claude McKay, Langston Hughes, and Carl Van Vechten favored the black common people whether urban hepster, the exotic rural folk, or primitives. The second branch, advanced by George Schuyler, firmly believed that only Africans could truly create black art because black Americans were merely black Anglo-Saxons without a distinct culture of their own. A third school of thought divided the group between racial integrationists and separatists. W.E.B. Du Bois and Marcus Garvey, the leader of the Universal Negro Improvement Association were the two chief spokesmen for this third position. Their ideologies were antagonistic, but both supported positive race uplifting literature and images. As a result, the Harlem Renaissance activists never achieved a consensus. The crisis gained renewed intensity with the emergence of the film *The Birth of a Nation* (1915).

D.W. Griffith's *The Birth of a Nation* was a cruel blow to the black image in the newly emergent medium of motion pictures. It perpetuated a great many negative black stereotypes, and its message reached unprecedented numbers of people. William Joseph Simmons, a fraternal organizer, after repeatedly seeing Griffith's film in Atlanta, organized a new urban Ku Klux Klan movement that mushroomed all over the nation.[2] The film had a permanent impact on Du Bois and the National Association for the Advancement of Colored People (NAACP) and resulted in a running battle with Griffith.[3] The film's message was that blacks during the Civil War and Reconstruction period used the North's military and political victory to force racial amalgamation on the South to improve inferior black genes through forced interracial marriages between blacks and whites.[4]

Du Bois complained that it was an "insidious and hurtful attack: the new technique of the moving picture had come to America and the world" in the hands of D.W. Griffith. "He set the pace for a new art and method. . . ." Griffith "deliberately used as the vehicle of his picture one of the least defensible attacks upon the Negro race, made by Thomas Dixon in his books beginning with the 'Leopard's Spots,' and in his play 'The Clansman.'" Du Bois bitterly noted that "there was fed to the youth of the nation and to the unthinking masses as well as to the world a story which twisted the emancipation and enfranchisement of the slave in a great effort toward universal democracy into an orgy of theft and degradation and wider rape of white women." What is more, the film caused lynching of blacks to jump to its highest level in a decade, charged Du Bois.[5]

Protest against the film bitterly divided blacks and their white allies. Du Bois lamented: "In combating this film, our Association was placed in a miserable dilemma. We had to ask liberals to oppose freedom of art and expression, and it was senseless for them to reply: 'Use this art in your own defense.'" Blacks did not have the resources.[6] Du Bois never resolved this dilemma, and it became a source of continual disagreement that prevented a consensus on the nature of blacks and art ideology during the Harlem Renaissance in the 1920s.

Blacks lost their rights to vote, serve on juries, run for and hold public offices, and lost access to public and private accommodations on an equal basis with white citizens and European immigrants at the turn of the century (1890 to 1915) when every Southern state passed rigorous discriminatory and segregation laws, and the United States Supreme Court in *Plessy v. Ferguson* in 1896 upheld authoritarian racial laws and practices. The federal government did not recognize or enforce Constitutional guarantees accorded black citizens during the Civil War and Reconstruction era. Many, like Du Bois, believed that racist art, literature, and films like Griffith's added to a white public opinion corrupted by racism. The battle over the status of blacks in America continued.

From the early twentieth century until World War II, black leaders and leaders of the Niagara movement and the National Association for the Advancement of Colored People struggled to protect and project a positive image of blacks in the battle for their civil rights. The struggle was many-sided—political, economic, social, cultural, and artistic. Black leaders and white allies united to launch a struggle for cultural pluralism and social equality that resulted in a close and critical scrutiny of the mass media and films and the racial images they reflected.

The battle over Griffith's film divided some blacks and whites because of the issue of censorship. Some whites felt blacks and their allies overreacted. Du Bois recognized this and, in 1921, cautioned blacks that they often overreacted to art dealing with the race problem or black images because they had been slandered so often. "We want everything that is said about us to tell of the best and highest and noblest in us. We insist that our Art and Propaganda be one." He admonished blacks, "This is wrong and in the end it is harmful." On the other hand, he said, "we have a right, in our effort to get just treatment, to insist that we produce something of the best in human character and that it is unfair to judge us by our criminals and prostitutes. This is justifiable propaganda."[7] He opposed the racist literature and art of the Rev. Thomas Dixon and D.W. Griffith. He approved of such white art as Edward Sheldon's *The Nigger* (1909), Ridgely Torrence's *The Rider of Dreams* (1917), and Eugene O'Neill's *The Emperor Jones* (1920) despite the fact that O'Neill found "even educated Negroes shrinking or openly condemning" it. Sheldon's play was repeatedly driven from the stage for its name alone by black protesters.[8] Moreover, Du Bois boasted that "Sheldon, Torrence, and O'Neill are our great benefactors—forerunners of artists who will yet arise in Ethiopia of the Outstretched Arm."[9] In other words, he thought black artists should follow their lead in writing and interpreting the black experience.

Du Bois keenly felt that black artists should take the lead in interpreting the black experience. In 1923 he said, "Negroes as actors and as dramatic writers have a wonderfully rich field to exploit in their own terrible history of experience."[10] He declared in 1924, "the Negro is primarily an artist" and he possesses a "spirit of gayety and the exotic charm which his presence has loaned the parts of America which were spiritually free enough to enjoy it."[11] Further, "the Negro has been one of the greatest originators of dancing in the United States and in the world." He created the "Cake Walk," the "Clog," the "Tango," and the "Turkey Trot." The last two dances, Du Bois claimed, were created by West Indies blacks.[12] He noted that Vernon and Irene Castle made these dances famous in the white world in the early twentieth century and always gave credit to their black creators.

William Ferris, a black nationalist, in 1913 declared, "when colored men write as colored men and not as white men, only then will they be interesting. In assimilating the culture and traditions of Anglo-Saxons, they must not lose their rich and luxuriant African heritage, they must not lose the barbaric splendor of the African imagination or the fervid eloquence of the native African. The charm of individuality is the charm of naturalness."[13] Both Ferris and Du Bois were aware of the Africans' culture of elaborate ceremony, dance, masks, costumes, music, and singing. They sought to preserve this tradition in writing by calling for a unique black tradition based on the African past and present traditions.

Ferris became a follower of black nationalist leader Marcus Garvey and a columnist for his newspaper, *Negro World* (April 30, 1921), where he voiced a view that gained widespread acceptance in black and white liberal intellectual circles: "The history and literature of any race are the credentials on which that race is admitted to the family of civilized men and are the indications of its future possibilities."[14] This perception added to the zeal for blacks to project positive images of themselves in the mass media.

Blacks and their white allies promoted "cultural pluralism" to gain recognition and respect for black culture. They rejected the pseudo-scientific racism of Victorian America, often associated with the Ku Klux Klan. Horace M. Kallen argued in his book, *Culture and Democracy in the United States* (1924), that "cultural growth is founded upon Cultural Pluralism." Moreover, "the alternative before Americans is Kultur Klux Klan or Cultural Pluralism." He said a powerful racist backlash had resulted from massive social and cultural upheavals brought on by World War I and the advances of science.

The Klan appointed itself the defender of traditional

American Victorian values and codes of conduct, which it claimed
were under a massive assault by immigrants, social and cultural
rebels, blacks, Jews, and other national minorities. The Klan
violently objected to cultural pluralism as un-American and
dangerous to American life and culture. Imperial Wizard Pro
Tem Brother Edward Clarke Young bitterly declared in September
1922 that the Klan "does here and now declare war to the bitter
end upon all those in America who are seeking in an insidious
but powerful manner to undermine the very fundamentals of the
Nation."[15]

Hiram Wesley Evans, Imperial Wizard, said the Klan
rejected liberalism. "The first and immediate cause of the break
with Liberalism was that it had provided no defense against the
alien invasion, but instead had excused it—even defended it
against Americanism. Liberalism is today charged in the mind
of most Americans with nothing less than national racial and
spiritual treason." Moreover, "liberalism has come completely
under the dominance of weaklings and parasites whose 'idealism'
reaches its logical peak in the Bolshevik platform of 'produce as
little as you can, beg or steal from those who do produce, and
kill the producer for thinking he is better than you.'" The Klan
preached race purity and rejected "interbreeding" for fear of
"mongrelization." He said "the Jew is a . . . complex problem"
because Western European Jews were productive but "quite
different are the Eastern Jews" because "anthropologists now tell
us that these are not true Jews, but only Judaized Mongols—
Chazars." Evans charged that they could not be assimilated into
American society.[16] His solution was segregation of the races.

Blacks needed to speak for themselves, declared Du Bois.
He believed that blacks could not rely on whites to defend their
interests or honor in race matters. Blacks had an obligation to
be the chief defenders of their image and life. George W. Cable,
Thomas Nelson Page, Thomas Dixon, Ruth M. Stewart, William
Dean Howells, and Thomas Wentworth Higginson wrote about
blacks, said Du Bois, but "the influence of the Negro here is a
passive influence and yet one must remember that it would be
inconceivable to have an American literature, even that written
by white men, and not have the Negro as a subject." Finally, Du
Bois asked, "in the minds of these and other writers how has
the Negro been portrayed?"[17] He felt blacks often suffered in

their dignity and status as human beings at the hands of insensitive whites or racists. Du Bois claimed that "in the days of Shakespeare and [Thomas] Southerne the black man of fiction was a man, a brave, fine, if withal over trustful and impulsive, hero. In science he was different but equal, cunning in unusual but mighty possibilities." The slave trade, slavery, and the Reconstruction experience saw blacks treated as Sambos, of no consequence. "And yet," declared Du Bois, "with all this, the Negro has held the stage. In the South he is everything. He is figured into everything. In the North and West he waits in the wings."[18]

Congressman Charles M. Stedman, from Greensboro, North Carolina, proposed in early 1924 "a bill (H.R. 6253) authorizing the erection in the city of Washington [a] monument in memory of the faithful colored mammies of the South, to the Committee on the Library."[19] C.H. Tobias, secretary of the International Committee of the Y.M.C.A., offered a telling black rebuttal to the movement to honor the black mammy: "It was not 'Black Mammy' who responded one-half million strong to the call to fight for the preservation of world democracy, but it was 'Black Mammy's' sons and grandsons. . . . "[20] Du Bois said, "Black Mammy" was "the most pitiful of the world's Christ" (because, in his view, she was crucified by white racists intent on keeping her in a slave-servant capacity). She helped to "uplift the South" and "from her great full breast walked forth governors and judges, ladies of wealth and fashion, merchants, and scoundrels who led the South." Du Bois cynically noted, "but a few snobs have lately sought to advertise her sacrifice and degradation and enhance their own cheap success by building on the blood of her riven heart a load of stone miscalled a monument."[21] These blacks felt insulted and saw the monument as a salute to slavery.

The mammy debate had raged earlier. The mammy tradition was a relic of plantation life and slavery. Mammy was held in slavery and Jim Crowed after slavery's demise, and racists presented her as a loyal retainer who did not aspire to freedom. In the view of racists, she relished her servant role. Blacks resented Thomas Nelson Page for romanticizing "The Old Time Negro" who was docile and accommodating. Nelson boasted that in the slave hierarchy, "among the first in station were the Mammy." He charged that the new Negro was belligerent and caused race

hatred rather than sympathy from whites.[22] Julia Peterkin, a white
novelist, in a letter to the editor, thought blacks had made a
mistake in their opposition to the erection of a "Negro Mammy
Memorial" because it was a positive move in recognition of blacks'
contribution to society.[23] But many thoughtful and race-conscious
blacks objected to the movement to build a monument in
recognition of a black mammy. Mammy was seen as a vicious
stereotype of black womanhood. Peterkin, as an outsider and
white woman, did not comprehend black values, especially in
regard to promoting a servile image of blacks as a positive social
recognition. It only perpetuated, in the views of some blacks, the
status quo.

Blacks suffered from censorship, said Du Bois, but racists
were published or their works were presented in the most
respectable circles and media. He complained that the nation
was unaware of black artists "for everything touching the Negro
has hitherto been banned by magazines and publishers unless
it took the form of caricature or bitter attack, or was so thoroughly
innocuous as to have no literary flavor." He noted, however,
"this attitude shows signs of change at last."[24] Du Bois wanted
to fight racist propaganda with pro-black propaganda. Some black
artists were mainstream and others were conscious race artists.
"There is without doubt a certain group expression of art which
can be called American Negro." Moreover, "already this art
expression is showing its peculiarities, its unique content." Black
artists in music were recognized and widely acclaimed.[25] But
blacks had to produce a credible literature that would gain them
recognition in the family of man. The opening up of various
media to blacks was crucial to the emergence of the Harlem
Renaissance because it meant that blacks and their white allies
could challenge racial stereotypes in the same media.

Du Bois encouraged black literary artists to develop
recognition through their art. He lamented, however, that "the
time has not yet come for the great development of American
Negro literature." He believed this was so because "the economic
stress is too great and the racial persecution too bitter to allow
the leisure and the poise for which literature calls." He boasted
that *The Crisis* had published most of the new black artists like
Claude McKay, Langston Hughes, Jean Toomer, Countee Cullen,
Anne Spencer, Jessie Fauset, and Abram Harris. Some became

famous Harlem Renaissance writers in the 1920s.[26] Du Bois was obviously proud that his journal first showcased the emerging black talent by providing a platform from which to launch their careers.

In 1924 a dinner was held at the Cafe Savarin in New York City upon Du Bois's return from Europe and Africa. Ridgely Torrence, a white whose two plays were produced on Broadway, one in 1914 with a white cast and another in 1917 with a black cast, read a poem written by Witter Bynner entitled "To Du Bois and his People." Heywood Broun, Walter Hampton, Robert Benchley, and the Lieutenant Governor of New York spoke. James Weldon Johnson read Zona Gale's tribute to Du Bois. Harry Burleigh sang spirituals. Eugene O'Neill, however, made the most telling comments. "It seems to me that to be a Negro writer today must be a tremendously stimulating thing." He added, "They have within them an untouched world of deep reality. What greater boon than their rare opportunity can a true artist ask of fate? They are fortunate." Blacks needed to write and reflect their own experience, to which so many whites were attracted and wanted to know about. O'Neill felt that blacks should be the natural and authentic interpreters of the black experience. Moreover, he thought that "it is to Dr. Du Bois more than to any other man they owe their good fortune; for by the sheer power of his own ability he has played a foremost part in convincing the world that it must await with genuine artistic respect the contributions of the Negro to modern literature."[27] Du Bois sought to press black artists into service for the civil rights movement. They were asked to counter negative black stereotypes fostered by white artists and propagandists who sought to maintain white supremacy and instigate contempt and hatred of blacks.

Charles S. Johnson of the National Urban League (NUL) in March 1924 took a momentous step when he invited artists, editors, and book publishers to the Civic Club in New York for a dinner to celebrate the publication of Jessie Fauset's novel *There Is Confusion*. She was literary editor of the NAACP's magazine, *The Crisis*. He invited Jean Toomer, Eric Walrond, Du Bois, Walter White, Gwendolyn Bennett, Countee Cullen, Langston Hughes, Alain Locke, T. Montgomery Gregory, the chairman of Howard University's drama department, poet Georgia Douglas Johnson, a dozen other poets, and many other blacks. Such prominent whites in the literary field as Oswald Garrison Villard, editor-owner of the *New York Evening Post*; Eugene O'Neill, playwright; H.L. Mencken, editor of *Smart Set* and the *American Mercury*; Mary Johnston, a fine Virginia novelist; Zona Gale, a novelist, short-story writer, dramatist, and poet; Robert Morse Lovett, an American literary critic, university professor of English and rhetoric; Ridgely Torrence, a playwright; Carl Van Doren, editor of *Century* magazine; Philadelphia pharmaceutical tycoon Albert Barnes, who boasted that he had a magnificent collection of African art; and Paul Kellogg, editor of *Survey Graphic*, were invited. More than 100 prominent whites and blacks attended. These artists, editors, businessmen, and publishers attempted to promote and guide the emerging interest in black arts as blacks and art about them came into vogue.[28]

At the dinner Carl Van Doren gave a seminal talk, "The Younger Generation of Negro Writers," which urged blacks to take advantage of the black experience and use it in their writings and art. He had "a genuine faith in the future of imaginative writing among Negroes in the United States." Moreover, he had "a feeling that the Negroes of the country are in a remarkable strategic position with reference to the new literary age which seems to be impending." He thought that "what American literature decidedly needs at this moment is color, music, gusto, the free expression of gay or desperate moods. If the Negroes are not in a position to contribute these items, I do not know what Americans are."[29]

Benjamin Brawley, a black scholar, was so impressed by the tempo of the gathering that he told James Weldon Johnson, an NAACP officer, "we have a tremendous opportunity to boost the NAACP, letters, and art, and anything else that calls attention to our development along the higher lines." Their efforts bore fruit.[30]

William H. Baldwin III, a white Urban League board member, spoke at the dinner too and used his influence to persuade Frederick Lewis Allen, editor of Harper Brothers book publishers, to support the movement by publishing black writers of talent. Editor Paul Kellogg of *Survey Graphic* proposed to devote a whole issue to blacks. Charles S. Johnson and Alain Locke were appointed to collect and edit the volume. They excluded lowbrow materials, which they thought projected a negative image of blacks. The published magazine materials were soon expanded and published in book form as *The New Negro* (1925). This became the bible of the emerging Harlem Renaissance. Allen and Johnson accepted black art expression as uniquely black. Johnson believed in "racial poetry" and the "new racial consciousness and self-conception" on which the Harlem Renaissance was based. Locke said that the black race, "having no sophisticated vent for its collective ambitions—since political participation and equal civic rights are the goal of its practical aspirations—has an enormous amount of accumulated energy to focus upon artistic expression and cultural self-determination."[31] Du Bois sought to direct this artistic energy.

The emergent Harlem Renaissance was recognized at this dinner with a view to undergird it with firm support from writers and publishers. Du Bois sought to control its direction in the interest of the NAACP and his vision of black art. He was not pleased with the direction of the movement. Two years after the dinner honoring Du Bois's return from Europe and Africa, in the March 1926 issue of *The Crisis*, Jessie Fauset got Carl Van Vechten to submit anonymously seven questions concerning blacks and the arts to gauge the movement's ideological temperament. *The Crisis* asked:

1. When the artist, black or white, portrays Negro character is he under any obligations or limitations as to the sort of character he will portray?
2. Can any author be criticized for painting the worst or the best characters of a group?
3. Can publishers be criticized for refusing to handle novels that portray Negroes of education and accomplishment, on the ground that these characters are no different from white folk and therefore not interesting?
4. What are Negroes to do when they are continually painted at their worst and judged by the public as they are painted?
5. Does the situation of the educated Negro in America with its pathos, humiliation and tragedy call for artistic treatment at least as sincere and sympathetic as 'Porgy' received?
6. Is not the continual portrayal of the sordid, foolish and criminal among the Negroes convincing the world that

> this and this alone is really and essentially Negroid, and
> preventing white artists from knowing any other types
> and preventing black artists from daring to paint them?
> 7. Is there not a real danger that young colored writers will
> be tempted to follow the popular trend in portraying
> Negro characters in the underworld rather than seeking
> to paint the truth about themselves and their own social
> class?[32]

These questions started a bitter and running debate among the
very artists, publishers, and editors who were interested in
promoting art about blacks.

Mary White Ovington, a white NAACP officer, and many
others responded to Van Vechten's questions in letters to *The
Crisis*, which Du Bois edited. She thought good books were
accepted by publishers and that positive portrayals of blacks were
emerging. Du Bose Heyward, a white author who wrote on black
themes in *Porgy* (1925) and *Mamba's Daughters* (1927), said artists
should be free to write as they wish. Blacks must write the "real
subjective literature" on the black experience. Carl Van Vechten,
critic and novelist (*Nigger Heaven*, 1926), thought that negative
black characters were portrayed "for a very excellent reason. The
squalor of Negro life, the vice of Negro life, offer a wealth of
novel, exotic picturesque material to the artist." He felt that the
black middle and upper classes were the same as whites and not
very interesting. "The question is: Are Negro writers going to
write about this exotic material while it is still fresh or will they
continue to make a free gift of it to white authors who will exploit
it until not a drop of vitality remains?"[33] He gave a direct rebuff
to Du Bois's aversion to portrayals of the black underclass and
their exotic lifestyles. He warned blacks that whites would benefit
from writing about black culture and gain cultural hegemony if
blacks didn't take advantage of the opportunities to get published.

H.L. Mencken wrote to *The Crisis* that "the artist is under
no obligations or limitations whatsoever. He should be free to
depict things exactly as he sees them." Moreover, "the remedy
of a Negro novelist is to depict the white man at his worst. Walter
White has already done it (in his novel, *Fire in the Flint* [1924])
and very effectively." Mencken advised Du Bois and black writers
that "the remedy of the Negro is not to bellow for justice—that
is, not to try to apply scientific criteria to works of art."[34] Mencken

rebuffed any movement to assert art ideological criteria because he feared useless propaganda would result, not art.

Langston Hughes's letter to *The Crisis* said that "the true literary artist is going to write about what he chooses anyway regardless of outside opinions." Joel E. Spingarn, a white founder and officer of the NAACP and one of its leading theoreticians, wrote that good works will find a publisher because "a work of genius will find some form of publication." Moreover, "from the standpoint of Negro culture it may be important that some writers should get a hearing, even if their books are comparatively poor. The culture of a race must have a beginning, however . . . simple, and imperfect books are infinitely better than a long era of silence." What is more, "the Negro race should not sniff at the Uncle Tom's Cabins and the Jungles of its own writers, which are instruments of progress as real as the ballot-box, the schoolhouse or a stick of dynamite." John Farrar, editor of *The Bookman*, wrote that the works of Octavus Roy Cohen, whom Du Bois especially deplored, were humorous and amusing.[35]

Book publisher Alfred A. Knopf simply responded to the questions in his letter to *The Crisis* with 1. No; 2. No; 3. Senseless; 4. Write books, supply the deficiency; 5. Yes; 6. "I doubt it"; 7. "I doubt it." William Lyon Phelps, critic, essayist, educator, and columnist for *Scribner's Magazine*, wrote that artists should write the "Truth." He was critical of those who took as typical the worst portrayals of blacks. He thought it absurd for publishers to reject material about assimilated blacks. He said correct black life in reality refuted the propaganda and caricatures. Walter White, a black officer in the NAACP, in his letter said that since blacks were getting published he was disturbed by divided opinion over what they should write. He rejected the notion that upper-class blacks were the same as whites. He offered an elaborate defense of upper-class blacks and their lives because much novel material resulted from their experiences in a racist and segregated society. Artists should be free to write whatever they pleased. He opposed artists who wrote only the worst or best characterizations of blacks, contending that they should seek balance. Black writers were obligated to correct the negative stereotypes of white writers.[36]

Vachel Lindsay, a white poet who played a key role in Langston Hughes's discovery, wrote a letter which said that writers were free to write whatever they wished. He thought they should seek balance in their characterizations. Publishers should accept materials on all social classes and black upper-class life, too. He said that the NAACP's *The Crisis* and the NUL's *Opportunity* magazines were outlets for blacks if whites rejected their material. Sinclair Lewis, a novelist, asked in his letter, should blacks write on blacks and others? Should they provide their own publishers and other outlets? In other words he, too, thought blacks should supply the deficiency rather than moan about it. Sherwood Anderson, an author, said a writer must be free to write what he pleased. "I do not believe the Negroes have much more to complain of than the whites in this matter of their treatment in the arts."[37]

Benjamin Brawley, a black author, wrote to *The Crisis* that "an artist must be free," but that blacks should protest negative stereotypes which instigate public ridicule and hatred of them. He thought that good material by blacks would be recognized. Robert T. Kerlin, a professor of English, stated in his letter that the artist of integrity must be free. Blacks should produce "first rate artistic works with which to kill travesties" that injured the black image. Moreover, "let the black artist not hesitate to show what white 'civilization' is doing to both races." Jessie Fauset, author and NAACP literary editor, wrote that the writer must be free and under no obligations or limitations on what he could portray, unless the intent was malicious. Blacks should protest negative stereotypes. Blacks needed to buy books by blacks to influence the publishers to meet the demand. To Du Bois's question, are young black artists in danger of imitating popular negative stereotypes to get a hearing, she answered, "emphatically. This is a grave danger making for a literary insincerity both insidious and abominable."[38] Fauset apparently agreed with Mencken that blacks should simply compete with whites in the production of art rather than whine and wage useless ideological battles.

More writers responded with letters. Georgia Douglas Johnson thought that black writers were oppressed and exploited. "The few who do break thru the hell-crust of prevalent conditions to high ground should be crowned, extolled and emulated." Countee Cullen, a black poet and novelist, believed the writer must be free as an artist. Black artists must correct negative stereotypes of the race. "Negro artists have a definite duty to perform in this matter, one which should supersede their individual prerogatives, without denying those rights." Julia Peterkin said writers must reject propaganda in art.[39] Her answer was to produce better art than the anti-black group of artists.

Otto F. Mack wrote from Stuttgart, Germany, responses to all seven questions posed by Van Vechten in *The Crisis*. He said no to 1; no to 2; yes to 3; and for number 4, artists must "be true to themselves"; for 5, "yes," educated blacks should be portrayed sincerely, "and more so"; to 6, "no," the continued portrayal of negative black types should not compel blacks to write in a similar vein; for 7, he felt young blacks were in danger of capitulating to negative black stereotypes to get attention and be published.[40]

The venerable and elder black writer Charles W. Chestnutt said that the writer must be free. "We want no color line in literature." Portrayals should have balance between negative and positive images. Publishers sought to sell literature and they would publish what would sell. Blacks should protest negative literature on blacks, but should write better literature themselves. Blacks should make up their own literature and model heroes. He did not think that the continual portrayal of stereotypes compelled black writers to follow the pattern. He did not think there was much danger of blacks following negative stereotypes. "He should not worry about his social class." He complained that "the colored writer, generally speaking, has not yet passed the point of thinking of himself first as a Negro, burdened with the responsibility of defending and uplifting his race." He felt "such a frame of mind . . . is bad for art."[41] Chestnutt's letter ended the formal debates in *The Crisis* over Van Vechten's seven questions. The ideological battle, however, raged on in other forums and in the literature produced.

George S. Schuyler, a black writer and critic, called the Harlem Renaissance "The Negro-Art Hokum" in an article in *The Nation* magazine June 16, 1926. He charged that "Negro art 'made in America' is . . . non-existent. . . ." Only Africans have truly black art. One need only to "realize that the Aframerican is merely a lampblacked Anglo-Saxon." He argued that "it is sheer nonsense to talk about 'racial differences' as between the American black man and the American white man." He bitterly charged that this was "the last stand of the old myth palmed off by Negrophobists" like the so-called "scientists" Madison Grant and Lothrop Stoddard, "the vociferous scions of slaveholders," and "the patriots who flood the treasury of the Ku Klux Klan," as well as most white Americans who think in terms of immutable race characteristics.[42] His view on race matters was that blacks were human beings with no special characteristics from other people in reaction to longstanding racist propaganda that blacks had inferior human instincts.

In Schuyler's satire, "Our Greatest Gift to America" (1929), he said the gift was "flattery" that made whites feel equal to one another and superior to blacks. This article was a counterargument to Du Bois's book, *The Gift of Black Folk: The Negroes in the Making of America* (1924), the Renaissance, and a view by thoughtful blacks who promoted a sort of black chamber-of-commerce race boosterism. Schuyler noted that some Harlem Renaissance writers made a nice living by flattering whites.[43] He stopped short of outright calling these blacks Sambos. He felt blacks as a group were assimilated by their environment and white neighbors. He feared that the Harlem Renaissance doctrine would backfire by keeping alive the old myths of immutable race differences that were used by racist white propagandists to justify segregation and discrimination. In his view, blacks and whites who accepted the notion of special racial characteristics, preached by the "New Negro" movement crowd, was nothing more than an ideological submission to white propaganda.

The poet Langston Hughes gave a rebuttal in the next issue of *The Nation* magazine, June 23, 1926, to Schuyler's attack ("The Negro-Art Hokum") in *The Nation* magazine on the Harlem Renaissance black art school of thought. Hughes argued that blacks trying to be white hindered the black poetry and art movement. He attacked assimilated blacks who avoided anything black. He derisively charged that it was ludicrous and impossible for blacks to acquire completely "Nordic manners, Nordic faces, Nordic hair, Nordic art (if any), and an Episcopal heaven. A very high mountain indeed for the would-be racial artist to climb to discover himself and his people." He also said elsewhere, "We younger Negro artists who create now intend to express our individual dark-skinned selves without fear or shame." What is more, "if white people are pleased we are glad. If they are not, it does not matter. If colored people are pleased we are glad. If they are not, their displeasure doesn't matter either."[44] The Schuyler-Hughes debate reflected respectively the assimilation ideology versus the modern movement for cultural diversity and democracy ideologies.

Du Bois launched a withering critique of the new black art and literature movement of the Harlem Renaissance near the end of "The Negro in Art" symposium in *The Crisis* after he became disturbed at an obvious consensus against art for propaganda to promote blacks' civil rights and positive images in the mass media. He first gave his talk in Chicago, and rumor about it swelled into a demand for copies of the speech, which was reprinted in the October 1926 issue of *The Crisis*. Du Bois wrote that many have asked "how is it that an organization of this kind can turn aside to talk about art?" Some thought it was a trivial pursuit. "The thing we are talking about tonight is part of the great fight we are carrying on and it represents a forward and an upward look—a pushing forward." Moreover, "we who are dark can see America in a way that white Americans cannot. And seeing our country thus, are we satisfied with its present goals and ideals?" He thought not. America was a racist and segregated society that degraded and oppressed blacks and painted a scandalous picture of the black experience. "And it is right here that the National Association for the Advancement of Colored People comes upon the field, comes with its great call to a new battle, a new fight, and new things to fight before the old things are wholly won; and to say that the Beauty of Truth and Freedom which shall some day be our heritage and the heritage of all civilized man is not in our hands yet and that we ourselves must not fail to realize."[45] Du Bois desperately wanted to control the black art and artists emerging and centering in Harlem.

In his article Du Bois acknowledged that recognition of black artists was growing. Blacks and whites as a result were "whispering: Here is a way out. Here is the real solution of the color problem. The recognition accorded Cullen, Hughes, Fauset, White, and others shows there is no real color line. Keep quiet! Don't complain! Work! All will be well!" Du Bois had serious doubts of the truth of this. "I will not say that already this chorus amounts to a conspiracy." He thought too many whites backed the younger generation of black writers because they believed their approach would "stop agitation of the Negro question. They say, 'What is the use of your fighting and complaining; do the great thing and the reward is there.'" What is worse, "many colored people are all too eager to follow this advice; especially those who are weary of the eternal struggle along the color line, who are afraid to fight, and to whom the money of philanthropists and the alluring publicity are subtle and deadly bribes. They say, 'what is the use of fighting? Why not show simply what we deserve and let the reward come to us?'"[46] Du Bois was pleading for ideologically oriented literature. Blacks should not allow their critics to go unanswered, which in his view, was virtual surrender.

Du Bois emphatically disagreed with the direction of the new Harlem Renaissance writers and their white allies. He concluded: "Thus all Art is propaganda and ever must be, despite the wailing of the purists. I stand in utter shamelessness and say that whatever art I have for writing has been used always for propaganda for gaining the right of black folk to love and enjoy. I do not care a damn for any art that is not used for propaganda. But I do care when propaganda is confined to one side while the other is stripped and silent."[47] Du Bois, in effect, threw down the gauntlet, not only against avowed enemies of black people, but friends as well whose art ideology excluded propaganda in the service of black civil rights and opportunity.

Carl Van Vechten published his novel *Nigger Heaven* (1926) and sparked a bitter debate and division among black and white intellectuals over its merits as art or as propaganda injurious to the black image. Du Bois reviewed it in *The Crisis*. "Carl Van Vechten's 'Nigger Heaven' is a blow in the face. It is an affront to the hospitality of black folk and to the intelligence of white." First he complained about the title: "a nasty, sordid corner into which black folk are herded, and yet a place which they in crass ignorance are fools enough to enjoy." Furthermore, "he masses this knowledge without rule or reason and seeks to express all of Harlem life in its cabarets. To him the black cabaret is Harlem; around it all his characters gravitate." What is more, "it is a caricature. It is worse than untruth because it is a mass of half-truths." Du Bois bitterly concluded, "I advise others who are impelled by a sense of duty or curiosity to drop the book gently in the grate and to try the Police Gazette."[48] Most of Van Vechten's novel did not deal with Harlem night life, but Du Bois knew that Van Vechten believed that the entertainment world was the crucial point where the races often met, and perhaps not on equal terms. Du Bois often saw the cabaret as a den of sin, vice, and crime.

Prominent black literary figures defended Van Vechten's role in the Harlem Renaissance and his book at various times over the years. The venerable James Weldon Johnson, also an NAACP officer, who was awarded the NAACP's Spingarn Medal in 1925, thought well of the book and said so in a 1926 review and his 1933 autobiography. Johnson said, "In this the author pays colored people the rare tribute of writing about them as people rather than as puppets." He completely disagreed with Du Bois's assessment of the book. "In the book Mr. Van Vechten does not stoop to burlesque or caricature. There are characters and incidents in the book that many will regard as worse than unpleasant, but always the author handles them with sincerity and fidelity." Moreover, Van Vechten had no malice and depicted the low life as well as genteel Harlem with class and sophistication. "Most Negroes who condemned 'Nigger Heaven' did not read it; they were stopped by the title."[49] Johnson felt critics who had not read the book were unable to judge it simply by its title.

Johnson thought that Van Vechten loved and respected black people, and had a "warm interest" in blacks long before Harlem came into vogue. His book "is full of propaganda. Every phase of the race question, from Jim Crow discriminations to miscegenation, is frankly discussed." This satisfied some critics, but Johnson believed that propaganda should be avoided in art. Johnson thought that Van Vechten "did more to forward" the Harlem Renaissance than anyone else.[50] Van Vechten promoted the reputation of Harlem worldwide. "Harlem was made known as the scene of laughter, singing, dancing, and primitive passions, and as the center of the new Negro literature and art; the era in which it gained its place in the list of famous sections of great cities." He believed that Van Vechten's *Nigger Heaven* (1926) and Claude McKay's *Home to Harlem* (1928) were largely responsible for Harlem's international reputation as a major social and cultural community.[51] Blacks, in his view, should take advantage of the recognition. Harlem night life boomed as white Americans and European celebrities started a steady trek to Harlem cabarets and entertainment centers. Harlem became one of the Western world's fun capitals.

In 1937 Claude McKay said of Van Vechten, "I found Mr. Van Vechten not a bit patronizing, and quite all right," after he had been warned in Europe of the criticisms leveled against him. Langston Hughes said in 1940, "The word nigger to colored people of high and low degrees is like a red rag to a bull." However, "Mr. Van Vechten became the goat of the New Negro Renaissance, the he-who-gets-slapped [a reference to Leonid Andreyev's *He Who Gets Slapped*]. The critics of the left, like the Negroes of the right, proceeded to light on Mr. Van Vechten, and he was accused of ruining, distorting, polluting and corrupting every Negro writer from then on, who was ever known to have shaken hands with him, or to have used the word nigger in his writings, or to have been in a cabaret. . . ." In reality, said Hughes, Van Vechten was a great promoter of the Harlem Renaissance and black artists and writers. He personally took materials to editors and book publishers on behalf of blacks and was successful in getting them published.[52] Hughes, like James Weldon Johnson and George S. Schuyler, argued that Van Vechten was a great benefactor to the black cause. Du Bois's ideology blinded him to the new opportunities opened up in publications and the international recognition of Harlem as an attractive and exotic community.

George S. Schuyler, a bitter critic of the Harlem Renaissance, argued, too, that "the Sage of Central Park West," Van Vechten, who had moved from West 55th Street after 1937, "has done more than any single person in this country to create the atmosphere of acceptance of the Negro." Van Vechten's goal was to "break the taboo on the highest levels and finally that process will seep down to the masses." He invited white cultural, political, and business leaders to his home, where their black counterparts, as well as working-class blacks, came by invitation as well, and they socialized, drank, danced, talked, and where entertainers— especially blacks—performed on a level of social equality with whites. As a result of his Central Park West gatherings and his earlier ones on West 55th Street, Schuyler said, "what was at first an innovation and a novelty soon became commonplace, an institution."[53] Van Vechten made it fashionable for some whites to socialize with blacks. But, as Du Bois well knew, it was not of much consequence as long as institutional segregation, discrimination, and constitutional racial authoritarianism remained the norm. What was worse, Du Bois sensed that Harlem was being turned into a red-light district for whites seeking to gratify their prurient proclivities.

The debates over the Harlem Renaissance and art ideology raged for years. Although H.L. Mencken thought that blacks had made rapid progress despite neglect and repression, in 1927 he accused blacks of not producing any great art or literature. This created a hot debate. "A roar naturally followed," he said. Many people sent proof of black works. After heated rebuttals, he conceded that "these I have now examined patiently and at great length. They induce me to modify my doctrine in only one particular." He recognized Professor H. Nathaniel Dett of Hampton University, who authored the splendid spiritual "Listen to the Lambs" which Mencken thought "a genuinely original and moving piece of work." Blacks had many popular musicians and composers but "it is not the Negroes but Jews who have turned it to more ambitious uses. In much the same way it is white novelists and dramatists and not Negroes who have best utilized the Negro as a dramatic figure. The imaginative authors of the race all seem to be hampered by a propaganda purpose." He advised blacks to purge themselves of superstition, useless rituals, expensive churches and manipulation, and gaudy fraternal groups that consumed valuable time and resources. Progress was being made in the arts and business, but more critical self-analysis was definitely needed.[54] Mencken saw the confusing effects the ideological battles raging over art versus propaganda were having on the Harlem Renaissance. He believed that works of merit would get recognized, but propaganda was useless.

Du Bois, naturally, responded to Mencken's criticism. He said Mencken was a fair man but rejected the charge that first-rate books by blacks since the Civil War did not amount to "a shelf a foot long." He said even that should cause blacks to be congratulated in the face of racist repression and obstacles. American whites had not done much better either. He concluded that "on the whole, then, despite a stimulating critic's opinion, we Negroes are quite well satisfied with our Renaissance. And we have not yet finished."[55] Du Bois felt blacks could produce works of art with propaganda as part of its content.

Du Bois and Alain Locke, however, were ambivalent about the Harlem Renaissance and its achievements. Locke said in 1928 that "the flood tide of the present Negro-phile movement" was at hand. It was only a fad that would soon pass. "The real significance and potential power of the Negro Renaissance may not reveal itself until after this reaction, and the entire top-soil of contemporary Negro expression may need to be ploughed completely under for a second hardier and richer crop." Moreover, on reflection, "to get above ground, much forcing has had to be endured; to win a hearing much exploitation has had to be tolerated."[56] Locke accepted the complexity and mixed motives and productions which came from the Harlem Renaissance. He only wanted to extend the possibilities of the undertaking.

John Henrik Clarke has noted that the Harlem Renaissance and the Marcus Garvey movements rose and declined about the same time. The Garvey movement, however, existed independent of white support and patronage. Garvey's Universal Negro Improvement Association was the largest black mass movement in the 1920s. In fact, many whites and some black leaders opposed it quite vigorously.[57] The Great Depression helped to kill the Harlem Renaissance while the federal government's prosecution, imprisonment, and exile of Garvey, as well as internal disputes and chaos in his movement, destroyed his influence.

William H. Ferris, a black nationalist who became a follower of Garvey, reviewed Du Bois's book, *Darkwater*, in 1920. He was very critical of the book although he thought it was a brilliant piece. He said, "We see in it the agony of soul of a Negro of mixed blood, writhing and twisting and turning in the cage in which the Anglo-Saxon has confined it. It is the white blood of Du Bois crying for its own." On the other hand, he noted, "the black and brown masses . . . are not as sensitive about social ostracism as Du Bois and the mulattoes, quadroons, and octoroons are."[58] Ferris believed that blacks did not want to integrate or socialize with their oppressors, but sought liberation from their oppressive grip.

In October 1923 Marcus Garvey declared in his paper, *Negro World*, in an editorial entitled "Appeal to the Soul of White America," that "the Negro will have to build his own government, industry, art, science, literature and culture, before the world will stop to consider him." He added, "The race needs workers at this time, not plagiarists, copyists, and mere imitators, but men and women who are able to create, to originate and improve, and thus make an independent racial contribution to the world and civilization."⁵⁹ He argued for blacks to create their own art, science, and culture, and not to slavishly follow white trends. Garvey's wife, Amy Jacques Garvey, said in an article in *Negro World* on March 6, 1927, entitled "The Value of Propaganda," that bold and subtle propaganda must be used in the black cause for liberation from European and American imperialism. "Truly propaganda is a wise investment," she declared.⁶⁰

On September 29, 1928, in another front page editorial in *Negro World*, Marcus Garvey lambasted Claude McKay's novel, *Home to Harlem* (1928). He noted that "our race, within recent years, has developed a new group of writers who have been prostituting their intelligence, under the direction of the white man, to bring out and show up the worst traits of our people." These white publishers only wanted, he declared, to circulate "the libel against us among the white peoples of the world, to further hold us up to ridicule and contempt and universal prejudice." He added, "This book of Claude McKay's is a damnable libel against the Negro. It is doing a great deal of harm in further creating prejudice among the white people against the Negro." Garvey said, "We want writers who will fight the Negro's cause. . . ."⁶¹ Garvey took a position similar to Du Bois and supported the use of propaganda in the arts to advance the race. His wife had argued such a position, also.

Du Bois reviewed the book, too. He declared, "Claude McKay's 'Home to Harlem' . . . for the most part nauseates me, and after the dirtier parts of its filth, I feel distinctly like taking a bath." He felt the book was not wholly a bad one, given McKay's obvious talent. McKay, he charged, "has set out to cater for that prurient demand on the part of white folk for a portrayal in Negroes of that utter licentiousness which conventional civilization holds white folk back from enjoying—if enjoyment it can be called."⁶² Garvey, his wife, and Du Bois were in agreement that positive racial propaganda should be used to uplift the race and negative propaganda, as they judged it, in the mass media should be denounced.

George W. Jacobs launched a scathing critique of Harlem Renaissance writers in 1929. He personally heard one black

Harlem writer declare as a defense of "negative" black characters, "authors must eat." Jacobs ruefully recounted that "the Negro writers of New York . . . plunged beneath the surface of their environment; they hoisted the sewer system to one's very nose and amid the jingling of many shekels, insisted that this was all that there was of black Harlem." Jacobs said that blacks had plenty of "opportunities" after World War I "of destroying the racial stereotypes" that plagued the race. They could have written literature that presented "a [more] polite form of amusement than that afforded by any of the Harlem night clubs" (which Van Vechten had portrayed in *Nigger Heaven*). Whites "trekked up to Harlem," Jacobs bitterly charged, "to show the little colored boys and girls the path to Parnassus; they redefined 'the literature of a people'" from varied joys and sadness and achievements and failures to "the literature of a people's shortcomings and its follies."[63] This "sewer sensationalism and misguided primitivism" were deplorable because "the prostitute is the high priestess of the first type. Negro primitivism is the creed of the second. Extremists both."[64] He was sadly disappointed with the results of the Harlem Renaissance black writers who, in his view, perpetuated slanderous racial stereotypes. In fact, the Du Bois faction had lost the Harlem Renaissance ideological battle, and therefore denounced it and any black writers, who, like whites, wrote for an audience who would buy their books. Polite and placid literature did not sell well to blacks or whites. Du Bois and Garvey reasoned that blacks had not been cultivated properly to appreciate good, race-uplifting literature. The Du Boisian school of thought, having lost the ideological battle, became bitter sideline critics.

In 1933 Du Bois complained, "Why was it that the Renaissance of literature, which began among Negroes ten years ago, has never taken real and lasting root? It was because it was a transplanted and exotic thing. It was a literature written for the benefit of white people and at the behest of white readers, and started out privately from the white point of view." What is more, "it never had a real Negro constituency, and it did not grow out of the inmost heart and frank expression of Negroes; on such an artificial basis no real literature can grow."[65] Du Bois did not graciously accept the end result of the Harlem Renaissance and his ideological defeat.

Locke, on the other hand, believed that "cultural chauvinism" was "ridiculous" and "would shut the minority art up in a spiritual ghetto and deny vital and unrestricted creative participation in the general culture." In 1940 Du Bois acknowledged that "my career as a scientist was to be swallowed up in my role as a master of propaganda."[66] In other words, Du Bois and Locke believed that the Civic Club dinner of 1924 where they had sought to undergird and direct the Renaissance had backfired because of the conflicting views over art and propaganda.

Locke lamented the propaganda aspect of the Renaissance as unwarranted and harmful. Du Bois and Locke agreed that the literary Renaissance had gone over the heads of most black readers. Black and white writers catered to white readers who were fascinated by the lurid and exotic lifestyles of the black entertainment world and underclass of Harlem; because they flouted—in their "jive" speech, in revealing, gaudy, and dandy dress codes and dance styles, and in their freewheeling sexual mores—conservative values and codes of conduct, which were under massive assault in the 1920s.[67]

Du Bois's ideological views had crystallized in the battle against Griffith's film, *The Birth of a Nation* (1915), which had devastating consequences for blacks. It encouraged violent and aggressive racial restrictions against blacks in every area of American life. Du Bois wanted black artists and their white allies to make bold statements and positive presentations on behalf of blacks to counter racist art, politics, and propaganda. His definition of art and propaganda was expressed many times in his speeches and writings, and most notably in the famous and controversial seven questions posed in *The Crisis* in 1926.

Du Bois had supported black artists before 1924, the year that Charles S. Johnson and others spearheaded a movement that undergirded the Harlem Renaissance. Du Bois defended the movement even while he voiced grave misgivings over the subject matter its black and white writers produced. He stridently opposed their ideological opposition to using art for propaganda in race relations while the racists did so without hesitation. The Harlem Renaissance writers never achieved a consensus on this point. Du Bois finally concluded that the Harlem Renaissance had not been a vehicle for a major assault against white supremacy and segregation. Politics, in his view, remained the principal avenue of protest and action for black liberation. Literature without a political guide, in his view, was not only useless, but harmful because he felt it supported negative black stereotype imagery that helped to maintain racial authoritarianism.

James Weldon Johnson still believed that racist art could be undone only by a counter, positive black art. He lamented, in 1934, the persistence of black stereotypes in books and on the stage, but he also noted "in the earlier years the motion pictures (most notably Griffith's epic film) carried on this tradition. . . . Now, just as these stereotypes were molded and circulated and perpetuated by literary and artistic processes, they must be broken up and replaced through similar means. No other means can be as fully effective. Some of this work has already been done, but the greater portion remains to be done—and by Negro writers and artists." He said that blacks cannot expect whites to do it. "What we need to do is to rear a group of Negro American writers and artists who can smash the old stereotypes, and replace them with newer and truer ones; who can produce work that will reach and affect many and many a white American who may never in a lifetime exchange a hundred words with a Negro; who can produce work that may affect people will never even see a Negro." He thought that blacks should buy more books by black writers to impress publishers.[68] In effect, he was looking for a second edition of the Renaissance with new artists committed to breaking up the old negative black stereotypes, rather than helping to perpetuate them in their own works. The Great Depression destroyed any hopes for another black Harlem literary renaissance.

Claude McKay, who tried to stay out of the race, art, and political infights, declared in 1937, "I was surprised when I discovered that many of the talented Negroes regarded their renaissance more as an uplift organization and a vehicle to accelerate the pace and progress of smart Negro society." He added, "I understood more clearly why there had been so much genteel-Negro hostility to my 'Home to Harlem' and Langston Hughes's primitive Negro poems."[69] McKay apparently rejected art for propaganda.

The Harlem Renaissance debates had a profound impact on both black and white artists, editors, publishers, and newspaper critics for many years after the formal debates had ended. These debates had been part and parcel of the search for a solution to end white-supremacy practices. Segregation often kept willing whites from associating with blacks out of fear of ostracism for associating with an allegedly inferior and debauched race. In many states, especially in the South, violence and legal sanctions were used to keep the races separated. Many blacks were convinced that racist white public opinion was undergirded by negative black stereotypes—and there was a substantial body of literature on the subject—that were used to maintain white supremacy and racial segregation and subordination.

W.E.B. Du Bois, Charles S. Johnson, and James Weldon Johnson sought to counter stereotypes with the Harlem Renaissance. Carl Van Vechten, many other white writers, and Langston Hughes saw beauty and dignity in the black folk and urban jive cultures judged as stereotypes by Du Bois. George Schuyler rejected even the notion that black art was possible. Garvey wanted art for propaganda in the cause for black liberation, like Du Bois, but Du Bois was for racial reconciliation and integration while Garvey sought racial separation from whites and a literature compatible with his views and high moral standards of a civilized black society.

Ideological differences divided the Harlem Renaissance writers and critics into several camps and prevented them from ever achieving a consensus. No camp was completely satisfied with the productions of the Harlem Renaissance writers and critics. Nevertheless, they did achieve a significant level of operational unity, with the exception of Garvey, until the Renaissance dissipated.

Although the Harlem Renaissance did not achieve the lofty goals its creators had envisioned, it remained a significant chapter in the American experience. It brought black and white writers and critics, magazine and book editors together in efforts that often resulted in social and racial integration. Blacks gained greater cultural and artistic recognition. The Harlem Renaissance helped crack the rigid hierarchical Victorian culture that ranked blacks at the bottom of the social and racial structure. This aspect of Victorianism had gained legitimacy as a result of the pseudo-scientific racism it fostered. Blacks, by helping to fragment Victorianism, made a major contribution to opening the door for cultural liberalism and social democracy.

Notes

1. Charles S. Johnson (address delivered to the National Conference of Social Work, Washington, D.C., 23 May 1923), in "Public Opinion and the Negro," *Opportunity*, I, No. 7 (July 1923), 201–202.

2. See Fred Silva, ed., *Focus on The Birth of a Nation* (Englewood Cliffs, N.J.: Prentice-Hall, Inc., 1971).

3. Dr. Bruce M. Tyler, "Racist Art and Politics at the Turn of the Century," *The Journal of Ethnic Studies*, 15, No. 4 (Winter 1988), 85–103.

4. Thomas F. Gossett, *Race: The History of an Idea in America* (New York: Schocken Books, 1968); Kenneth T. Jackson, *The Ku Klux Klan in the City, 1915–1930* (New York: Oxford University Press, 1967), p. 4.

5. W.E.B. Du Bois, *Dusk of Dawn* (New York: Schocken Books, 1968 [1940]), pp. 239–240.

6. *Ibid.*

7. Du Bois, "Negro Art" (orig. pub. in *The Crisis*, June 1921), in Meyer Weinberg, ed., *W.E.B. Du Bois: A Reader* (New York: Harper Torchbooks, 1970), pp. 239–240.

8. *Ibid.*

9. *Ibid.*

10. "Can the Negro Serve the Drama" (orig. pub. in *Theatre*, July 1923), in Weinberg, ed., pp. 241–246.

11. W.E.B. Du Bois, *The Gift of Black Folk: The Negroes in the Making of America* (New York: Washington Square Press, 1970 [orig. pub. 1924]), pp. 158–159.

12. *Ibid.*, p. 161.

13. William H. Ferris, "For an Afro-American Literature" (orig. pub. in his *The African Abroad, or, His Evolution in Western Civilization Tracing His Development under Caucasian Milieu*, 2 vols. [New Haven: Tuttle, Morchirise & Taylor, 1913], Vol. I, pp. 267–268), quoted in Herbert Aptheker, ed., *A Documentary History of the Negro People in the United States, 1910–1932*, Vol. 3 (Secaucus, N.J.: The Citadel Press, 1977 [1973]), pp. 65–66.

14. William Ferris, "The Arts and Black Development" (orig. pub. in *Negro World*, April 30, 1921), in Theodore G. Vincent, ed., *Voices of a Black Nation: Political Journalism in the Harlem Renaissance* (San Francisco: Ramparts Press, Inc., 1973), p. 327.

15. Horace M. Kallen, *Culture and Democracy in the United States* (New York: Boni and Liveright, 1924), pp. 43, 34–35; Stanley Coben, "The Assault on Victorianism in the Twentieth Century," in Daniel Walker Howe, ed., *Victorian America* (Philadelphia: University of Pennsylvania Press, 1976), pp. 160–181; Jackson, *The Ku Klux Klan in the City, 1915–1930*.

16. Hiram Wesley Evans, "The Klan's Fight for Americanism," (orig. in *The North American Review* [March 1926], 136–145), in George E. Mowry, ed., *The Twenties: Fords, Flappers & Fanatics* (Englewood Cliffs, N.J.: Prentice-Hall, Inc., 1963 [pbk.]), p. 140.

17. Du Bois, *Gift of Black Folk*, pp. 161–162.

18. *Ibid.*, pp. 162–163.

19. Congressman Charles M. Stedman, Greensboro, North Carolina, *Congressional Record, 68th Congress, 1st Session,* Vol. 65, Part 2, pp. 1019–2050, 16 January to 7 February 1924, 26 January 1924, p. 1516.

20. C.H. Tobias, "Good-By, Black Mammy," in Robert T. Kerlin, ed., *The Voice of the Negro* (New York: Arno Press and *The New York Times,* 1968 [1920]), p. 29.

21. W.E.B. Du Bois, *Gift of Black Folk*, pp. 188–189.

22. Thomas Nelson Page, *The Negro: The Southerner's Problem* (New York: Charles Scribner's Sons, 1904); Thomas Nelson Page, "The Old Time Negro," *Scribner's Monthly,* XXXVI (November 1924), 522–532.

23. Du Bois, "The Negro in Art," *The Crisis*, 32, No. 4 (August 1926), 193–194; *ibid.*, 32, No. 5 (September 1926), 238–239.

24. Du Bois, *Gift of Black Folk*, p. 169.

25. Du Bois, "The Social Origins of Negro Art" (orig. pub. in *Modern Quarterly* [October–December 1925]), in Weinberg, ed., pp. 247–250.

26. Du Bois, *Gift of Black Folk*, p. 169; Du Bois, *Dusk of Dawn*, p. 270.

27. Du Bois, *In Battle for Peace & The Story of My 83rd Birthday* (New York: A Masses & Mainstream Publication, 1952), pp. 7–8.

28. David L. Lewis, *When Harlem Was in Vogue* (New York: Vintage Books, 1981 [pbk.]), pp. 89–94.

29. *Ibid.*, pp. 93–95; Alain Locke, ed., *The New Negro* (New York: Atheneum Books, 1970 [1925]).

30. Lewis, p. 92.

31. *Ibid.*, pp. 89–94; Alain Locke, *The New Negro*.

32. See Bruce Kellner, *Keep A-Inchin' Along: Selected Writings of Carl Van Vechten about Black Art and Letters* (Westport: Greenwood Press, 1979), pp. 64–65; Du Bois (Jessie Fauset edited the art section, but since Du Bois had the most sweeping reaction and was editor of the journal, I use his name), "The Negro in Art: How Shall He Be Portrayed; A Symposium," *The Crisis*, 31, No. 5 (March 1926), 219 (hereafter cited as Du Bois, "The Negro in Art").

33. Du Bois, "The Negro in Art," pp. 219–220.

34. *Ibid.*

35. Du Bois, "The Negro in Art," 31, No. 6 (April 1926), 278–280.

36. *Ibid.*

37. Du Bois, "The Negro in Art," 32, No. 1 (May 1926), 35–36.

38. Du Bois, "The Negro in Art," 32, No. 2 (June 1926), 71–73.

39. Du Bois, "The Negro in Art," 32, No. 4 (August 1926), 193–194; *ibid.*, 32, No. 5 (September 1926), 238–239.

40. Du Bois, "The Negro in Art," 32, No. 4 (August 1926), 193–194.

41. Du Bois, "The Negro in Art," 33, No. 1 (November 1926), 28–29.

42. George S. Schuyler, "The Negro-Art Hokum," *The Nation*, 122, No. 3180 (16 June 1926), 662–663.

43. George S. Schuyler, "Our Greatest Gift to America," in V.F. Calverton, *Anthology of American Negro Literature* (New York: The Modern Library Publishers, 1929), pp. 405–408.

44. Langston Hughes, "The Artist and the Racial Mountain," *The Nation*, 122, No. 3181 (23 June 1926), 692–694.

45. See Du Bois, "Criteria of Negro Art," *The Crisis*, 32, No. 6 (October 1926), 290–297; also as "Criteria for Negro Art," in Meyer Weinberg, ed., pp. 251–260.

46. *Ibid.*

47. *Ibid.*

48. Du Bois, "Books: 'Nigger-Heaven'" *The Crisis*, 32, No. 2 (December 1926), 81–82.

49. James Weldon Johnson, "Romance and Tragedy in Harlem—A Review," *Opportunity*, 4, No. 40 (October 1926), 316–317, 330; James Weldon Johnson, *Along This Way: The Autobiography of James Weldon Johnson* (New York: The Viking Press, 1968 [1933]), p. 382.

50. Johnson, *Along This Way*, p. 382; Johnson, "Romance and Tragedy in Harlem," pp. 316–317, 330.

51. Johnson, *Along This Way*, pp. 380–381.

52. Claude McKay, "From A Long Way from Home," quoted in introution to 1971 edition of Carl Van Vechten, *Nigger Heaven* (New York: Harper Colophon Books, 1971 [1926]), pp. xi–xii; see Claude McKay, *A Long Way from Home* (New York: Arno Press and The New York Times, 1969 [1937]), p. 319, for original quote; Langston Hughes, "From The Big Sea," in Van Vechten, *Nigger Heaven*, pp. xvi–xviii.

53. George S. Schuyler, "Phylon Profile, XXII: Carl Van Vechten," *Phylon*, XI, No. 4 (1950), 362–368.

54. H.L. Mencken, "The Dark America," *Chicago Tribune*, 25 September 1927.

55. Du Bois, "Mencken," (orig. pub. in *The Crisis*, October 1927) in Weinberg, ed., pp. 261–262.

56. Alain Locke, "1928: A Retrospective Review" (orig. pub. in *Opportunity*, January 1929, 351–353), in Theodore G. Vincent, ed., *Voices of a Black Nation*, pp. 353–357.

57. John Henrik Clarke with the assistance of Amy Jacques Garvey, *Marcus Garvey and the Vision of Africa* (New York: Vintage Books, 1974), pp. 180–188.

58. William H. Ferris, "Darkwater" (orig. appeared in *African and Orient Review*, June 1920), quoted in Theodore Vincent, ed., *Voices of a Black Nation*, pp. 344–345.

59. Marcus Garvey, "Appeal to the Soul of White America" (orig. pub. in *Negro World*, October 1923), quoted in Amy Jacques Garvey, *Garvey and Garveyism* (New York: Collier Books, 1974 [1968]), pp. 24–25.

60. Amy Jacques Garvey, "The Value of Propaganda" (orig. pub. in *Negro World*, 6 March 1927), quoted in Theodore G. Vincent, ed., *Voices of a Black Nation*, p. 74.

61. Marcus Garvey, "'Home to Harlem,' Claude McKay's Damaging Book, Should Earn Wholesale Condemnation of Negroes," *Negro World* (29 September 1928), 1.

62. W.E.B. Du Bois, "Home to Harlem and Quicksand" (orig. pub. in *The Crisis*, June 1928), quoted in Theodore G. Vincent, *Voices of a Black Nation*, pp. 359–360.

63. George W. Jacobs, "Negro Authors Must Eat," *Pittsburgh Courier*, 22 June 1929, sec. 1, p. 12, col. 3.

64. *Ibid.*

65. Du Bois, "The Negro College" (orig. pub. in *The Crisis*, August 1933), and excerpts from an address at Fisk University, June 1933, in Weinberg, ed., pp. 177–186; Du Bois, *Dusk of Dawn*, pp. 270–271.

66. Du Bois, *Dusk of Dawn*, p. 94; Alain Locke, "The Negro's Contribution to American Culture," *The Journal of Negro Education*, VIII, Chapter XXI (1939), 521–529, esp. 522.

67. See Walter E. Houghton, *The Victorian Frame of Mind* (New Haven: Yale University Press, 1964 [1957]); Stanley Coben, "The Assault on Victorianism in the Twentieth Century," in Daniel Walker Howe, ed., *Victorian America*, pp. 160–181; Robert A. Bone, *The Negro Novel in America* (New Haven: Yale University Press, 1970 [1958]).

68. James Weldon Johnson, *Negro Americans, What Now?* (New York: The Viking Press, 1934), pp. 91–94.

69. Claude McKay, *A Long Way from Home*, pp. 321–322.

FROM HARLEM TO HOLLYWOOD

In the middle 1930s, after W.E.B. Du Bois and Charles S. Johnson proclaimed the literary Harlem Renaissance dead, black newspaper editors and writers took up the issue of the image of blacks in the mass media. While these new critics continued the ideological battles started by the Harlem Renaissance writers and critics, the focus of the movement shifted decisively toward the images projected by Hollywood films.

A militant group of black Los Angeles professionals and community leaders adopted—although some for different reasons—the Du Boisian position. Blacks never forgot the image etched by *The Birth of a Nation*. Black critics attacked Hollywood film producers for continuing to project negative black stereotypes in films. These harmed black efforts to advance because racial stereotypes undergirded a racist public opinion which, in turn, supported a Jim Crow social order.

Charles S. Johnson made a trip to Los Angeles in 1926 to survey black labor conditions. While there, he organized "California's large colony of race writers into a formal group entitled the 'Ink Slingers.'" They became a West Coast version of the Harlem Renaissance but never gained artistic recognition for lack of any significant works of art. The Ink Slingers were prominent in community affairs and had family and business connections across the country. They were the community-minded black middle and upper classes and their influence was pervasive in black Los Angeles.

The original members of the Ink Slingers were California State Assemblyman Fred B. Roberts, a Republican and editor of the *New Age Dispatch*; Noah Thompson, a writer for a white newspaper, the *Evening Express*, and later business manager of *Opportunity*, the organ of the National Urban League; and Catherine Barr, secretary of the Urban League. She started an employment business, later called the Tuskegee Industrial Society, which about 1920 became the Los Angeles branch of the National

Urban League. Garland Anderson, who wrote the play "Appearances," which was promoted by Al Jolson and shown in San Francisco and on New York's Broadway in 1929, was also a member.[1] Artistically, he was the most successful.

Other founding members of the Ink Slingers were Henry L. Jones and Emma Lue Sayers, writers for the *Pittsburgh Courier*. Sayers was a sister of Jessie L. Terry, whose husband was a building contractor in Los Angeles. Jessie Terry was active in Democratic Party politics. She was the first woman and black to serve on the board of the Los Angeles City Housing Authority. She later resigned to manage Pueblo Dio Rio, a housing project. Other members brought a wide range of abilities and experience to the Ink Slingers. George S. Grant was self-employed in real estate and had a reputation for public speaking at many black forums. He also was an author. Leroy Hart was an author and newspaper reporter. Fay M. Jackson Robinson and William Borders were writers for the *Pacific Defender*. Fay Jackson was married to a black physician, John Robinson, the son of a doctor who practiced in Texas well into his nineties. John Robinson was a graduate of the University of California, Berkeley. His academic scores and performance were so high that he was given a letter recommending him for internship at Los Angeles County Hospital despite the fact he was black. He was the first to break that color bar.[2]

Alderman Byer joined the Ink Slingers as did Eloise Bibb Thompson, the wife of Noah Thompson who apparently was related to Joseph D. Bibb, a writer for the *Chicago Defender*, the *Chicago Whip*, and the *Pittsburgh Courier*. Gladyse Greenaway— a popular clubwoman who organized The Doll League, which held an annual party to which patrons brought dolls for girls and gifts for boys to be given away at Christmas—became a member. Harry Levette was a writer for the *Defender* and the *Pittsburgh Courier*.[3] This group represented the black professional class who provided leadership for the black community in Los Angeles. Apparently, they were not serious writers or artists, but probably read the Harlem writers and discussed their works.

This core group inspired other Los Angeles black activists to join their struggle against negative stereotypes in the mass media and in the Hollywood film industry. The influence of this powerful group of blacks—powerful at least in black affairs in

Los Angeles—and their family and business ties spread across the country. Taking up the struggle begun with the Harlem Renaissance, they emerged as militant critics of Hollywood and its anti-black stereotypes.

The Ink Slingers were influenced by Loren Miller and Langston Hughes who leaned to the left in politics and departed for the Soviet Union in June 1932 to make a radical race film with a group of twenty other black Americans. The German Meschrabpom/Film Company, an affiliate of the Workers' International Relief, invited this group to go to the Soviet Union to make a picture titled *Black and White* about black workers in Birmingham, Alabama. Hughes noted, "Of the twenty-two Negroes headed for Moscow, most were youthful intellectuals— recent college graduates curious about the Soviet Union—or youngsters anxious to see Europe, but whose feet had never set foot on any stage and whose faces had never been before a motion-picture camera. There were only two professional theater people in the group."[4] The disparate motives of many in this group later led to bitter disappointment to some and attacks on the Soviet Union.

The film script had to be translated into English. When Langston Hughes read it, he said, "At first I was astounded at what I read. Then I laughed until I cried. And I wasn't crying really because the script was in places so mistaken and funny. I was crying because the writer meant well, but knew so little about the subject and the result was a pathetic hodgepodge of good intentions and faulty facts."[5] He added, "I simply took the scenario back to the Meschrabpom officials the next morning to tell them that, in my opinion, no plausible film could possibly be made from it since, in general, the script was so mistakenly conceived that it was beyond revision."[6] After convincing officials of the errors, half the film staff was fired. Hughes declared he could not write the script because he had never lived in the South or worked in a steel mill.[7]

A violent controversy broke out among the blacks after the film was postponed and then cancelled. "Two members of our group," noted Hughes, "claimed that Colonel Raymond Robbins had urged them weeks ago, over drinks in the Metropol Bar, to withdraw from the cast of a motion picture which, in the colonel's opinion, would be a black mark against the United States."[8]

Apparently, this incident, blown up by some of the disgruntled blacks and an anti-Soviet international press, was the source of the rumor that the Soviet Union had cancelled the film in a bid to gain diplomatic recognition from the United States.

The international press carried the story of the cancellation and distorted the facts, falsely claiming the blacks had been abandoned and were destitute. Eighteen of the group led by Hughes and Loren Miller denied the press's lies. Four other blacks in the group attacked the cancellation of the film as a betrayal of the blacks because the Soviet Union was seeking diplomatic recognition from the United States.[9] In fact, the film was cancelled because it simply did not have a plausible script and Hughes was unable to write a new one.

Disenchanted, four of the twenty-two blacks left abruptly and published critical and distorted accounts on the postponement and cancellation of the film. Louise Thompson replied to this group and the outright lies printed in the international press by saying that technical problems and weather conditions led to the postponement. Meanwhile, the pro-Soviet group led by Hughes and Miller traveled in the Soviet Union and sent back long dispatches telling the truth about the film and the status of the black Americans in the Soviet Union. United Press correspondent Eugene Lyons refused to forward the pro-Soviet press releases to the United States. Louise Thompson boasted that the Soviet Union's national policy was "the right of self determination for minor nationalities, the economic development of their backward regions, and the encouragement of national culture." She was disturbed "that four Negroes, who, for the first time in their lives enjoyed complete equality in Soviet Russia, should walk into the trap of becoming the weapons against the Soviet Union of those capitalist forces that oppress them in America."[10] The flap over the film was used, Thompson believed, to discredit the Soviet Union and its stated policy of racial democracy. With this view in mind, she defended the Soviet Union and attacked the four blacks who did not, in her view, fully appreciate the Soviet's experiment with racial democracy.

Nevertheless, newspaper columnist George S. Schuyler, writing for the *Pittsburgh Courier*, insisted upon distorting the facts by charging that Joseph Stalin of the Soviet Union had halted work on the film to avoid jeopardizing his efforts to win diplomatic recognition from the West. The film would have been resented as an embarrassment to the United States because, he charged erroneously, the script by Langston Hughes and German director Karl Junghaus was to show "the horrors of the slave trade and so-called lynch terror in the capitalist world in general and the United States in particular."[11] Schuyler had become a militant anti-Communist and used the crisis for his own advantage and to protect, in his view, black Americans from the taint of Communist radicalism. He was a long-time associate and writer for the National Association for the Advancement of Colored People (NAACP) which had waged a bitter fight over the legal defense in the 1930s of the Scottsboro boys charged with raping a white woman in the South. The NAACP had increasingly come under attack as a Communist-front group by white racists who resented its legal attacks on racial authoritarianism, especially in the South.[12]

Loren Miller of Los Angeles, a young attorney and newspaperman, emerged as one of the city's first radicals on the cultural front against Hollywood film stereotypes of blacks. He and Langston Hughes had driven nonstop for six days from California to New York to join the twenty blacks headed for the Soviet Union to make the ill-fated *Black and White*. Miller and Hughes were embittered by Hollywood's negative stereotypes of black and non-European people. Hughes was told by a Meschrabpom executive, "Don't mention Hollywood in the same breath with the film industry of the Workers' Socialist Republics. That citadel of capitalist escapism—Hollywood! Bah!"[13] Miller, already disenchanted with Hollywood, became a strident critic of Hollywood and activist upon his return from the Soviet Union.

Miller saw the film "Trader Horn" produced by Metro-Goldwyn-Mayer at a "Negro theater" and was outraged because blacks applauded the white hero when he came to the rescue of whites against "savage . . . Africans." He thought blacks "must stop applauding for such imperialistic jingoism as Trader Horn." He believed that "Negroes themselves fortify their inferiority complex by seeing themselves always cast as the underdog to be laughed at or despised." He lamented that even the newsreels ridiculed blacks and their religious revivals and Christian faith as superstitious. He charged that "the cumulative effect of constant picturization of this kind is tremendously effective in shaping racial attitudes." The world over, people "depend almost entirely on the movies for their knowledge of Negro life." Moreover, "the Hollywood portrayal of Negro life is so out of focus that it is in effect rabid anti-Negro propaganda. . . ." It instigated hatred and violence against blacks and made "the breakdown of racial chauvinism more difficult."[14] Miller also chastised blacks who patronized Hollywood films and considered them a major stumbling block in the fight against stereotypes. Moreover, the NAACP, in his view, was not committed to mass action which was a critical tool for radical activists in the 1930s.

Miller felt that blacks were without allies, since this was a black issue and the NAACP had failed to mobilize the black masses, while key Hollywood magnates were allied with the Franklin D. Roosevelt administration and their films reflected its status quo attitude toward blacks. Blacks had several options. Making their own films was not very promising. Oscar Micheaux tried to produce black films, he said, but "the run-of-mill films produced by Negro companies fail miserably because their producers simply ape white movies." He thought that a "little movie" movement with 16-millimeter films might take off like the "little theater" movement. He believed that "the second move lies in protest." Moreover, "protest to be of its greatest value must be inculcated in the great mass of Negro people." They must be taught to resent anti-black films and object at the ballot box. Another line of attack was film criticism. "Criticism of the movies is in a deplorable state at the present time." Moreover, "the Negro masses will adopt a critical attitude only if organs of opinion and Negro leadership establish an adequate critique for their guidance." He noted, too, "Negro newspapers have pages devoted to the theater and the film, but those pages are jokes, or worse." Finally, Miller indicated to blacks that "it's time we took up arms on the Hollywood front. We might get in some telling blows just now when the movie makers are already under fire."[15] The central problem facing such radicals as Miller was how to politicize the black masses in order to get them to boycott Hollywood films depicting black stereotypes.

Miller believed that the NAACP not only had failed to mobilize the black masses, but had no will to do so. He noted that the Chicago branch of the NAACP at the 1933 national convention in St. Louis, Missouri, had denounced what it called the "self-perpetuating oligarchy" that ran the organization. Discrimination and repression of blacks had increased in the last twenty-five years. He charged that circulation of *"The Crisis* [the NAACP's magazine] dropped from more than 106,000 in 1920 to less than 20,000" in 1934! The NAACP listed twenty-three new branches in 1934 and 85,000 members in 404 branches around the country. Some were inactive but were still on the list. Its dues intake, however, came to a mere $20,000. If the membership figures were correct, it should have been twice that amount. A distraught W.E.B. Du Bois resigned after his program calling for blacks to take "advantage of segregation" was repudiated by the NAACP as a capitulation to Jim Crow. Miller claimed it was the "old dream of a petty-bourgeois utopia in which an assured clientele would be guaranteed to the professional and business man" who benefitted by a black captive market.[16]

Miller charged that Walter White and attorney Charles Houston of Washington, D.C., were part of the oligarchy which needed to be replaced. Miller and the other Los Angeles insurgents never were able to oust White and Houston in order to develop radical direct-action boycott of Hollywood by mobilizing the black masses. One reason Miller failed was because many critics were also supporters of Hollywood's black film stars who simply wanted more jobs and a variety of roles.

Earl J. Morris, entertainment and theatrical editor for the *Pittsburgh Courier*, had a view different from Miller's about the black press's treatment of black entertainers. Black stars "cost the hundred-odd Negro newspapers nearly $50,000 a year." Moreover, "the Negro press, in order to glorify their sepia celebrities, spends thousands a year in reproducing photos for newspaper use." On the other hand, the theatrical pages of the national papers "don't carry five cents worth of advertising to pay for all this linage." He added, "Most Negro newspapers devote true whole pages to the theatre." He concluded, "Don't knock" the black press's treatment of black stars and entertainment.[17] Morris's career as an entertainment editor for the black press was based on promoting black stars. Entertainment and black entertainers were widely appreciated in the black community and were a major avenue to fame and wealth. Moreover, black entertainers, critics, and columnists for the black press never achieved a consensus over what were appropriate black film roles. The Harlem Renaissance debates, as a result, continued unabated, but over Hollywood films.

The *Pittsburgh Courier* and many other black newspapers had followed the graphic art example set by Du Bois to counter stereotypes because of the refusal of the white press to use positive pictures of blacks. Du Bois said that *The Crisis* from 1916 to 1919 "expanded enormously" with a paid circulation of 100,000. By 1910, more than four and a half million copies had been sold. With this wide circulation, Du Bois said, "I sought to encourage the graphic arts not only by magazine covers with Negro themes and faces, but as often as I could afford, I portrayed the faces and features of colored folk. One cannot realize today how rare that was in 1910." He noted, too, that "the colored papers carried few or no illustrations; the white papers none." *The Crisis* "published large numbers of most interesting and intriguing portraits."[18] The black press followed the pattern established by Du Bois.

The black press recognized that readers often bought the publications for their entertainment news and gossip. Black entertainment writers often praised black stars and criticized negative stereotypes as demeaning to them and blacks as a group. They wanted more jobs and a variety of roles. They were not necessarily committed, like Miller, to class and racial war against Hollywood.

Blacks were ambivalent toward Eugene O'Neill's play and film, *The Emperor Jones*. Some liked the film and roles blacks played. Others found both distasteful. Films with blacks often were judged with the view of how it might affect the image of the blacks as a group. Some critics found themselves praising blacks' acting but damning the film roles blacks played and derogatory race names. The film version of *The Emperor Jones* opened in September 1933 at the Rivoli and Roosevelt theaters in Harlem. Paul Robeson's acting was applauded by many blacks and whites. "The constant recurrence of the word 'nigger' is one of the reasons for Harlem's lack of interest," reported the *Philadelphia Tribune*. Another critic, Ed R. Harris, said that O'Neill's "plays have all been for the classes and not for the masses." He doubted that the film version would have wide appeal as a result. Some Harlemites were not pleased that Jones was portrayed as a brute and a mean dictator.[19] Harris was disturbed; to "hear giggling and chortling while some highly emotional actor is playing a very sad and touching scene is just a bit disconcerting and always annoying. The laughs that greet the sacrifice of a mother or a sweetheart often make me wonder whether the colored mother or sweetheart would do the same thing." He thought these scenes and blacks' reaction to them were bringing to the surface deep-seated feelings of self-contempt and hostility.[20]

These criticisms were a continuation of the Harlem Renaissance debates. Harris was perturbed, as was Loren Miller, at black audiences for either patronizing such films or for their so-called uncouth behavior in the audience. Miller and Ed Harris failed to create an organization to replace the NAACP that could lead the mass boycott of Hollywood which they envisioned would be the solution to negative black stereotypes. As a result, they largely played the roles of strident critics of Hollywood and films with black stereotypes, and were angry at black patrons of these films.

J.A. Rogers, too, applauded the fine acting of Charles Gilpin in 1921 in the play of *The Emperor Jones* and the acting of Paul Robeson in the film version in 1933, but he objected to the way blacks were portrayed. "The Emperor Jones represents defeat and pessimism, which is not true of the Negro, for in spite of persecutions that would crush many other people, he presses buoyantly on, hoping and working for a better day." He objected to the black ghetto criminality and vice portrayed in the film. It was an insult to hear "the refrain of nigger, nigger, nigger, which runs through the whole piece from beginning to end," complained Rogers. The film was designed to appeal to the prejudices of whites and to stereotype blacks as ghetto riffraff. Rogers scathingly denounced the film: "The play is on the whole but a repetition of the things said by Thomas Dixon, [Mississippi Governor James K.] Vardaman, [South Carolina Governor Ben "Pitchfork"] Tillman and others of a generation ago who harped so much on this single string. These writers and politicians used to boast of their friendliness for Negroes, and unless I am mistaken, so does O'Neill."[21] Moreover, he thought any self-respecting black should refuse to play such roles. Blacks should develop their own films and theaters to counter negative stereotypes.[22] Rogers, too, thought that such plays and films projected the worst traits of blacks. His ambivalence was reflected by praising the black actors' ability but denouncing the roles they portrayed.

Edgar Dale wrote a scholarly article, "The Movies and Race Relations" (1937) and cited other sources that indicated the negative impact ethnic stereotypes had on children and adults. Films reached some seventy million people a week and racial stereotypes were the norm. Blacks were often portrayed as clowns and brutish rapists. Famous black actors such as "Louise Beavers, Stepin Fetchit, Clarence Muse and Hattie McDaniel repeat the same role endlessly—devoted doglike servant, lazy good-for-nothing, meek and happy," he charged. A *March of Time* newsreel caricatured black religion and Father Divine, and fanned the notion that one third of 300,000 black Harlemites were under the spell of a current "voodoo" craze, said Dale.[23] The mass media catered to the wild and exotic in black life and thereby helped to maintain racism and ostracism of blacks as uncouth and uncivilized, and subsequently, unworthy of citizenship rights and respectability.

The radicals did have some impact because the problem became a primary concern of a number of civil-rights groups. A newly organized film consumer group called Associated Film Audiences was organized in 1937—affiliated with twenty organizations such as the Emergency Peace Campaign, American Youth Congress, the League for Industrial Democracy, the National Urban League, and the National Association for the Advancement of Colored People. It published *Film Survey* bimonthly to monitor and protest ethnic stereotypes and cheap thrillers in films. Black protest, however, was hampered because there were only 232 Jim Crow movie houses in the United States. They amounted to only 1/2 percent of all of the seats in the country.[24] Whites, however, had many more theaters to attend, and they featured blacks in "bit" parts that were often negative racial stereotypes.

Despite this problem, blacks organized to protest film stereotypes. The *California Eagle* newspaper in Los Angeles carried a headline on January 20, 1938, which read: "Film Society Is Launched to Aid Protection of Race Dignity in Screen Portrayals." Fay M. Jackson, a studio correspondent and theatrical editor of the *Eagle* and an original member of the Ink Slingers, founded the "Cinema League of Colored Peoples" of Hollywood.

Interracial membership was sought from such world centers as Paris; London; the Gold Coast, West Africa; Trinidad, West Indies; Honolulu; and British Guiana "to raise the status of colored people in films." Earl Dancer of Hollywood originated the idea. He, Fay M. Jackson, attorney Thomas L. Griffith Jr., president of the Los Angeles NAACP and son of the influential minister of the Second Baptist Church in Los Angeles, famous Los Angeles architect Paul R. Williams; John Gray, a graduate in Pedagogy from the Ecole Normal, Paris, France, and an authority on black music; the Rev. S.M. Beane of the Los Angeles Ministerial Alliance; and Charlotta A. Bass, editor of the *California Eagle*, joined this group as charter members.[25] All were influential in black Los Angeles affairs and assumed leadership roles.

Jackson said, "In many cases coming under my observations, Negroes are cast in an inferior light" from ignorance "and lack of" direct cooperation of intelligent blacks. She noted with "disgust" a case in which a "studio bootblack" was consulted by a "production manager" on a serious issue of black history for a film.[26] This was unacceptable and distorted black history. The black educated middle class insisted that it be consulted on the race's history and culture. Hollywood, however, was not about to produce only or largely black documentaries to suit some of its black critics.

Jackson said that informed blacks and their organization intended to serve as a clearing house and censorship board for black history in regard to films. "One of the main objectives of this league will be to serve as a clearing house for the helpful exchange of ideas and facts pertaining to Negro people offered in solution of the motion pictures in which they are cast." She complained that "on the various censorship boards" every race, religion, and political group was represented "but the Negro. Yet, there is as much to defend, we feel, in racial self respect, and in the colored man's contributions to civilization and to the progress of films as in any other phase of organized groups working with the industry."[27] This group's views were fully in line with the ideology laid down by Du Bois.

The *California Eagle* ran an article on March 10, 1938, by Harry Levette, an Ink Slinger, which asked, "Should Negro film heads be branded as 'stooges' of white capitalists?" It was felt that no all-black company had the capacity for continuous output of films. Maceo Sheffield, a black former lieutenant of detectives with the Los Angeles Police Department, made successful films like *Harlem on the Prairie* (1937) with white backers. He complained, however, that "every Negro connected with the production of so-called all-Negro motion picture companies is no more than a stooge fronting for whites for whom the bulk of the profit goes." He was only a "supervisor" in the Juld (often called Jed) Buell Film Company but the names of people like Ralph Cooper and Clarence Brooks and others were used as fronts. Blacks did not have the money for films so they turned to white backers. Sheffield demanded that the "race" support black motion picture producers to solve the problem. Moreover, he complained, "I, for one, was inveigled into one of these companies with pretty promises and a glowing future. I find, now, that it was all poppy-cock and simply a bait to use in the exploitation of our artists and the goodwill of the Negro public at large."[28] In other words, some independent black film companies were a sham and any positive images of blacks were certainly not a result of black autonomy and commitment to uplift the race.

Sheffield invited Eastside blacks to form a "Committee for the Promotion of Colored People in Motion Pictures." Charlotta A. Bass, Fred C. Williams, George Randol (who had made five short films for RKO and advocated black cooperatives for films), Vernon McCalla, Clarence Brooks, Daniel Shaw, Flournoy E. Miller, attorney Walter Gordon Jr., Terry Brown, and Emory Crain joined with Sheffield. They planned to develop "race capital" for black films. Meanwhile, Sheffield signed a five-year contract as Mantan Moreland's manager and joined with Art Wallace in several business ventures.[29] But this group, like others, failed to replace the preeminent position of the NAACP in the struggle against Hollywood's stereotypes.

Raising "race capital" proved to be an uphill battle that bore little fruit. Their role as watchdogs, critics of films' black images, managers of Hollywood's black actors, and employment promoters remained their main function. Many in this group such as Sheffield; Flournoy E. Miller, a comedian who was an important figure (along with Aubrey Lyles and Eubie Blake) in the famous all-black musical *Shuffle Along* that ran on New York's Broadway for a couple of years in the early 1920s; Herb Jeffries, a singer and actor; Spencer Williams Jr.; Connie Harris, who worked in the Paradise Cafe in Yuma, Arizona; and many others who starred in the black film *Harlem on the Prairie* (1937) were "an interesting cross-section of the upper crust of Los Angeles' South Central Avenue (Negro district)," noted a reviewer of the film.[30] They had joined with the Los Angeles NAACP, black professionals, civil-rights activists such as Loren Miller, Charlotta A. Bass, and other black newspaper writers to confront Hollywood and protest the images projected on the screen.

Black critics charged film producers with racism. Earl J. Morris wrote in the *Pittsburgh Courier*, "American Whites, Negroes Being Shoved into Background in Movies by Jewish Film Owners." Earl Dancer wrote in the *California Eagle*, "Hollywood Jews Use Southern Prejudice as Smoke Screen" to deny blacks opportunities and to maintain racial stereotypes.[31] Dancer was quite distraught because he was an ambitious man whose career as a promoter and producer had apparently collapsed. He did master-of-ceremonies work at night clubs in the Los Angeles area, where he managed black entertainers and provided choirs for Hollywood films. Morris charged that "Negroid types like Martha Raye, who are brimming with the Negro's style of song delivery, get the jobs. A Negro is cut out of pictures wherever possible." Moreover, he bitterly charged, "the motion picture and theatrical professions are for the most part controlled by a few Jews." And this "handful of Jews, drunk with power, are stirring up hatred against all the Jewish people." Their racial stereotypes kept the North and South divided by flaming old sectional hatreds. Whenever racial "progress is attempted, these Hollywood producers come forth with a Civil War picture (a reference to *Gone With the Wind*) and undo all the progress that has been made. It is an American tragedy," lamented Morris. He and Dancer approached Aubry Blair, the executive secretary of the Screen Actors Guild, and John Dale, its attorney, for an interview concerning these matters but were told to see Will Hays, president of the Motion Picture Producers and Distributors of America. Thus rebuffed, Morris accused Jewish Hollywood magnates of being "Hollywood Hitlers."[32]

Hollywood, naturally, rebuffed strident critics who sought to restrict its independence in artistic choices or be dictated to in what it should produce. Also, Hollywood understood, apparently, that some blacks were attempting to get employment for themselves under the cover of being critics. Earl Dancer was an obvious example of this type. He had for years been trying to maneuver himself into a position as a manager of black talent and conduit into the Hollywood film pipeline. Also, he wanted to write and direct films, especially his film or documentary on Crispus Attucks. This is not say, however, that Dancer was not sincerely concerned with the eradication of negative stereotypes.

Earl Dancer charged that "Hollywood Jews Use Southern Prejudice as Smoke Screen" in order to deny blacks roles other than as "Uncle Toms and Topsys." He said the white South accepted black entertainers and film stars without prejudice. To say otherwise "is the most vicious lie ever perpetrated." For example, "the white South has received Cab Calloway in Dallas, Texas, where 10,000 whites and blacks attended together a concert and dance. This same South applauded Ethel Waters in an all-white production, *As Thousands Cheer*."[33] The South recognized Jesse Owens, Marian Anderson, and Roland Hayes, he claimed. Jobs and recognition of black talent were at stake, he said. "This is an economic problem, one [against] which no Negro can sit idly by and not raise a real protest. The Hollywood Jews want everything for the Jews. We, the Negro race, who contribute $50,000,000 or more annually to the motion picture industry, demand something from Hollywood for the Negro actors." If necessary, blacks should boycott every Hollywood film until their demands were met, Dancer said.[34]

Dancer and other blacks in Los Angeles promoted the same program, "Don't Buy Where You Can't Work," that Chicago and Harlem blacks had adopted earlier to win substantial gains in jobs, recognition, and respect from white employers. Dancer overstated his case that the South had received black stars. They performed under rigorous segregation rules and often in humiliating circumstances. Because whites patronized some black entertainers did not indicate they were according blacks social equality or equal opportunity. Blacks were also still rigorously segregated in the North and in Harlem social circles and entertainment.

Tensions between blacks and Jews over economics and ideological differences had been building for years. J.A. Rogers, a black Jamaican journalist widely read in the black press, said as early as 1933, "Negroes Suffer More in U.S. than Jews in

Germany." He alleged that Jews received justice but blacks were victims of mobs, lynchings, and shootings. Hitler's claim to racial superiority over other whites "sounds strikingly like the frothings of a Southern cracker," Rogers said. He believed that "Hitler, at his worst, is but a poor imitator of cracker methods" in the United States in repressing blacks.[35] He believed that "the Nazi treatment of the Jew is brutal and unjustified," but, nevertheless, doubted that the truth was coming out of Germany because "most of what is told about Jewish treatment in Germany is propaganda, since the Jews control to a great extent the international press." He thought that Jews, unlike blacks, had enough power to defend themselves. Rogers concluded, "The injustices suffered by the Jew in Germany are insignificant when compared with those inflicted on Aframericans. Yet the Jew's slightest injustice seems far more enormous to him than the Aframerican's greater ones to the Aframericans."[36] In September of 1941, Rogers reversed himself. He still maintained that "we have Hitler here" but "the Hitler in Europe is the worse of the two." Moreover, he believed that "conditions are improving here" in the United States.[37]

W.E.B. Du Bois had written on December 1936 a view contrary to Rogers's 1933 analysis that blacks were treated worse than Jews. Du Bois noted that German prejudice toward Jews was "instinctive." Hitler organized German hatred by use of the state and propaganda. As a result, noted Du Bois, "there has been no tragedy in modern times equal in its awful effects to the fight on the Jew in Germany. It is an attack on civilization, comparable only to such horrors as the Spanish Inquisition and the African slave trade."[38] Du Bois much earlier had recognized the full significance and the completely new factor in race hatred and violence in Germany, a view Rogers finally recognized.

Blacks in the 1930s had launched economic campaigns with the slogan, "Don't Spend Your Money [Buy/Patronize] Where You Can't Work." Some Jewish merchants became a target of this campaign. Even in black communities where they did not dominate the economic activity, Jews had high visibility, and some blacks apparently expected much from the Jews because of their historical suffering at the hands of white Protestants, who had a long history of ethnic chauvinism against both blacks and Jews.

Threats and charges of abuse broke out between blacks

and Jews. Sufi Abdul Hamid, "a black bearded, green uniformed mystic," emerged in Harlem and accused Jews of exploiting blacks. He was the first to advocate in the 1930s the doctrine of job picketing against white employers who did business in black communities but refused to employ blacks. He claimed that he was born in Egypt but admitted he was from Boston (actually, Lowell, Massachusetts) after he was threatened with deportation. He had organized successful boycotts in demanding that Chicago merchants employ blacks, and he had the support of the community. In Harlem, he organized a group called the "Aframerican Federation of Labor." He threatened and picketed white businesses along Harlem's main thoroughfare, the 125th Street. The *Daily News* dubbed him "The Black Hitler" and "The Fuhrer of Harlem" because of his "vitriolic anti-Semitic speeches." In 1934, Hamid was jailed for twenty days for inciting to riot. His activity won "scores of jobs" for blacks. Many of the merchants were Jews, and they were the first to start hiring blacks. Hamid's activities were a contributing cause of the Harlem riot of 1935. He was killed in 1938 when his airplane ran out of gas in flight.[39]

To seize the initiative from Hamid's group, Dr. Adam Clayton Powell Sr. and Dr. William Lloyd Imes organized the Greater New York Coordinating Committee for Employment with Harlem's 300,000 blacks and more than 200 black organizations. They worked out an agreement with the uptown Chamber of Commerce that reserved for blacks one-third of the white-collar jobs in the Harlem and 125th Street area.[40] These gains were impressive, but frightened whites felt that black radicals must be side-stepped in favor of black moderates. Powell and Imes shared the NAACP united front concept against racism. Hamid and other radicals often saw Jews as just another group of selfish white racists. Even Langston Hughes voiced this view.

In response to a continued undercurrent of tensions between blacks and Jews, Powell noted in *New Currents* (1943), that "there is not now, nor has there ever been any pronounced or widespread anti-Semitic feeling among Negroes." He added, "Jews have been great benefactors to Negroes all over America" in many areas of life. Furthermore, the black "is partial to the Jews and has been through the years." A "People's Committee" was organized which included "all of the major white and Negro organizations of a labor, civic, professional, or fraternal character in greater New York" in 1943. The Rev. Ben Richardson, Powell's assistant at the Abyssinian Baptist Church, was elected by the People's Committee "to make a study of concrete ways in which a program of Negro and Jewish cooperation can be established to the mutual benefit of both and to the defeat of local fascist forces who would have it otherwise." Richardson was also the religious editor for the New York *People's Voice* newspaper and wrote two articles, "Negro, Jew United thru History by Persecution" and "Jews Gave the World Wealth," and concluded in one of them that "They're Damned," referring to strident black critics of Jews.[41] Powell and Richardson wanted to maintain a united front of blacks and Jews as minorities fighting against racism at home and abroad. They rejected the apparent racial chauvinism of Rogers and Hamid.

Walter White, sponsored by "the Non-Sectarian Anti-Nazi League," of which Samuel Untermyer was president, spoke over radio station WMCA on "Nazism and the Negro." White said minorities must unite to oppose the inflammation of racial hatreds. He noted that a German paper, *Der Welkamp*, denounced the use of black troops in World War I and that it ran an article titled "Schmeling's Victory a Cultural Achievement," in reference to Joe Louis's defeat by German boxer Max Schmeling.[42] White rejected the black nationalists' separatist tendencies and strident attacks on Jews and recognized the need for allies in the struggle against the rampant racism which had become a crucial factor in mob violence at home and the war in Europe.

In 1938, a black editor in Chicago published a small give-away newspaper called *Dynamite*. His activities resulted in some blacks "staging anti-Jewish campaigns" over ownership of apartments and stores on the Southside, where most blacks lived. The editor made several anti-Jewish speeches at rallies and fought a running editorial war against Jews. Other blacks broke with him because of his intemperate language and threatening behavior, but on the issue of employment a few black extremists emerged in some major cities, Chicago and New York's Harlem. The *Pittsburgh Courier* and the NAACP attacked black mobs in Chicago and New York, charging that their behavior aided Hitlerism.[43]

The *New York Amsterdam News*, however, noted that "anti-

Semitism is regrettable but the Jew, himself, is its author insofar
as it concerns the American Negro. To stop its spread, the Jew
must go beyond written appeals to the Negro leadership and
press and make a decided about-face in his tactics toward the
race." Nevertheless, the June 1938 issue of *The Crisis* hastened
to add that there was no deep-seated or widespread anti-Semitism
among blacks. "Negroes have . . . been puzzled and disturbed
at times over the actions of some Jewish individuals and groups."
It cited cases of outright discrimination and insults to blacks.
"Certain Jewish philanthropists have made substantial
contributions to the financing of programs for Negro advancement
and improvement. . . . But the Jewish middle class (upper class
and lower), the shopkeepers and merchants and the landlords,
in many cases and in many localities, leave much to be desired."
The NAACP, nevertheless, supported the Martin Dies
Committee's investigation of German-inspired anti-Semitism in
the United States.[44]

Langston Hughes charged that "there is a good deal of
anti-Semitism among Negroes in the big American cities,
seemingly because many of the merchants in Negro communities
are Jewish where (as with gentile merchants) higher prices are
charged. . . ." Many Jewish businessmen refused to hire blacks
as clerks and many landlords or their agents exacted higher rents
in black neighborhoods than in white ones, he charged. He added
that many Southern Jews "support just as assiduously as the
majority of white gentile Southerners, the segregation and lynch-
law systems below the Mason-Dixon line." Hughes asked how
whites could justify the fact that "both Jews and Gentiles in
America . . . act strongly like Hitlerian Aryans in many parts of
our staunch democracy—when it comes to colored folks?"[45]
Hughes believed all Jews were not free of racism and
discrimination and exploitation of blacks. He blamed them for
the rise in blacks' resentment toward Jews.

An article in the NAACP's *The Crisis* (October 1939) pointed
out that the Germans justified their treatment of the German
Jews by saying that they were only following the example of the
United States in treatment of national minorities who were viewed
as undesirable. *The Schwartz Korps*, organ of the German secret
police, wrote that: "This solution follows a documented
democratic example." The United States "does not permit [in] its

State citizens with equal rights with a darker hue to sit, much less sleep, next to a white person, even if the white is only a sewage worker and the black a world boxing champion (a reference to Joe Louis) or other national hero. The colored people will be relentlessly driven by an equally colored conductor into their own rolling kraal." The NAACP again called for a united front of national minorities.[46] The Jewish press launched a "systematic campaign to improve relationships between Negroes and Jews" after members of the Jewish press met with black organizations.[47] Some felt a united front should be developed or maintained in the struggle against racism.

These tensions over Jewish economic advantages in black communities and employment carried over into Hollywood where the "Big Eight" film producers were largely owned and run by former Eastern European Jews. Black critics also promoted a "Don't Buy Where You Can't Work" campaign against Hollywood for both its employment practices and negative racial stereotype images. Earl Dancer, J.A. Rogers, and many Los Angeles radicals, among others, were leaders of this campaign.

J.A. Rogers wrote a scathing critique of Hollywood in May 1937. The headline read: "Rogers Attacks Anti-Negro Propaganda of Movie Industry: Says Hollywood Is Unfair, Uses Race in Effort to Belittle." He charged that "in the matter of anti-Negro propaganda Hollywood took the lead with *Birth of a Nation* and has kept ahead ever since." Moreover, "whilst the Negro is working hard to win the esteem of white America, Hollywood is working as hard to undo it. Shamelessly it continues its campaign of belittlement." Rogers believed this was true despite the fact that "Hollywood has a vast corps of research historians."[48] He asked some of his white friends what they thought of this state of affairs. One, who was Jewish, said, "I am ashamed to think that some of these motion picture magnates are Jewish. They would not dare to malign Jews like that. The Jewish actor who played such roles would be ostracized by his people. Have Negroes no self-respect?" Rogers advised blacks to boycott theaters that showed anti-black stereotype films.[49] He did not think that a black-Jewish united front against racism was possible as long as Hollywood Jewish film moguls produced, in his view, anti-black films, fanning the flames of racial hatred against blacks.

The *Chicago Defender* ran an editorial in April of 1940

boasting about the success of the Chicago "Don't Spend Your Money Where You Can't Work" consumer boycott campaign led by A.C. McNeal and Joseph Bibb. It noted that the movement was not immediately imitated but had eventually led to "pickets and protests for jobs in white downtowns. Now students at black colleges are debating the new tactics." It added, "Time after time Race citizens have found the boycott technique successful in opening jobs that had long been closed." Finally, "again the picket lines have appeared before motion picture houses in efforts to build sentiment against other discriminatory practices."[50] The protest at film theaters apparently related to employment since there was no mention of anti-black stereotypes in the editorial.

Earl Dancer, along with Los Angeles radicals and writers for the *Pittsburgh Courier*, emerged as a leader of the protest movement in Los Angeles against Hollywood. Dancer sought to use the movement to advance his personal ambitions in entertainment and Hollywood. Apparently, he became quite frustrated in his own drive to break into film producing, script writing, and directing. He fervently believed that his own career had been held in check by anti-black racism rather than a lack of competency in some areas, like script writing. His script on Crispus Attucks, the famous black American of Revolutionary War fame, for example, was rejected by Hollywood.

Dancer had risen to fame as Ethel Waters's manager in the 1920s. He kept telling her "that you oughta go on the white time." That is, cross over from entertaining blacks to whites in order to perform in the big clubs and earn more money. Waters recalled, "Earl Dancer pushed me into the white time." She said, "For a long time Earl Dancer had wanted to be a producer." He told her, "Someday, you will see in lights the words, 'Earl Dancer presents. . . .' Oh, if I could only get hold of a backer." Waters told him he had no material or money for a show. Finally, Otto H. Kahn, a Wall Street banker and philanthropist who in years past had given Mike Gold, a Communist, $10,000 for a proletarian theater in Greenwich Village in New York and had invited the world-famous black tenor Roland Hayes to his New York home to sing for him and guests, fronted $10,000 and Dancer took a tab show called *Miss Calico*, embellished it, and renamed it *Africana* (Dancer tried to revive it in 1943 and it was a dismal failure). It opened at Daly's Sixty-third Street Theatre on New York's

Broadway. Waters claimed it was well received there and on the road. The owner of Daly's took Dancer and Waters to court for breach of contract and to prevent their moving the play to the National Theatre on West Forty-first Street.[51]

Dancer put on another show at the Apollo Theater for Jack Schiffman who said Dancer was "a competent manager and brilliant producer." The show featured Edith Wilson and Earl "Snakehips" Tucker. Dancer fled with the money without paying the cast. Schiffman politely refused to deal with him again.[52] Dancer moved to Hollywood, where he attempted to rebuild his reputation and start a new career. He flayed Hollywood Jews because he felt they perpetuated negative stereotypes that restricted black, and his, attempts to break into the "white time."

Increasingly, blacks from every part of the nation and New York especially, seeking fame and fortune, came to Los Angeles. In 1931 Buck Clayton, a jazz trumpeter, arrived. Eddie Beal played with him. In 1934 Clayton performed with the Mills Brothers at the Paramount Theatre on Sixth Street in downtown Los Angeles. He formed his own group called "Buck Clayton and His Harlem Gentlemen." Beal said, "We dressed up, with high hats and so on" imitating the high class style of the Cotton Club and New York blacks. Moreover, recalled Beal, "We were negotiating to do a motion picture, just as a sideline, and it didn't work because they had taken a bunch of white musicians and put blackface on them. I was then backing a guy named Earl Dancer, who was strictly a showman and not a musician. . . ."[53] This rebuff was a bitter blow to Dancer's ambitions as a promoter who attempted to push blacks into Hollywood's film industry.

Dancer still made headway. He managed a black choir that sang and performed in a number of motion pictures. He managed Jeni LeGon who came from Chicago, and as her agent negotiated one of the first major multi-film contracts for a black actor with M-G-M for the fantastic sum of $1,500 a week. In late 1934, during a slack period, he broke her M-G-M contract and signed her in London with C.B. Cochrane, an English producer, to perform in the production *Follow the Sun*, which ran for six months. Upon her return in late 1936, LeGon was able to sign contracts with Universal Studio and others for three or four films.[54] LeGon continued to appear in numerous Hollywood films in the years after. Dancer, despite his work in Hollywood, remained a strident critic of Hollywood's film producers whom he blamed for negative racial patterns of employment and stereotypes for blacks. As Hollywood work dried up, he turned into a disappointed and bitter critic of Hollywood's Jewish moguls.

Miss Joyce Dancer, a native of Los Angeles and the niece of Earl Dancer, was a student of modern dance who was discovered by Artie Mason Carter, one of the founders of the Hollywood Bowl. She attempted to enroll in Mills College of the Dance in July of 1938 but was rejected "because of her color." An outraged *California Eagle* editorial carried a huge picture of Joyce Dancer with the caption, "What Nerve, Mr. Jim Crow; What Nerve!" It noted that Earl Dancer was the *Eagle's* theatrical editor and he and the paper obviously took the rebuff as a personal affront. Joyce Dancer enrolled in a dance school in Detroit.[55] Dancer and his niece were bitter over their rebuffs in Los Angeles and Hollywood. Personal, family, and group racial rejections resulted in Earl Dancer's bitter criticisms of the Hollywood entertainment industry and its Jewish moguls in his quest for recognition and employment.

Many black supporters and beneficiaries of Dancer's management, promotion, and organizational skills agreed that he also had an uncanny ability to undo himself and wreck his own achievements. He often gambled at the racetrack and played dice at illegal Central Avenue joints and lost his and "other people's money," charged Mae Alice Harvey and Alfred LeGon. Dancer gained a reputation "as a spendthrift," said LeGon. He made a lot of money and spent or gambled it away.[56] Apparently, he attacked Hollywood moguls for real wrongs against the black race as well as attempting to recoup gambling losses to pay off his debts and prove to blacks that he could deliver on his promises as an experienced producer, promoter, and manager.

Isadora Smith, writing in the *Pittsburgh Courier*, protested Broadway's refusal to make a film with an all-star cast of blacks and Europeans with Paul Robeson because the "Managers Believe PIC(ture) Shows Too Much Racial Equality." *Big Fella* was a hit in England and broke all attendance records in London. But when Frank Schiffman of the Apollo Theatre tried strenuously to bring the show to the United States, get the rights to it, and distribute it throughout the country because he thought every black American should see it, he was unsuccessful.[57] Integrated shows with a hint of social equality were offensive to racist whites in every section of the nation. It seemed theater operators thought *Big Fella* was too advanced for race conscious viewers.

When Margaret Mitchell's book, *Gone With the Wind*, sold for an unprecedented $50,000 for a first publication and was immediately accepted for filming, the NAACP reacted strongly. The subject had been considered taboo by Hollywood because the Civil War and race had been a sensitive issue since the continuous battle waged by blacks and liberal whites against the showing of *The Birth of a Nation*. The NAACP said that unless some scenes depicting blacks in Mitchell's film version were changed, blacks would boycott and picket the film. Many whites, however, fretted over the casting, and sent letters making suggestions and warnings not to tamper with the book when translating it to film. Southerners were jubilant over the impending film about their region and the hallowed "Lost Cause."[58]

George S. Schuyler wrote a review of the book for *The Crisis* in 1937. He charged, "Margaret Mitchell's 1037-page novel may be a Pulitzer Prize Winner to white America but it is just another Rebel propaganda tract to the colored citizen who knows our national history and knows the South." It romanticized the slaves. "It is also the South of a prize crew of Uncle Tom house servants who denounce freedom and identify themselves with the Confederacy and what it stands for. They are faithful old dogs ready to die for 'Ole Massa.'" He concluded, "But it is eminently readable, bolsters [the] southern white ego, is an effective argument against according the Negro his citizenship rights and privileges and sings Hallelujah for white supremacy."[59] Schuyler, like Loren Miller and other blacks and some whites, deeply resented epic films which distorted history and portrayed blacks as happy and carefree slaves.

Gone With the Wind's world premiere in Atlanta on December 15, 1939, at the Grand Theatre was made a special holiday by Governor Ed Rivers, the press reported. Mayor William Hartsfield held a three-day festival with costumes and the city was decked out with "Christmas and the Confederacy combined in the street decorations." People lined the streets for seven miles listening to "Dixie" while viewing the arrival of Clark Gable and Vivien Leigh and other notables who stayed "at Atlanta's

hallowed Georgian Terrace Hotel." The film won an
unprecedented ten Oscars with Vivien Leigh as best actress and
Hattie McDaniel as the best supporting actress and the first black
ever to win an Oscar.[60] The South and the nation loved the
romanticized Southern plantation civilization and its loyal slave
retainers. Such films were entertaining and drew large crowds
to the theaters. McDaniel's Oscar held up the romantic image of
the loyal Black Mammy that white Southern women earlier had
sought to venerate with a monument movement in Washington,
D.C., but which failed because of strident opposition by blacks
who saw it as a pro-slavery monument.

Dan Burley in 1940 attacked the film in the *New York
Amsterdam News*: "Gone With the Wind: Subtle Propaganda of
Anti-Negro Film Told by Reviewer." Burley charged that "at
once it tells every Negro in this country that he is still a chattel
slave in the eyes of his former masters, and at the same time tries
to convert to this viewpoint through various devices the millions
of the various races who will see it."[61] He, too, felt that plantation
epics injured blacks' reputation and promoted stereotypes of the
happy slaves. *The Birth of a Nation* (1915) had left a bitter legacy
to blacks concerned about their public image because it
encouraged vicious historical distortions and undergirded legal
racial authoritarianism. *Gone With the Wind* was seen as another
racist plantation epic.

David Selznick, the producer of the film, thought otherwise
and defended his film in the press during the controversy
preceding its release. "I personally feel quite strongly that we
should cut out the Klan entirely." Moreover, he stated, "I, for
one, have no desire to produce any anti-Negro film either." He
was well aware of the black reaction to Griffith's epic. "A year
or so ago I refused to consider remaking 'The Birth of a Nation',
largely for this reason." He wrote a letter to *Film Survey* April
2, 1937, that said, "The treatment of the Negro characters will
be with the utmost respect for this race [and] with the greatest
concern for its sensibilities."[62] However, some blacks resented
any slavery or plantation epics that appeared to romanticize
slavery, the plantation, and the South, no matter how
sympathetically or dignified blacks were portrayed or however
much the role of the Klan was down-played.

Blacks feared again that white and world public opinion

was being marshaled against them and that they were being held up to public ridicule. The Ku Klux Klan had been reborn in Atlanta in 1915 with David Griffith's epic film by an inspired William Joseph Simmons and Atlanta became the "Imperial City" that exercised a disproportionate share of power in national Klan affairs.[63] Blacks, understandably, were apprehensive over the grand celebration for *Gone With the Wind* in Atlanta and throughout the nation because it generated the same type of national and Southern hoopla that *The Birth of a Nation* had in 1915. Some felt that this resulted in more national racial repression. Blacks were well aware of the impact films had on people, public policy, and race relations. White citizens, artists, and public officials also were cognizant of the power of films. Southerners promoted and supported films—especially Civil War, Reconstruction, and old plantation epics—that viewed their area and culture favorably.

Walter White of the NAACP was concerned with the images of blacks projected by Hollywood. Wendell Willkie, the Republican Party candidate for President in 1940, had made strong overtures to White to back his candidacy. White refused, pointing out that the NAACP was a non-partisan organization. Willkie was a lawyer, the chairman of the board of Twentieth Century-Fox, a special counsel to the NAACP, and had represented the motion picture industry in the Senate hearings in 1940 that investigated its alleged role in propaganda encouraging the United States to join the war in Europe. He and White discussed blacks and Hollywood at a luncheon in New York City. Said White, "I pointed out that the most widely circulated medium yet devised to reach the minds and emotions of people all over America and the world was perpetuating and spreading dangerous and harmful stereotypes of the Negro." Willkie replied, "Let's go out to Hollywood and talk with the more intelligent people in the industry to see what can be done to change this situation."[64] The portrayal of blacks on the screen became a priority with White and the NAACP as directly related to civil rights and black progress.

Willkie was invited to speak before the Annual Award Dinner of the Motion Picture Academy at which the Oscars were awarded. He brought White along with him to Los Angeles. They met with Walter Wanger and Darryl Zanuck of Twentieth

Century-Fox and discussed how to influence producers, writers, directors, and actors about the "justice of picturing the Negro as a normal human being instead of as a monstrosity." Wanger was "in the forefront of Hollywood's crusade for social consciousness" and was "Hollywood's No. 1 anti-dictator producer by making *Blockade*," a film about the Spanish Civil War and fascism, reported *Time* magazine.[65] He was receptive to Willkie's and White's agenda. The presence of White and Willkie at the Biltmore Bowl dining room, which was packed to capacity, put Hollywood on notice to correct racial stereotypes.

In 1942, at the Thirty-first Annual Conference of the NAACP in Los Angeles, Willkie gave the closing address. He told blacks that the war then raging was not racial because China was an ally and Japan an enemy. It was a war between democratic and authoritarian societies. He deplored America's domestic "race imperialism" against blacks. Among the attendees were Clarence Muse, a black actor; Hollywood producer Walter Wanger, who met and spoke with A. Philip Randolph, the black leader of the "March on Washington Movement" for racial democracy; actor Walter Houston; film star and Oscar winner Hattie McDaniel; and film star Joan Bennett. Willkie declared, "We will not abandon our fight for racial justice during the war." It was at this conference that Willkie and White became familiar with the full range of black grievances, including those of the more strident critics within the black ranks who charged Jewish indifference to the image of blacks projected by Hollywood.[66]

Walter Wanger and Darryl Zanuck used the occasion to host White and Willkie at the plush Cafe de Paris on the Twentieth Century-Fox lot. At that luncheon it was reported in the press that "one of the most select groups of producers, writers, directors, and heads of the important motion picture guilds ever assembled in the moving picture capital" were present. Wanger introduced White to make the opening statement. White said the power of the motion picture was awesome and that he knew Southern state boards of censorship demanded that blacks be depicted only as comic and menial characters. He deplored Hollywood's "slavish following of these stereotypes" because they feared the loss of patrons and money. Blacks and darker races around the world resented Hollywood's "racial caricatures." What is more, "I urge Hollywood to have courage enough to shake off its fears and taboos and to depict the Negro in films as a normal human being and an integral part of the life of America and the world."[67] In other words, White said, stop the stereotypes and comic roles accorded blacks as typical reflections of black life and behavior, show them as normal human beings.

Willkie spoke next. He said that on his "recent world tour" he had discovered that the darker races keenly resented Hollywood's depiction of them. Moreover, many Hollywood people belonged to groups that were "the target of Hitler" and that "they should be the last to be guilty of doing to another minority the things which had been done to them." White noted that Willkie's comments were so sensitive that "few men could have made this latter statement without giving offense." Willkie, however, was roundly cheered.[68] Willkie and White bolstered the charges that had been made by J.A. Rogers, Loren Miller, and others that racial stereotypes had a harmful impact at home and abroad in encouraging warmongers who used race to murder perceived enemies and attack certain ethnic groups.

Willkie had won Hollywood's admiration in 1940 with his deft defense of Hollywood producers and writers in Senate hearings investigating alleged pro-war propaganda in the motion picture industry believed aimed at getting the United States involved in the war because Jews from conquered countries dominated the film industry. He was especially well liked by those who had been direct targets of the investigation. Willkie was chosen unanimously to receive the annual silver cup given by the Jewish War Veterans of the United States at their mid-year conference in Louisville, Kentucky, in February 1941 for his "outstanding example in leadership in the promotion of Americanism and democracy."[69] Willkie's reputation and credentials were impeccable in Hollywood circles.

In March he reminded Jews that "wherever Hitler moves in, the first victims, the first to suffer, are the Jews." Moreover, "You must remember that Hitler is the enemy of all progressive elements in the world and the destructive force endeavoring to annihilate all liberal forces. He is the arch enemy of democracy and liberty." He added, "Jews are known the world over for their faith in the Bible, for their spirituality, for their love of peace and their hate of wrong and ruthlessness. They are fanatical advocates of liberty. This is really one of the most important

reasons why Hitler considers the Jews in particular as the enemies
of Nazi ruthlessness. Hitler's desire is to destroy all the Jews of
the world."[70] Willkie made it clear that stereotypes injured Jews
and Hitler's murderous program was an example of how the
German people were whipped into war hatred and hysteria over
racist stereotypes, largely directed at Jews. His reasoning and
facts were unassailable and made a deep impact on his audience.

A large portion of the audience stayed after the luncheon
to ask questions to try to determine what they could do to
implement White's and Willkie's proposals to destroy anti-black
stereotypes. A few said their errors had been "of the head rather
than of the heart, and arose from the lack of unbiased and
authoritative sources of information." White said, "Two producers
suggested that the NAACP establish a Hollywood bureau for
which the funds would be contributed by producers." He and
Willkie were cautious and thought that "he who pays the piper
calls the tune." Nevertheless, for the future, said White, "it is still
the hope of the NAACP to establish an independent Hollywood
bureau so competently and objectively conducted as to make it
influential in changing the movie stereotypes of Negroes which
influence scores of millions of human beings all over the earth."[71]
White wanted to be sure that he could remain an outside critic
and not be charged with making a deal with Hollywood moguls
because black radicals were already suspicious of him and the
effectiveness of the NAACP after the organization had failed to
mobilize a mass boycott of Hollywood films.

White and Willkie found an abundance of evidence from
their Hollywood contacts that "constantly" proved how
Hollywood was intimidated into depicting racial stereotypes.
There was "evidence of the terrifying power to intimidate
Hollywood which a few people possessed," said White.
"Repeatedly producers told us frankly that they dared not risk
offending boards of censorship in Southern states." He was told
that one man controlled five Southern states and he "belligerently
objected to any Negroes in moving picture films unless they
played roles in conformity with his own prejudices." White noted,
however, that these five states generated only 1.25 percent of the
estimated income from any pictures made in Hollywood.[72] Still,
film producers' sales departments were sensitive to the racist
feelings and pressures from the South which rejected any hint

of racial equality in films. White did not believe this, and the evidence available to him did not give full credibility to the exaggerated fears of Hollywood moguls. Of course, Hollywood was under tremendous political and social pressures by interest groups hostile to its artistic freedom. This included the South and its theaters and viewers as well as a nation still committed to racial authoritarianism which rigidly circumscribed blacks in every area of life, including the arts.

The South did have some influence over films and Hollywood. Despite the modest success of the film *The Green Pastures* in 1935 with its all-black cast, two sequels were squashed because of objections from the South. Joseph I. Breen of the Motion Picture Producers and Distributors of America told the film company RKO that "you may want to give some further thought to these scenes before actually shooting them. It is certain that audiences in the South will not like such scenes, and your studio is likely to be deluged with letters of protest." White obviously was not completely impressed with the Hollywood producers' explanation for the prevalence of racial stereotypes in films. Sales departments, however, were intimidated and counseled against radical changes. White nevertheless pressured Hollywood to defy the South.[73] Hollywood producers were aware that their actions could result in powerful political repercussions such as the recent Senate hearings that threatened to destroy alleged Jewish domination and manipulation of films for their selfish ends. Blacks, too, had developed a tradition of criticism of Hollywood movies that persisted and reached a watershed in 1942 with the NAACP's Walter White and Hollywood moguls.

The black press reported the meetings of Wilkie, White, and Hollywood moguls and their deliberations. They agreed to democracy on the screen "by correcting the misinformation which is the basis of the entire problem of the Negro race. By avoiding the perpetuation of the stereotypes and broadening the treatment, you can lessen the load of misunderstanding from which the Negro is suffering," said the *Pittsburgh Courier*.[74] Jack Warner of Warner Brothers Pictures said his latest film, *In This Our Life*, gave blacks positive roles, and "we have several other films in which we will definitely portray the Negro the same as any other human being is portrayed." Fred W. Beetson, executive vice president of the Association of Motion Pictures Producers, said,

"I feel every producer who was at the meeting was greatly impressed and will undoubtedly find ways and means of helping to put into effect some of the suggestions offered." Sidney Buchman of the Screen Writers' Guild added, "I have taken the matter deeply to heart and shall act in every way possible to further this vital education." A.L. Litchman, vice president of M-G-M, chimed in: "I am thoroughly in accord with the efforts being made for the Negroes. I will do my utmost in whatever way I can in helping this cause. I think the program is a very intelligent one." Even Will Hays, president of the Motion Picture Producers and Distributors of America, spoke up. "I agree completely with your outline of procedure." Samuel Goldwyn and Harry M. Warner supported the new program. Sal Lesser of Principal Artists Productions supported the program as well, and film writers were instructed to follow it.[75] Some of Hollywood's moguls saw the need for a new departure in how they portrayed blacks.

White issued a manifesto that he apparently hoped would quiet such strident black critics of Hollywood as Charlotta A. Bass, Earl Dancer, Dan Burley, Maceo Sheffield, Fay M. Jackson, attorney Thomas L. Griffith, and Earl Morris of the *Pittsburgh Courier*. He dedicated his manifesto "to the Negro public, particularly in Los Angeles," and he published another pamphlet, "Race—A Basic Issue in This War." Both were couched in language suggesting that the new roles were part of the war effort.[76] Indeed, the Office of War Information (OWI) intervened in Hollywood to build morale and participation by persuading Hollywood film producers, thus reducing blacks' criticism and protest. Walter Wanger wrote the Office of War Information's domestic director, Gardner Cowles Jr., in the summer of 1942 that "the American film is our most important weapon as no country has developed its film industry to compete with ours." He boasted that film could reach the illiterate and teach and train with a minimum of difficulties. He was merely restating a position he had published in 1939 entitled "120,000 American Ambassadors" in which he pointed out that there were "50,025 theaters wired for sound" abroad for which and the United States supplied 600 pictures a year at 200 prints each or 120,000. This had a tremendous influence on people abroad. Despite nudging and pioneering efforts, by 1945 the OWI had not been very successful in erasing black stereotypes.[77] New patterns had been established and new opportunities, over time, did emerge.

Walter Wanger supplied evidence as to why Hollywood did not completely erase stereotypes. Domestic and foreign critics constantly attacked Hollywood and its productions. As a result, "Hollywood leadership, due to its tremendous preoccupation in actual picture-making, has retreated too far before the winds, and imagined winds, of public opinion. The time has come to say to pressure-group minorities: 'Go fuss at someone else. We are going to make strong pictures, and let the public judge them and us.'"[78] Hollywood film moguls, therefore, were ambivalent about critics in general and sought to accommodate them, but they refused to be intimidated or dictated to. Then, too, many blacks and whites were not in agreement on what constituted stereotypes. Many wanted to work, and so-called stereotype roles were some actors' stock-in-trade. Some blacks believed that so-called stereotype roles had reached a laudable art form and should be respected as such.

In May 1942 nine blacks were named to the Hollywood Victory Committee to promote pro-war enthusiasm and participation. They were Hattie McDaniel, Leigh Whipper, Eddie Anderson, Louise Beavers, Ben Carter, Fayard Nicholas, Lillian Randolph, Nichodemus Stewart, Mantan Moreland, and Wonderful Smith. None of the black radicals was part of this group. Blacks were, as in the Harlem Renaissance, divided into several factions. In the film industry, some blacks wanted merely to work; others wanted positive roles and opportunities for social mobility in the industry itself as producers, directors, and filmmakers. Edward Arnold of the Screen Actors Guild spoke to the black members of the committee at McDaniel's home in an effort to include blacks and build their morale.[79] This group tended to get more film jobs and often so-called stereotype characters were their stock-in-trade. The radicals excluded from their inner circle were critical of this group and the roles they played, which probably explains why they were excluded.

The blacks on the Hollywood Victory Committee reminded Arnold that White had told Hollywood film magnates that stereotypes not only injured blacks but "colored peoples throughout the world, as it constantly holds the Negro up to ridicule and disparagement." Hattie McDaniel said that blacks had made "tremendous progress in the film industry down through the years" and "we will continue to make more. It takes time, and I don't believe that we will gain by rushing or attacking to force studios to do anything they are not readily inclined to do." Mantan Moreland added, "Let's quit acting like clowns on the streets and they'll soon stop showing us as such." Ben Carter thought things were on the upswing for blacks in Hollywood. He played a cook (in the film *Crash Dive*) as just one of the crew on a submarine at a time when blacks were excluded or rigidly segregated in the Navy, especially in regard to close-quarter living arrangements. He agreed that changes were needed, especially from the comedian roles so many blacks played.[80] Again, many blacks were critical of their own group's public behavior and there was no consensus on what constituted negative black roles.

Los Angeles's black cinema radicals and critics did not agree with the blacks on the Hollywood Victory Committee. Things were not changing rapidly or dramatically enough to suit them. The Los Angeles *Sentinel*'s editor, Leon Washington, threatened to march on theaters that showed films with black stereotypes. He charged that these images caused mayhem and instigated murder against blacks. He attacked the nine blacks on the Hollywood Victory Committee for their conservatism and defense of black stereotype roles. "If degrading pictures such as *Cabin in the Sky*, *Porgy and Bess*," were made, he would march on the theaters in protest. "Our fight is to broaden the scope afforded the Negro actor. Negro actors of every type and hue must be used in every scene of democratic life. Hollywood's answer in the past has been to give employment to large numbers of Negroes through such 'Uncle Tom' pictures as *Green Pastures*, *Hearts in Dixie*, so that the employed Negroes would use pressure to hush up the militant Negroes. Despite our protests, Hollywood continues to merrily shove us around."[81] Washington considered the new departure in Hollywood as more Uncle Tom roles, which were a form of bribery by employment to divide the employed blacks against the unemployed. He thought nothing had changed as how blacks were to be depicted.

Billy Rowe of the *Pittsburgh Courier* thought Hollywood was making dramatic changes. "On the less belligerent home front in the professions to which these pages are dedicated, talented artists went beyond discrimination and prejudice to achieve great and lasting things. Among them, Lena Horne opened the way for our beautiful girls in Hollywood and smashed the bars against our performers in the swank Cafe Lounge of the Savoy-Plaza Hotel." Moreover, he praised Warner Brothers for its release of the film *In This Our Life,* in which Ernest Anderson won fame. Anderson's career did not lead anywhere despite Rowe's claim that he had won "fame." The producer, Arthur Freed of M-G-M, Rowe noted, had "disregarded the voices of prejudice and is bringing *Cabin in the Sky* to the screen."[82] The blacks could not expected to mobilize the black press either for a mass boycott of Hollywood films with such writers as Rowe in support of the White, Willkie, Wanger, and Hollywood accords. Again the Los Angeles black radicals were left fuming on the sidelines.

By this time, Billy Rowe, Walter White, and the blacks on the Hollywood Victory Committee were now squarely pitted against the Los Angeles radicals because the former saw progress while the latter did not. Rowe and White had a huge stake in the new departure. Rowe made his living reporting on and promoting black entertainment and artists. It sold papers in the black community, which often admired and cheered on these artists because of the glamour surrounding their lives and the magic of the silver screen. Blacks in film were considered successful and respected. Nevertheless, White was under pressure to produce results. He was an old Harlem Renaissance man who understood the role of blacks in the arts and how blacks' civil rights and public image were affected by the mass media. Plus, some individuals and the Chicago NAACP threatened revolt.

Billy Rowe wrote in January 1943, "Tinsel City Seems Ready to Receive Our Best Artists" (referring to the black New Yorkers who some Los Angeles blacks felt were threatening to push them to the sidelines). He felt euphoric because he believed "that '43 should find the race coming into its own in Hollywood." Moreover, "because of it, the race is slowly coming into its own on several fronts. Hollywood, no exception to the rule, has spiced this desire with action."[83] He boasted, "Bringing democracy to the screen, the film industry seems well on its way towards full integration of the great talent that is to be found among Negroes in the world of incandescent glare."[84] He, like Walter White, was persuaded that the new roles for blacks in Hollywood were part of the war effort to raise black morale and acceptance of the Double V program, the one that sought to have racial democracy and pluralism here and abroad as part of the war goals. Powerful groups like the Hollywood Victory Committee and the Washington-based Office of War Information were taking steps to include blacks in their mobilization for the war. The *Pittsburgh Courier*, as a founder and enthusiastic supporter of the black Double V, had a huge stake in the success of this new venture. Black moderates like White and the black Hollywood Victory Committee group now had institutional support for their own program and goals in Hollywood and Washington.

Rowe noted with pleasure, "Eastern Performers Start Western Trek for 20th Century-Fox Film." Bill Robinson, Lena Horne, Cab Calloway, Katherine Dunham, Fats Waller, Dooley Wilson, and others left New York for Hollywood. They were to star in *Stormy Weather* and *Cabin in the Sky*, among other films. Hy Kraft, who wrote one of the films' scenarios, said those stars' performances would make an "outstanding contribution of the race to entertainment."[85] Leigh Whipper, a member of the Hollywood Victory Committee's black group, said the film industry was large enough for all and blacks should stick together. He was not happy at the infighting between the two black factions. "The actors can change the roles given them on the screen by just speaking up." He noted, for example, that "Rochester" (black actor and comic Eddie Anderson) in the film, *Meanest Man in Town*, starring Jack Benny, "got the star to take out a line that would have hurt the race's feelings."[86] These were small victories, yet blacks who protested roles feared they might not get work.

The Los Angeles faction tended to be more Victorian and wanted genteel black characters—an old Du Boisian position. White and Rowe stood to gain from the impending changes because they had considerable influence with black New York artists who, like whites, had been making the steady trek to Hollywood to star in films. With *Cabin in the Sky* and *Stormy Weather* and many other films scheduled for production, New York artists would star and overshadow Los Angeles blacks who, naturally, resented this New York-led hegemony. They responded with rigorous artistic criticism and a defense of genteel imagery over plantation and cabaret cultural models that *Cabin in the Sky* and *Stormy Weather* were sure to project. Los Angeles blacks not only demanded more employment, but insisted on black directors, writers, and producers. They criticized blacks who they believed had sold out their principles for employment opportunities—especially if those opportunities were in demeaning roles that in their view injured the race.

The *Pittsburgh Courier* boasted, "200 Race Artists Working in Film" at Twentieth Century-Fox—the largest number employed by the company—on *Stormy Weather* based on the life of tap dancer Bill "Bojangles" Robinson. It was pleased to note that *Stormy Weather* is "a cavalcade of Negro music and . . . is to be the greatest all-colored cast picture ever produced in Hollywood." Edward W. Bailey, president of Musicians' Local No. 767, the segregated all-black musicians A.F.L. branch, said the film portrayed black life as it was, that prejudice caused divisions over complexion among blacks.[87] He revealed the undercurrents among blacks who squabbled over jobs and roles while Hollywood mobilized to produce a series of all-black musicals and parts in regular films.

The *Pittsburgh Courier* noted again the NAACP's approval of Hollywood's new direction as a result of the 1942 gentlemen's understanding with Walter Wanger and Darryl Zanuck and others in Hollywood with the press title, "Our Role in Movies Better, NAACP Notes."[88] Actually, Edward Bailey, Billy Rowe, and Leigh Whipper were trying to quiet fears among some blacks—especially the Los Angeles faction—that they would be left out or get only minor roles in the batch of impending new major films featuring New York's black stars who had won fame in cabarets and in the recording industry. They feared that divisions over what constituted stereotype roles and films, and over the impact of light- and dark-skin color jealousies among blacks within the film colony, might stall, if not jeopardize, the whole enterprise. They wanted to respond with unity to this unprecedented show of goodwill by Hollywood producers.

Hollywood films with major and minor black characters meant employment for all. Stereotype roles, plantation nostalgia, urban musical jubilees, and jive films that portrayed blacks in an unfavorable light would be gradually phased out. Then, too, the old unresolved Harlem Renaissance art and propaganda debate over what actually constituted stereotypes versus reality and balanced portrayals of blacks waxed hot in these divisions as well. The Los Angeles radicals, led for the moment by *Sentinel* editor Leon Washington, threatened to boycott the Hollywood productions starring New York's old Cotton Club black entertainers.

Los Angeles blacks, Earl Dancer with his Crispus Attucks hero film script, Maceo Sheffield as a promoter and producer, and their organizations, were superseded by the New York blacks led by Walter White, who deftly promoted a new departure and New York blacks' cultural expansionism and hegemony. Los Angeles's black radicals deeply resented this invasion but could not directly attack White, the NAACP, and the nationally famous black entertainers. Loren Miller had done so in an article to no effect. Leon Washington threatened a mass boycott of Hollywood films which never materialized. The Chicago branch threatened and pleaded for more militant tactics to no avail. Meanwhile, White and Rowe built up a consensus to work with Hollywood moguls, put as many blacks to work as possible, and to work within the system. They were not about to employ a radical labor-type strike strategy used by the Congress of Industrial Organizations. This was the model the radicals had in mind. All black artists wanted to work; some without stereotype roles and others with any roles.

Los Angeles blacks, failing to mount a mass boycott, fought Hollywood and New York blacks led by Walter White by retrenchment into militant ideological art standards that had been established by Du Bois, and with the addition of labor strike methods. They attacked the studio owners for their alleged duplicity and theater operators with threats of boycotts. Lacking influence, they were contemptuous of black actors who acted stereotype roles and black audiences who patronized the theaters and applauded. The radicals never built an organization to carry out their threats to boycott Hollywood. Agitation and criticism remained their main weapons.

Los Angeles blacks had good reason to be apprehensive over White's hegemony in the fight over Hollywood producers' imagery of blacks in films. Mayor Fiorello H. La Guardia of New York City launched a major campaign to lure the film industry back to New York. He visited the studio plant of Walter Wanger in Hollywood in September 1938. He and Wanger had flown together in Italy as pilots in World War I. La Guardia was impressed as he listened to the New York Philharmonic Orchestra under Jascha Heifetz playing a film sound track live while he watched the filming in progress. He told Wanger he wanted to keep the "cheap thrillers" out of New York neighborhoods. "I don't believe they do our young people any good." In New York, he warned theater owners they would be cited for letting in underaged children. Wanger told him about the difficulties with the censorship of film movement then under way. La Guardia said he supported freedom of the screen and press.[89] He thought that better-quality films would quiet parental and community fears and black protest.

The following year La Guardia spoke to 250 people at the fall convention of the Society of Motion Picture Engineers at the Hotel Pennsylvania in New York City. "I can't see why the motion picture producers don't make pictures here." He said New York had beaches, lakes, mountains, urban areas, and all the location characteristics of California and the Hollywood area. Moreover, "we have a city here. This is the art center of the world. There is more music here than any place in the world. We can give you every kind of casts." He subtly touched on the problem of stereotypes that blacks and others were concerned with: "Then, too, we have our own libraries and some of the little historical slip-ups in the movies wouldn't happen if you had these libraries and museums." To underscore his seriousness, he concluded, this is "not small-town talk or chamber of commerce talk—I mean it."[90] La Guardia wanted to get the new business Hollywood would provide for the city, more employment for its entertainment industry, capital for Broadway, undergird the black New York entertainers, and quiet the protest over racial stereotypes which concerned many blacks, including Walter White of the NAACP.

La Guardia met with Nicholas M. Schenck, the president of Metro-Goldwyn-Mayer and Loew's, Inc., at City Hall to discuss his plans to attract the motion picture industry to New York City as part of his overall effort to bring new businesses there. His Deputy Commissioner of Sanitation, Clendenin J. Ryan Jr., resigned and drafted employees from other city departments for the city's new Department of Commerce with offices at Rockefeller Center, "donated by Nelson Rockefeller" to support La Guardia's campaign. Schenck told the Mayor that $20,000,000 was invested in studio plants and it was impossible to move. Schenck invited La Guardia to see M-G-M's new film, *Gone With the Wind*.[91] He sought to quell the mounting black protest against the film as a slanderous *Birth of a Nation* follow-up. He knew that La Guardia was well regarded by blacks and that he and Walter White (White and the NAACP national headquarters were located in New York City) enjoyed a close partnership on race and political matters.

La Guardia boasted that New York City's museums, libraries, and talent pool—and singers and entertainers both black and white—could be used to check much, if not all, of Hollywood's excesses in cheap thrillers and racial stereotypes that generated so much unrest and censorship crusades. There were tremendous advantages that the advanced leadership of White and Mayor La Guardia and their offices, along with their command of the respect of the entertainment and art communities, had to offer the film community.

A brief flap occurred when NBC banned La Guardia from speaking on a national radio broadcast to be held before the annual awards banquet of the New York Critics' Association because Abel A. Schechter, director of special events for NBC, had told William Boehnel of the *World-Telegram* and chair of the New York Critics' Committee on Arrangements that "the chances are La Guardia will talk about bringing the movies to New York" and that was too political. He feared he would be compelled to "invite the Mayor of Hollywood to speak also." He said it was the policy of NBC to ban a "political figure" from speaking. La Guardia phoned David Sarnoff, president of Radio Corporation of America (of which NBC was a subsidiary), and received permission to speak. The New York Film Critics' Association meanwhile had voted to use another network rather than allow censorship of La Guardia's speech. Sarnoff had smoothed things over with La Guardia, who gave his talk without any restrictions as to what he might say.[92]

La Guardia pushed his plan because as Hollywood's problems multiplied it appeared possible that producers might seriously consider moving into a more sophisticated and protective environment like New York's. Hollywood had labor problems. A ten percent wage increase had been won by 35,000 stagehands against the wishes of the producers after a strike call. The film companies expected to reopen talks again in three months after they had perfected a united front, and a strike was feared that would further injure the economic well-being of Hollywood producers.[93] La Guardia wanted to take advantage of the economic woes facing Hollywood.

The European war had devastated the market for Hollywood films and many profit margins were jeopardized. It was difficult to get any money out of Europe because of the new war restrictions. The United States Ambassador to Great Britain, Joseph P. Kennedy, had held a "secret meeting" with fifty of Hollywood's leading producers in 1937 and advised them to keep a low profile to avoid charges that Hollywood's Jewish film producers were conspiring to force the United States into the war because that could lead to serious complications for them and the Roosevelt administration. He devised a plan to get around the British restrictions on the outflow of capital.[94] Hollywood, in part, defended its interests with limited concessions to blacks to compensate for the war-constricted market in Europe.

Hollywood was threatened with further economic disaster when the Allied States Association of Motion Picture Exhibitors organized to protest Hollywood's policy of "block-booking." This policy compelled independent theater owners to lease films in blocks in order to get the one film they wanted. It also contained "blind selling" whereby exhibitors had to lease a film before it was produced or the content known. The association also had to compete with Hollywood producers who owned many big theaters in metropolitan areas which showed double-feature films that reduced the independents' profit margins. The exhibitors wanted to force Hollywood film producers to be divested from theater ownership. Thurman Arnold filed a suit in New York to force the "Big Eight" film producers to divest.[95] Hollywood went on the defensive, very uneasy over these attacks, and sought to placate some of its critics, including blacks who attended theaters in significant numbers. Hollywood also sought to widen the black market as the European market constricted.

The United States Senate held hearings in 1939 before a Subcommittee of the Committee on Interstate Commerce to investigate "compulsory block-booking and blind selling in the leasing of motion picture films in interstate and foreign commerce." Senator Sheridan Downey of California told the committee "everything humanly and practically possible to produce films . . . acceptable to the public with the very highest standard and quality" was being done.[96] He pleaded in defense of Hollywood: "It is amazing to me that within 30 years a totally new industry of the world has come to be one of our greatest industries. In the history of the world we have not had a similar development in any art."[97] He did not want to see Hollywood destroyed. It was a major industry not only in California, but in the nation.

Downey defended Hollywood against American Firsters and their allies, who asserted Hollywood Jews were trying to force the United States into World War II through the use of film propaganda. These critics resented what they called Jewish influence, wealth, and power. They used political and racist attacks on Hollywood and its Jewish moguls who, they said, used their political influence against the interests of the United States. In 1941 Downey told another Senate Subcommittee of the Committee on Interstate Commerce holding hearings on "A Resolution Authorizing an Investigation of War Propaganda Dissemination by the Motion-Picture Industry and of Any Monopoly in the Production, Distribution, or Exhibition of Motion Pictures," that "we should, I think, be wary of using the ill-defined term 'propaganda' as an excuse for censorship or harassing investigation."[98] America Firsters and militant anti-war advocates charged that Hollywood was dominated by Jews who used Hollywood films to whip up pro-war passions. Ambassador Kennedy's warning that such accusations were possible and could have dire results had come to pass.

The *Pittsburgh Courier* ran an editorial on the Senate hearings and noted that even Willkie admitted Hollywood was anti-Hitler. It charged that "the movies are anti-Negro and have been carrying on white supremacy propaganda ever since their inception." Moreover, "the great crime of the motion picture industry has been that colored people have been consistently portrayed only as clowns, servants and savages, the roles in which they flatter the egos of white people and bolster the international propaganda of white supremacy." It rejected Willkie's assertion that race was not a factor in order to participate in the film industry, saying that blacks had limited job opportunities in Hollywood because of their race. What is more, "the fact that there is a large number of Jewish directors and officials in

Hollywood has not helped Negro employment there nor lifted the Negro out of the clownish-servant-savage roles in films." Then it added, "The industry may despise Hitler's racial discriminations but it certainly does not despise America's Racial discriminations, if we are to judge by the barring of Negroes from Hollywood hotels and restaurants, and its failure to produce a single film even touching upon the persecutions, exploitation and discrimination to which 13,000,000 Americans are subjected." The editorial concluded that blacks should consider boycotting all Hollywood films until the situation changed.[99]

The *Pittsburgh Courier* and Loren Miller had long argued that blacks should hit hardest when Hollywood was under attack from other sectors of society. A mass boycott never materialized because, Miller charged, Walter White of the NAACP had refused to promote such a drastic measure but had chosen negotiations, seen as ineffectual by the radicals and Miller, with Hollywood rather than militant confrontation.

Some black leaders had threatened mass protest during World War II to protest discrimination in employment, housing, public accommodations, and against a segregated military system. A. Philip Randolph was the major leader of this movement. He rejected President Roosevelt's and the American Communist Party's opposition to protest in favor of their policy to "win-the-war-first." Black radicals had learned from bitter experience that the American government and people were not committed to a racial democracy. Du Bois had long argued that only constant agitation and protest would bring any progress. In fact, the *Pittsburgh Courier* and black World War I veterans had organized in 1937 to protest, when they saw World War II unfolding in Europe, to insure that blacks got a better deal than they had during and after World War I. They had been bitterly disappointed because black leaders then had pursued a "wait till after the war" protest campaign and were met with race riots and government repression. Black radicals did not want to repeat the World War I mistake of putting protest on hold because whites did not respond to black patriotism or offer significant goodwill gestures for radical changes in support of racial democracy.

Hollywood found little sympathy among many black critics. Willkie responded to Hollywood's black critics by making a

special appeal to Jewish moguls. He, Walter White, and Mayor
La Guardia of New York tried to solve the problem by attempting
to entice the film industry back to New York where they could
work their brand of racial pluralism and cinema democracy on
the industry and thereby influence the entire nation in a similar
direction. This program took precedence over the mass-boycott
option advocated by the radicals. Willkie, White, and La Guardia
sought to take advantage of Hollywood's political problems and
promote the advantages to be gained in a New York setting.

Hollywood was beset with financial, legal, moral crusades,
labor unrest, and censorship problems. La Guardia tried to
capitalize on these troubles. A movie spokesman said: "Sure, the
industry can be moved to New York if the easterners are willing
to spend the money, but it would be some moving day!" Except
for two, every major film studio was located in Hollywood. Film
producers had $100,000,000 in studio plants, regularly employed
30,000 people, and many more thousands part time. Also, 150,000
more people were dependents or servants of Hollywood workers.
The residential investment amounted to $350,000,000 and the
yearly payroll came to $90,000,000 to $100,000,000. Hollywood's
product value amounted to $350,000,000 yearly. Film rentals by
theaters came to thirty-five percent of the $1,000,000,000 in paid
admissions. Hollywood's productions ranked higher than factory
production in some twenty states. Moreover, many still felt that
Hollywood's and California's diverse environments and weather
conditions were superior to anywhere else and were a crucial
factor in not relocating.[100] These factors indicated Hollywood
simply had too much at stake to pack up and move to New York
City.

New York's Broadway was in the doldrums from 1936 to
1939. In an effort to procure Hollywood capital, Broadway
supported La Guardia's efforts to induce Hollywood to relocate
to New York. Broadway dramatists had won a contract with
managers that made it difficult for Hollywood to buy screen
rights for dramatic works. In retaliation, Hollywood boycotted
the dramatists for several years. Broadway revenue declined
alarmingly. European capital was not available any longer because
of the war. Broadway producers preferred not to invest all of
their money in shows and turned to Hollywood. The war resulted
in a surge of United States patrons seeking escape, distraction,

and entertainment offered on Broadway. The Broadway boom attracted Hollywood stars. Broadway backed Mayor La Guardia's efforts to entice Hollywood to the city as timely and essential. One commentator said, "These are some of the reasons why Hollywood gold is so welcome and why its return is important enough to be registered here."[101] Broadway's support of La Guardia's program was encouraging.

A mass movement by blacks to support La Guardia's plan never developed because some venerable blacks had lost faith in Hollywood's possibilities to change and offer blacks a better deal. The venerable Alain Locke attacked Hollywood's black stereotypes in 1939. "Hollywood particularly, in spite of a new medium, is still snared in a reactionary groove and prostitutes genuine Negro talent to perpetuation among the masses of reactionary social and racial stereotypes of character and situation." He firmly believed that blacks must continue to fight for "the ultimate goal of cultural democracy, the capstone of the historic process of American acculturation." He thought the Federal Theatre Project with its black plays and dramas, or adaptations of a black cast and style, in such dramas and plays as "*Macbeth, Haiti* and the *Swing Mikado*, have been among the ranking successes," and the *Swing Mikado* was a commercial success. They might turn out "to be a crucial factor in so vital a general matter [and] will be a cultural contribution of supreme importance." Moreover, he thought that the Federal Theatre should be "used as an instrument for social enlightenment and constructive social reform" because of the "experimental natures of the powerful appeal of Negro idioms in dignified and unstereotyped contexts—a lesson Broadway and Hollywood have yet to learn."[102] Locke had written off Hollywood and failed to join the effort to relocate Hollywood to New York City.

Locke's attitude is perhaps understandable because the Federal Theatre in its heyday, noted a *Time* magazine reviewer who was impressed with the "all-Negro cast" in the *Swing Mikado*, had switched its scene from Japan to the "South Sea Island setting and swing interpolations" and "became a smash hit overnight." The reviewer also noted that it "in five months broke all Federal Theatre records by playing to 250,000 people and clearing $35,000 at a $1.10 top." Michael Todd and Alfred de Liagre Jr. planned to make it a Broadway show with Bill Robinson. The Chicago show immediately closed down and opened in Manhattan three weeks ahead of the Todd and Liagre show. It opened "to the splashiest and most exciting opening night in Federal Theatre history" and in "flocked jitterbugs, Nosey Parkers, Harlem, Cafe-Society," said the *Time* review. Even more impressive, Eleanor Roosevelt came down the aisle for one of her first nights out since her husband became president. The audience stood and applauded her. She pointedly attended two nights at the "Harlempress" to see Ethel Waters in *Mamba's Daughters* and "the all-Negro *Mikado*" as a rebuke to the Daughters of the American Revolution in the wake of their ban on Marian Anderson's singing in Constitution Hall. The musical "on Broadway, as in Chicago . . . became overnight a smash hit." This reviewer concluded, "The Federal Theatre boldly moved *The Mikado* from Japan to the South Seas. It should have been bolder still and moved it, shag and shaggage, to Harlem."[103] The Federal Theatre held out such promise that it becomes clear why Locke and others ignored Hollywood.

The entry of the United States into World War II killed the Federal Theatre, but Hollywood boomed. Locke had put too much faith in the New Deal art program and failed to see the new approach in which Water White, Mayor La Guardia, and Wendell Willkie were engaged with Hollywood.

Nevertheless, Locke and many of the Harlem Renaissance ideologists were still active and inspired many followers to take up the social and cultural struggle to demolish the anti-black stereotypes judged to undergird Jim Crow by cultivating a racist public opinion among whites. The NAACP and the Urban League formalized their attack on Hollywood as part of the Associated Film Audiences's effort, but individuals, scholars, and especially black newspapers' crusader columnists, took up the battle against Hollywood as well. Some, like Locke, had despaired of Hollywood and looked elsewhere for relief. Others, like the Los Angeles radicals, were not very effective, although they did put pressure on White to act and confront Hollywood.

The radicals, especially those in Los Angeles, were side-stepped by the deft moves of White, Willkie, and Mayor La Guardia of New York, who worked strenuously to bring Hollywood's film industry to New York. White and La Guardia were close personal friends and political allies who worked together to advance black concerns. Hollywood stereotypes, cheap thrillers with their impact on race relations, and the relocation of the motion picture industry to New York were high on their agenda. La Guardia and White each offered New York City's economic and cultural advantages as well as racial art policy direction to Hollywood to further its economic and artistic interests.

New York City was, for blacks and whites, the cultural capital of the United States. Its cultural authority was well respected in many sections of the nation. The return of the film industry to New York held out, to those concerned with creating a political and economic racial democracy by cultural means, a potentially vital and vast new instrument that Walter White, Mayor La Guardia, Charles S. Johnson, W.E.B. Du Bois, Alain Locke, and the Harlem Renaissance artists and their white allies had been searching for since the 1920s.

So few blacks understood or had faith in Hollywood that they apparently were oblivious to the full significance of the White, Willkie, and La Guardia moves on Hollywood between 1938 and 1942. A few black film critics understood some aspects of the program, but apparently did not grasp the full significance of what was happening. They pushed for more roles in Hollywood. Hollywood producers felt more comfortable in dealing with Walter White. White stood ready to accommodate Hollywood with a policy of reasoned prodding and patience. He and La Guardia avoided alienating the film moguls by rejecting the mass boycott in favor of a more ambitious program of relocation to New York City. White was able to move and operate within powerful circles with whites because of his political and personal associations that were out of the reach of the Los Angeles blacks. Despite the skills of White, Willkie, and La Guardia, their goal to get Hollywood to relocate was not realized.

In the final analysis, the economics of moving the film industry studios and people, as well as the location and weather advantages it already enjoyed in California, ruled out the possibility of Hollywood relocating. La Guardia thought it possible that pressure and inducements might persuade Hollywood moguls to relocate. Harsh political repression might compel Hollywood to shut down and move—which was not altogether an impossibility considering the constant censorship

movements and Congressional investigations from the 1920s to
the 1950s. This possibility encouraged Wendell Willkie and New
York's Walter White and Mayor Fiorello La Guardia to stand
ready to receive Hollywood with an agenda that included the
wildest dreams of the Harlem Renaissance ideologues. Not to be
outdone, however, Walter White and Billy Rowe promoted New
York's Harlem black entertainers and encouraged them to make
the trek to Hollywood in order to gain hegemony and move the
Hollywood film industry toward racial democracy and cultural
pluralism. New York blacks, and some ambitious Los Angeles
blacks, promoted a powerful "Harlem in Hollywood" movement
with these goals in mind.

Notes

1. "Survey of the Month," *Opportunity*, 4, No. 48 (December 1926),
398; Miriam Matthews (retired Los Angeles City librarian), telephone
interview, 17 December 1988; obituary of Eloise Bibb Thompson,
Opportunity, 6, No. 2 (February 1928); Noah D. Thompson, business
manager, *Opportunity*, 6, No. 7 (July 1928), 193; Langston Hughes and
Milton Meltzer, eds., *Black Magic: A Pictorial History of the Negro in
American Entertainment* (Englewood Cliffs, N.J.: Prentice-Hall, Inc., 1967),
pp. 220, 223, 338.

2. "Survey of the Month," p. 398; Miriam Matthews telephone
interview, 17 December 1988.

3. Miriam Matthews, telephone interview, 17 December 1988;
"Survey of the Month," p. 398.

4. Langston Hughes, *I Wonder as I Wander: An Autobiographical
Journal* (New York: Hill and Wang, 1968 [1956]), pp. 69–70.

5. *Ibid.*, p. 76.

6. *Ibid.*, p. 77.

7. *Ibid.*, pp. 77, 79.

8. *Ibid.*, p. 96.

9. Louise Thompson Patterson, "With Langston Hughes in the
USSR," *Freedomways*, 81, No. 21 (Spring 1968, Second Quarter), 152–158,
esp. 156–157; see Arnold Rampersad, *The Life of Langston Hughes: I, Too,
Sing America*, Vol. I, 1902–1941 (New York: Oxford University Press,
1988 [pbk. 1986]), pp. 246–249.

10. Louise Thompson, "The Soviet Film," *The Crisis*, 40, No. 2 (February 1933), 37, 46.

11. George S. Schuyler, *Black and Conservative: The Autobiography of George S. Schuyler* (New Rochelle: Arlington House Publishers, 1966), pp. 205–207.

12. See Wilson Record, *The Negro and the Communist Party* (New York: Atheneum, 1971 [1951]), and his *Race and Radicalism: The NAACP and the Communist Party in Conflict* (Ithaca: Cornell University Press, 1966 [1964]).

13. Hughes, *I Wonder as I Wander*, p. 75.

14. Miller, "Uncle Tom in Hollywood," *The Crisis*, 41, No. 11 (November 1934), 329, 336; David L. Lewis, *When Harlem Was in Vogue* (New York: Vintage Books, 1981), pp. 288–289.

15. Miller, "Uncle Tom," pp. 329, 336.

16. Loren Miller, "How 'Left' Is the N.A.A.C.P.?" *New Masses*, 16 July 1935, pp. 12–13.

17. Earl J. Morris, "Grandtown: I Wish You a Merry Christmas," *Pittsburgh Courier*, 24 December 1938, p. 21, col. 4.

18. W.E.B. Du Bois, *Dusk of Dawn* (New York: Schocken Books, 1968 [1940]), pp. 271, 258.

19. "Harlem Not Pleased with Emperor Jones," *Philadelphia Tribune*, 28 September 1933, p. 2, col. 2; Ed R. Harris, "The Scannin' Acts," *Philadelphia Tribune*, 28 September 1933, p. 2, col. 3.

20. Harris, "The Scannin' Acts," p. 2, col. 3; "Harlem Not Pleased with Emperor Jones," p. 2, col. 2.

21. J.A. Rogers, "O'Neill's Masterpiece, 'The Emperor Jones,' Flayed by J.A. Rogers as Portraying False Negro Type; Appeals to Nordic Prejudice," *Pittsburgh Courier*, 30 September 1933, sec. 2, p. 1, col. 2.

22. *Ibid.*

23. Edgar Dale, "The Movies and Race Relations," *The Crisis*, 44, No. 10 (October 1937), 294–296, 315–316; for original quote see Archer Winsten, "The Negro Stereotype in American Pictures," *New York Post*, 7 April 1937, p. 16, col. 2.

24. Dale, pp. 294–296, 315–316.

25. J. Cullen Fentress, "Film Society Is Launched to Aid Protection of Race Dignity in Screen Portrayals," *California Eagle*, 20 January 1938, p. 7-A, col. 4.

26. *Ibid.*

27. *Ibid.*

28. Harry Levette, "Should Negro Film Heads be Branded as 'Stooges' of White Capitalists?" *California Eagle*, 10 March 1938, p. 9-A, col. 6; "The New Pictures: Harlem on the Prairie," *Time*, XXX, No. 24, (13 December 1937), 24.

29. "Form Film Committee," *California Eagle*, 31 March 1938, p. 5-A, col. 5; Earl J. Morris, "Grandtown Day and Night: Happy New Year, Folks," *Pittsburgh Courier*, 31 December 1938, p. 17, col. 1.

30. "The New Pictures: 'Harlem on the Prairie,'" *Time*, XXX, 24 (13 December 1937), p. 24.

31. Cited in Lunnabelle Wedlock, *The Reaction of Negro Publications and Organizations to German Anti-Semitism* (Washington, D.C.: Howard University Press, 1942), p. 161.

32. Earl J. Morris, "American Whites, Negroes Being Shoved into Background in Movies by Jewish Film Owners," *Pittsburgh Courier*, 27 August 1938, p. 20, col. 3; Earl J. Morris, "Grandtown Day and Night: Happy New Year, Folks," *Pittsburgh Courier*, 31 December 1938, p. 17, col. 1.

33. Earl Dancer, "Hollywood Jews Use Southern Prejudice As Smoke Screen," *Pittsburgh Courier*, 18 August 1938, p. 7-A, col. 1.

34. *Ibid.*

35. J.A. Rogers, "Negroes Suffer More in U.S. than Jews in Germany," *Philadelphia Tribune*, 21 September 1933, p. 3, col. 1; George S. Schuyler, *Black and Conservative*, pp. 142–143.

36. J.A. Rogers, "Negroes Suffer," p. 3.

37. J.A. Rogers, "Rogers Says: Of All the Hitlers, Adolf Is the Worst Threat to American Negroes," *Pittsburgh Courier*, 27 September 1941, p. 7, col. 1.

38. W.E.B. Du Bois, "Race Prejudice in Germany," *Pittsburgh Courier*, 19 December 1936, p. 1, sec. 2, p. 8.

39. "Harlem 'Hitler' Killed," *Pittsburgh Courier*, 6 August 1938, p. 1, col. 4; David L. Lewis, *When Harlem Was in Vogue*, pp. 300–301; Ted Fox, *Showtime at the Apollo* (New York: Holt, Rinehart and Winston), 1983, pp. 136–137; Jack Schiffman, *Uptown: The Story of Harlem's Apollo Theatre* (New York: Cowles Books Co., Inc., 1971), p. 188.

40. "Negroes Win Right to Jobs in Harlem," *The Christian Century*, LV, No. 34 (24 August 1938), 1004–1005.

41. "Deny Negroes Are Anti-Semitic," *Pittsburgh Courier*, 25 September 1943, p. 12, col. 4; Adam Clayton Powell Sr., "What Negroes Think of Jews," *New Currents*, 20 September 1943, pp. 15–16.

42. "Hitler's Racial Bigotry Scored," *Pittsburgh Courier*, 3 October 1936, sec. 1, p. 10, col. 4.

43. "Danger Seen in Race's Anti-Jewish Attacks," *Pittsburgh Courier*, 20 August 1938, p. 6, col. 1; Wedlock, pp. 23–24, 27.

44. Wedlock, pp. 23–24, 27; "Danger Seen in Race's Anti-Jewish Attacks," p. 6, col. 1; "Sagacious Sayings," *California Eagle*, 1 September 1938, p. 4-B, col. 5; "No Anti-Semitism among Negroes, Says 'The Crisis,'" *California Eagle*, 16 June 1938, p. A-4, col. 4.

45. The League of American Writers, *We Hold These Truths* ... (New York: The League of American Writers, 1939), p. 58.

46. "White Racialism in America," *The Crisis*, 46, No. 10 (October 1939), 308.

47. Released by the American Jewish Committee, "The Jewish Press and the Jewish-Negro Problem," *Pittsburgh Courier*, 9 December 1939, p. 18, col. 2.

48. J.A. Rogers, "Rogers Attacks Anti-Negro Propaganda of Movie Industry," *Pittsburgh Courier*, 1 May 1937, p. 14, col. 1.

49. *Ibid.*

50. David Ward Howe, "The Observation Post," *Chicago Defender*, 20 April 1940, p. 16, col. 3.

51. Ethel Waters with Charles Samuels, *His Eye Is on the Sparrow: An Autobiography* (Garden City: Doubleday & Co., Inc., 1951), pp. 173–175, 186–189; George S. Schuyler, *Black and Conservative*, pp. 159-160; David H. Pierce, "Is the Jew a Friend of the Negro?," *The Crisis*, 30, No. 4 (April 1925), 184; "Sues Over 'Africana' Production," *New York Times*, 26 August 1927, p. 15. col. 4.

52. Schiffman, *Uptown*, p. 146.

53. Paul Bullock, "A Conversation with Eddie Beal," *Jazz Heritage Foundation*, V, No. 4 (November–December 1984), 13–15.

54. Alfred LeGon (brother of Jeni LeGon), Los Angeles, telephone interview, 9 August 1988.

55. "What Nerve, Mr. Jim Crow; What Nerve!," *California Eagle*, 14 July 1938, p. 1-A, col. 2.

56. Mae Alice Harvey, Los Angeles, telephone interview, 24 December 1988; Alfred LeGon telephone interview, 9 August 1988.

57. Isadora Smith, "Broadway Turns 'Thumbs Down' on Robeson Film: Managers Believe PIC Shows Too Much Racial Equality," *Pittsburgh Courier*, 31 December 1938, p. 17, col. 3.

58. Norman Zierold, *The Moguls* (New York: Coward-McCann, Inc., 1969), pp. 53–54.

59. George S. Schuyler, "Not Gone With the Wind," *The Crisis*, 44, No. 7 (July 1937), 205–206.

60. *Ibid.*; Frank Daniel, "Cinderella City: Atlanta Sees 'Gone with the Wind,'" *The Saturday Review of Literature*, XXI, No. 9 (23 December 1939), 10–12.

61. Dan Burley, "Gone With the Wind: Subtle Propaganda of Anti-Negro Film Told by Reviewer," *New York Amsterdam News*, 6 January 1940, p. 16, col. 2.

62. Rudy Behlmer, ed., *Memo from David O. Selznick* (New York: The Viking Press, 1972), p. 151, quoted in Edgar Dale, "The Movies and Race Relations," *The Crisis*, 44, No. 10 (October 1937), 294–296, 315–316, esp. 315.

63. Kenneth T. Jackson, *The Ku Klux Klan in the City, 1915–1930* (New York: Oxford University Press, 1967), p. 29.

64. Walter White, *A Man Called White: The Autobiography of Walter White* (Bloomington: Indiana University Press, 1970 [1948]), pp. 198–199; Thomas Cripps, "Movies, Race and World War II: Tennessee Johnson as an Anticipation of the Strategies of the Civil Rights Movement," *Prologue*, 14, No. 2 (Summer 1982), 49–67, esp. 58.

65. White, *A Man . . .*, pp. 199–200; "Stagecoach (United Artists-Walter Wanger)," *Time*, 13 March 1939, pp. 30, 32.

66. White, *A Man . . .*, pp. 200–201; "Willkie Speech in Los Angeles," *The Crisis*, 49, No. 9 (September 1942), 296, 298–302.

67. White, *A Man. . . .*, pp. 200–201.

68. *Ibid.*, pp. 201–202.

69. "Propaganda in Motion Pictures," *Hearing Before a Subcommittee of the Committee on Interstate Commerce, United States Senate, 77th Congress, 1st Sess., on S. Res. 152*, September 9–26, 1941 (Washington, D.C.: United States Government Printing Office, 1941); "Americanism Cup Awarded to Willkie: Jewish War Veterans Honor Republican," *Louisville Courier Journal*, 17 February 1941, p. 8, col. 4; "Jewish Veterans Honor Willkie's 'Americanism,'" *New York Times*, 17 February 1941, p. 7, col. 4;

70. "Willkie Warns of Jews' Plight: Pressure on Them Will Spread to All Parts of World if Hitler Wins, He Says," *New York Times*, 8 March 1941, p. 10, col. 7.

71. White, *A Man . . .*, pp. 202–203.

72. *Ibid.*

73. *Ibid.*; Thomas Cripps, "Movies, Race and World War II," p. 54.

74. "Movie Moguls Study Plan to Improve Negro Roles: Wendell Willkie and Walter White Meet with Film Magnates over Issue Championed by the Courier," *Pittsburgh Courier*, 1 August 1942, p. 20, col. 5.

75. "Night Clubs Get Big Play; Break in Movies Arrives: Decision Comes after Visit by NAACP Head," *Chicago Defender*, 29 August 1942, p. 13, col. 7.

76. Thomas Cripps, "Movies, Race, and World War II," p. 58; also see Clayton R. Koppes and Gregory D. Black, *Hollywood Goes to War* (New York: The Free Press, 1987).

77. "OWI Goes to the Movies: The Bureau of Intelligence's Criticism of Hollywood, 1942–1943," *Prologue*, 6, No. 1 (Spring 1974), 44–59.

78. Walter Wanger, "120,000 American Ambassadors," *Foreign Affairs*, 18, No. 1 (1939), 45, 59.

79. "Name Nine Race Artists on Movies' Victory Committee," *Pittsburgh Courier*, 30 May 1942, p. 21, col. 5.

80. Herman Hill, "Change of Attitude in Hollywood Observed: Walter White Is Winning His Fight for Better Roles," *Pittsburgh Courier*,

8 August 1942, p. 20, col. 3; Donald Bogle, *Toms, Coons, Mulattoes, Mammies, & Bucks: An Interpretive History of Blacks in American Films* (New York: Bantam Books, 1974 [pbk.]), p. 196.

81. Herman Hill, "Change of Attitude . . .," p. 20, col. 3.

82. Billy Rowe, "Rowe's Notebook," *Pittsburgh Courier*, 9 January 1943, p. 20, col. 1.

83. Billy Rowe, "Tinsel City Seems Ready to Receive Our Best Artists," *Pittsburgh Courier*, 9 January 1943, p. 21, col. 1.

84. Billy Rowe, "We Should 'Arrive' in Hollywood in '43—Rowe," *Pittsburgh Courier*, 9 January 1943, p. 21, col. 1.

85. Billy Rowe, "Eastern Performers Start Western Trek for Twentieth Century-Fox Film," *Pittsburgh Courier*, 9 January 1943, p. 21, col. 4.

86. Billy Rowe, "Leigh Whipper, Famed Character Actor, Sees '43 as Best Movie Year," *Pittsburgh Courier*, 16 January 1943, p. 21, col. 3.

87. "200 Race Artists Working in Film," *Pittsburgh Courier*, 30 January 1943, p. 12, col. 3.

88. "Our Role in Movies Better, NAACP Notes," *Pittsburgh Courier*, 20 February 1943, p. 21, col. 3.

89. "La Guardia Visits First Film Studio: Discussing Censorship, He Links Freedom of Screen and Press," *New York Times*, 22 September 1938, p. 25, col. 7; "Warns Theatres on Child Law," *New York Times*, 6 November 1938, p. 38, col. 5.

90. "Mayor Asks Film Industry to Return to New York Where It Started," *New York Times*, 17 October 1939, p. 27, col. 7.

91. "Making Films Here Put Up to Schenck: Producer Tells Mayor He Has $20,000,000 Invested in Hollywood Studios," *New York Times*, 8 December 1939, p. 33, col. 4.

92. "NBC Bans La Guardia Then Reverses Itself in Hectic Day over Film Critics' Program," *New York Times*, 29 December 1939, p. 1, col. 2, p. 10, col. 4.

93. "Labor Angles: Three-Month Truce," *Business Week*, 2 December 1939, p. 32.

94. Ben Hecht, *A Child of the Century* (New York: Simon and Schuster, 1954), p. 520; Stephen Birmingham, *The Rest of Us: The Rise of America's Eastern European Jews* (New York: Berkley Books, 1985), pp. 256–258.

95. "Movie Trade Bemoans Unhappy Lot," *Business Week*, 29 June 1940, pp. 22–23.

96. "A Bill to Prohibit and to Prevent the Trade Practice Known as 'Compulsory Block-Booking' and 'Blind Selling' in the Leasing of Motion-Picture Films in Interstate and Foreign Commerce," *Hearings Before a Subcommittee of the Committee on Interstate Commerce, United States*

Senate, 76th Cong., 1st Sess. on S. Res. 280, April 3 to 17, 1939 (Washington, D.C.: United States Government Printing Office, 1939), pp. 1, 513.

97. *Ibid.*

98. "A Resolution Authorizing an Investigation of War Propaganda Disseminated by the Motion-Picture Industry and of Any Monopoly in the Production, Distribution, or Exhibition of Motion Pictures," *Hearings Before a Subcommittee of the Committee on Interstate Commerce, United States Senate, 77th Cong., 1st Sess. on S. Res. 152,* September 9 to 26, 1941 (Washington, D.C.: United States Government Printing Office, 1942), p. 207.

99. "The Movie Probe," *Pittsburgh Courier,* 20 September 1941, p. 6, col. 1.

100. "Hollywood Misses Cue: Mayor La Guardia Offers Picture Industry Chance to Brag, but Producers Slow on Uptake," *Business Week,* 16 December 1939, p. 24.

101. Brock Pemberton, "Broadway Is Hit-Happy Again," *New York Times Magazine,* 5 November 1939, p. 6, col. 1, pp. 7, 20.

102. Alain Locke, "The Negro's Contribution to American Culture," *Journal of Negro Education,* VIII (1939), 521–529, esp. 529.

103. "Mikado-deo-do," *Time,* XXXIII, No. 11 (13 March 1939), 57–58; Alain Locke, "The Negro's Contributions to American Culture," pp. 528–529.

HARLEM MEETS HOLLYWOOD

Starting in the 1920s and reaching a watershed during World War II, black New York artists and entertainers made a steady trek to Hollywood. Fame and fortune could be won in Hollywood, and one stood a better chance in Hollywood if he or she had won a reputation elsewhere, especially in New York. Blacks who had already gained fame, if not fortune, in New York, Harlem, and the Cotton Club increasingly looked to the new entertainment capital. In 1925 George S. Schuyler said that "today I believe it fair to say Negro America looks to New York for advanced leadership and opinion."[1] Harlem was the home of the Harlem Renaissance, W.E.B. Du Bois, and Walter White, and the NAACP's national headquarters was located in New York. From Harlem to Hollywood became the road to success.

Black and white critics continued to debate the images and performances of blacks who themselves were divided over what constituted anti-black stereotypes in films. The struggle for cultural democracy and racial pluralism in the film industry still remains a central issue for blacks and some whites. During the Great Depression, blacks in Los Angeles looked especially to Hollywood for employment. Black leaders demanded more jobs in the film industry, especially in non-stereotype roles. They argued that stereotype roles limited employment opportunities for blacks. Increasingly, blacks looked to Harlem's renowned entertainers to come to Hollywood to challenge and alter black caricature images.

James Reese Europe had built a fine jazz tradition in New York that continued to blossom under Duke Ellington, Fletcher Henderson, Cab Calloway, and many others. The Cotton Club, the Savoy Ballroom, Smalls' Paradise, and the Apollo Theatre were located in Harlem, and all shared an international reputation for high-quality entertainment and lavish floor shows with beautiful chorus line girls, dancers, and exotically dressed performers and patrons.

Walter White and Mayor Fiorello La Guardia worked together to promote civil rights and cultural pluralism in New York, which became a model for the whole nation. As a result, New York's Harlem emerged as the political, social, fashion, literary, and cultural capital of black America in the 1920s and remained so until the end of the 1940s.

Harlem's pervasive influence during that time had a dramatic impact on blacks in Los Angeles who looked to Harlem for political and cultural leadership. The proximity of black Los Angeles to Hollywood led to a keen desire among many blacks to imitate the already established and highly acclaimed social and cultural achievements of Harlem, with its proximity to Broadway, in order to break into Hollywood films. In fact, blacks in Los Angeles and around the country, especially New York, went to Hollywood seeking fame and fortune. Reputations earned in New York on Broadway or in the exclusive night clubs in Harlem carried more weight in Hollywood because of the high state of the performing arts and traditions there. Hollywood also maintained its connections with New York's entertainment world. The emergence of Hollywood as an entertainment center opened the door to blacks who had gained international recognition in the performing arts or those just entering the field.

Hollywood and theaters around the country employed musicians for movie scores. Motion picture musical scores exploded from 1928 onward after the success of the talking film *The Jazz Singer* (1927) starring Al Jolson. His singing of one song in blackface indicated Hollywood's interest in jazz. Jazz music had a different style than music associated with films. Joseph Carl Breil, a white man, had scored the music for *Queen Elizabeth* (Sarah Bernhardt) in 1912, *The Birth of a Nation* (1915), and *Intolerance* (1916). His attitude embodied a style of music opposite to that of the jazz style. He said, "Motion picture music is essentially program music, for it is a commentary and illustration of the play, entirely subservient to the action presented. It should be subtle, suggestive, and seductive.[2] Jazz as played by most blacks was just the opposite. It was often described as hot, frantic, and with a biting attack.

Hollywood producers hired musicians who played at such local Los Angeles theaters as Grauman's, Clune's Auditorium, the Orpheum, Kinema, and Miller's California. They played the type of music described by Breil. In 1918 Hollywood employed 100 musicians.[3] German music tended to dominate the classical music field and theaters, but World War I led to a powerful backlash. Los Angeles staged a downtown parade to celebrate the ending of the war. Bands and paraders sang. Some displayed signs with inscriptions as: "To Hell with the Kaiser" and "Goodbye France, Hello Broadway" as a signal to reject foreign influences and praise everything American. American music and black spirituals experienced a dramatic revival.[4] The rise of a formal musical community in Los Angeles and the rise of Hollywood as a movie and radio empire made the city a mecca for entertainers of every race, creed, color, sex, and national origin.

Los Angeles's musical community matured rapidly and developed the Los Angeles Philharmonic Orchestra and the Hollywood Bowl. Len E. Behymer conducted the Philharmonic between the two world wars. He supplied artists from his orchestra to the Southwestern states. The Shrine Auditorium was built in 1927 and offered another outlet for musicians and concerts. Behymer supplied the major motion picture studios with musicians from 1928 onward after Hollywood shifted to sound following the success of *The Jazz Singer* (1927) with Al Jolson. Behymer signed with Fox Film Corporation to provide its film musical scores. He served as a "master press agent" for Hollywood studios, and his work and musicians (for whom he served as a hiring agent) were in high demand. He performed for the Los Angeles Olympic Games in 1932.[5] Black musicians were not included in Behymer's group because of the prevalent racism.

The advent of the sound picture also led Hollywood's Sunset Boulevard and Vine Street to become an industry center for radio broadcasting. Earle C. Anthony, owner of the first big radio station in Los Angeles, announced a broad musical policy on January 15, 1923: "In the musical end we want to be able to broadcast from opera to jazz. . . ."[6] Musicians often played live on radio, which also used recorded music. This shift in musical policy proved hospitable for black jazz artists who made records or played live on the radio.

In 1927 and 1928 the advent of the sound picture led many theater operators to fire their bands and organists. About 5,000 musicians across the nation lost their jobs as a result. Joseph N.

Weber, president of the American Federation of Musicians, was alarmed. He went to Los Angeles to organize and supervise the deluge of unemployed musicians converging on Hollywood studios for work. He established minimum wages and maximum hours as work standards. He told musicians to share the work. He said in June 1929 that a musician "should willingly lend his aid that more musicians be employed instead of a mere handful earning huge wages."[7]

Behymer and his well-trained classical orchestra musicians early monopolized Hollywood studio film work because of their superior training and organization. Hollywood grew rapidly and so did jobs for studio musicians. The competition was fierce. Racism limited blacks in the competition and blacks had a small number of formally trained musicians compared to whites.

The Harlem Renaissance and Hollywood boomed at the same time in the 1920s. Hollywood for blacks became one of the few outlets—and the most lucrative—and offered the greatest exposure for artists. Harlem artists started going to Hollywood in the 1920s just as New York Broadway stars did in search of fame and fortune. These black and white New Yorkers set the standards which many others imitated in their attempts to break into show business. Competition grew fierce among blacks as opportunities exploded in Hollywood, Harlem, and on Broadway. The entertainment industry expanded to accommodate escapism, and jobs became lucrative and plentiful in the black entertainment market. Many blacks in Los Angeles caught the Harlem and Hollywood fever for the performing arts in quest of fame and fortune.

Central Avenue was the main street and residential area where blacks clustered. It became an important cultural and entertainment center, and its connection with Hollywood films resulted in its most spectacular growth and recognition. It looked to Harlem and its Renaissance as a model to imitate. Hollywood provided a crucial outlet for black entertainers in need of employment.

In the 1920s, Charles Butler became one of "the original talent agent[s] and scout[s] for Hollywood" to recruit blacks primarily for "G-string and African" native roles, "cottonfield" workers, and menial labor roles. Butler had an office at 1315 E. 12th Street, a few steps off Central Avenue, the heart of the black residential and entertainment community. He and his wife Sarah dominated the "cattle calls" (calls for work as "extras" who usually played background scenes or "bit" talking roles) for large numbers of blacks to play bit parts in Hollywood films. Butler positioned himself to take advantage of managing. He later moved his business to his residence in the 1100 block of East 52nd Street. Butler's wife was a pioneer as a minister of a church in the middle 1930s. Undoubtedly, because she and her husband recruited black choirs to sing spirituals and songs in films, it was an advantage to maintain a church and choir for film roles. Since most blacks lived and socialized in the Central Avenue district, it was convenient and easy to spot blacks who might fit a casting-type for certain film roles. For example, Darby Jones, a tall black native of Los Angeles, got frequent calls to play African warrior and buck roles because of his appearance. "Mammy types," "African bucks," and blacks with "a certain look" often received "cattle calls." Maids and butlers were considered prestigious roles by blacks in the 1920s because they were casting-types in regular demand and, therefore, provided the most days of employment. Earl Dancer became an agent and worked as a master of ceremony in the Central Avenue night spots. He moved in with his aunt, Bertha Dunigan, a native of Columbia, Texas, who had lived in Los Angeles since 1918. Since she lived at 840 Birch Street, just two blocks east of Central Avenue, Dancer wanted to take advantage of the talent and blacks who frequented the area as potential recruits for Hollywood "cattle calls." Besides, his aunt was well known in social circles. Earl Broady, who delivered mail to the Butler and Dancer residences, remembered Dancer as "an impresario for plays and actors."[8] Dancer used his family connections and his own experience in New York to promote his career in the entertainment world of Central Avenue and Hollywood.

It was a distinct advantage to live near Central Avenue, the black social and entertainment section of the black community. Promoters and entertainers worked the clubs and talent scouts looked to Central Avenue to hire blacks for Hollywood films. Hollywood periodically hired large numbers of blacks from Los Angeles's "Black Broadway," Central Avenue, as film extras. "Hollywood Movie Colony Studios Resembles League of Nations: Cosmopolitan Air Vogue at Smart Film Colony; Race Actors Are

Plentiful," a black newspaper reported in 1929. It noted that Hollywood and Los Angeles had settlements of almost every race, ethnic group, and talent from around the world. Hollywood's Central Casting Bureau recruited Orientals for the film *Dr. Fu Manchu* from Chinatown in Los Angeles. Also, "Seventy-five Negroes appear in a Harlem Cabaret scene of George Bancroft's new starring picture, *Thunderbolt*, as well as varied types of Americans. The Negroes were recruited from Central Avenue, Los Angeles," reported the *Pittsburgh Courier*.[9]

Harlem's racial, economic, and political trends developed early among blacks in Los Angeles and affected the way blacks perceived Hollywood. In 1921 in Los Angeles Noah Thompson led a majority splinter group out of the Universal Negro Improvement Association of Marcus Garvey, a Pan-Africanist, whose headquarters was located in Harlem. Garvey and Booker T. Washington developed plans to develop the economy of the black community. Thompson organized his group into the Pacific Coast Negro Improvement Association in November 1921. He and anti-Garvey crusader Chandler Owen in 1924 organized The California Development Company as a cooperative economic venture. They bought an apartment building in the black community which they called "the Harlem of Los Angeles." Other blacks started businesses that resulted in the emergence of a number of substantial black business institutions modeled on Garvey's plans and Booker T. Washington's National Negro Business League, which also was located in New York City.[10] Blacks in Los Angeles continued to imitate Harlem trends, especially in entertainment. During the Great Depression, Los Angeles blacks copied Harlem and Chicago demands for employment by verbal protests, threat, and boycotts first initiated by black militants.

Curtis Mosby, a Los Angeles musician, made the sound track for an obscure movie called *Thunderbolt* (1919) by George Bancroft. He played sound tracks for other film shorts in this period as well. His band played and appeared in the first all-black film musical, *Hallelujah* (1929), which starred Daniel Haynes and Nina Mae McKinney. Mosby's band played "Introduction," "Swanee Shuffle," and "Blue Blowers Blues" on the sound track. His regular band was called "Curtis Mosby and His Dixieland Blue-Blowers." Black Hollywood actress Nina Mae McKinney also sang with his regular band. Benjamin "Reb" (for rebel) Spikes, another black Los Angeles musician and businessman, had a group called Spikes' Seven Pods of Pepper Orchestra. They recorded in 1922 and the late 1920s. Les Hite played with this group, then formed the house band for Frank Sebastian's prestigious Cotton Club (named after the famed Harlem club) on Washington Boulevard in Culver City, a suburb of Los Angeles and a center of Hollywood film studios.[11] Black musicians performed at Sebastian's club but could not enter as patrons because it practiced racial discrimination and segregation. Black musicians and a few select notables, however, were allowed to sit on the bandstand as observers as a courtesy of the management.[12]

King Nina Mae McKinney's life epitomized the from-country-to-urban trek, the from-Harlem-to-Hollywood phenomenon, and the eventual rise to stardom when she made her first film, *Hallelujah*, in 1929. "I was born in South Carolina on the estate where our family had lived several generations. My grandmother was an old and trusted servant of this household." She "reared me until I was about 12 years old. Then my father, who was in New York, sent for me." She recalled, "Imagine my delight at this big metropolitan city. I was constantly thrilled by the wonder unfolded to me. Its skyscrapers, its parks, the theatres, anything, everything was a veritable fairyland, and I beheld its glories in wide-eyed amazement."[13] She dreamed, danced, and play-acted before her mirror. Three years later, "I joined the chorus of 'Lew Leslie's Blackbirds of 1928.'" She had taught herself to dance. "The phenomenal success of Florence Mills and Josephine Baker stimulated me. I longed to hold a place in the hearts of the world as they did."[14]

King Vidor, a Hollywood director, saw McKinney in the Broadway musical hit *Blackbirds* and called her to Memphis, Tennessee, where he was shooting *Hallelujah*. He had studied Louisiana's black countryside and religion in order to make his film. McKinney said, "I was thrilled. There I began the fascinating work of acting for the movies." She played the role of cabaret dancer "Chick," who seduced "Zeke" (Daniel Haynes), an evangelical minister. The film became a hit. McKinney praised Vidor and Hollywood for the 2,000 black extras who were hired for the film from the Memphis area plantations. One scene used the whole black population of a town of 500. Vidor said, "I am trying to do for Negro talent what we did for the doughboys in the *Big Parade*": Make them respected heroes. And he added, "Much depends upon the Negro pioneers in this field of art." McKinney was impressed. "He is very sympathetic to us."[15] Thus some blacks felt they had a future in films.

The *Chicago Defender* reported that the success of *Hallelujah* led to talk of another producer making another "race epic," boasting that "many of our group are finding steady employment in the pictures, not only in character, but as members of mob scenes in which their racial characteristics may not be seen."[16] Thus very early blacks appreciated employment in films and recognition.

Hallelujah's plot starkly revealed that the black, rural folk culture, including its ministry, quickly collapsed when confronted with the urban culture symbolized by the cabaret. King Vidor discovered that cabaret culture was so pervasive in black society that its exact counterpart existed in the most rural and backward regions of the South. Urbane hustlers preyed on the rural blacks by using exotic women, gambling, liquor, and jazz music to cheat them out of their wages. Country girls used hustling to escape a life of poverty and drudgery in the countryside. One reviewer noted that "the fate of Zeke (played by Daniel Haynes), a contented cotton picker and eldest son of a large family, is analogous to that of any country boy who enters the city 'green' as far as experience is concerned [and] whose pockets were lined with 'greenbacks,' representing his year's labor." He was cheated out of his money by the urbane McKinney and her pimp.[17]

The cabaret symbolized urban life and the Harlem which Carl Van Vechten in his novel, *Nigger Heaven* (1926), and Claude McKay in *Home to Harlem* (1928), had made famous, leading many whites to trek to Harlem to enjoy its entertainment. Vidor made the rural cabaret famous with *Hallelujah*. Cabaret and entertainment culture emerged early in Los Angeles, too. Hollywood's proximity to Central Avenue encouraged blacks to seek fame and fortune in entertainment and cabaret culture. McKinney and many other blacks went to Los Angeles to pursue acting and entertainment careers.

In the 1920s Mosby and Spikes both had music stores on Central Avenue, at 2315 and 1203 South Central respectively.

The Spikes brothers, Benjamin and Johnny, sold their records but concentrated on selling music publications from their record-store firm called Sunshine Record Company. Their biggest hit was "Someday Sweetheart" (1919), which they sold to the Melrose brothers (Melrose Avenue was named after them) in 1924. The Spikes brothers wrote the lyrics and music for the musical comedy *Steppin' High* (1924), which went on the road and disbanded in Amarillo, Texas, in December of 1924. Benjamin Spikes also used his record store as a referral service for musicians, placing them in night clubs around the city and elsewhere. In November 1924 Reb's Legion Club Forty-Fives recorded a tune, "Sheffield Blues," in tribute to Maceo Sheffield, a feared Los Angeles black police officer who became an actor, "supervisor," and management agent for actors. Mosby and various local musicians were among the first blacks to record sound tracks for Hollywood films. William Rogers Campbell "Sonny" Clay was born in Phoenix, Arizona, on May 15, 1899, but moved to Los Angeles around 1915. He organized Sonny Clay's Plantation Orchestra, a popular Los Angeles band. He was the most recorded black in Los Angeles in the middle and late 1920s. Clay claimed his band appeared in sixty-five films in his heyday.[18]

Lawrence "Speed" Webb and his Hollywood Blue Devils started out in Toledo, Ohio, in 1926 as a jazz band. They played in three films, *Riley the Cop*, *Sables and Furs*, and *On with the Show*, from 1927 to 1929 while in Los Angeles for ballroom engagements. Webb made a record with a flashy front cover that played up his Hollywood film connections: "Speed Webb and His Nationally Famous Hollywood Blue Devils"; "America's Smartest Colored Band"; "Direct from Warner Bros., M-G-M and Fox Studios"; "14 Radio and Screen Artists."[19]

Lionel Hampton, a drummer then, went to Los Angeles in 1927 and built his reputation at Frank Sebastian's Cotton Club in Culver City. Paul Howard's Quality Serenaders was regarded as the "most musical band" in Los Angeles in the 1920s. Howard came from Steubenville, Ohio, and formed his quartet at the Quality Cafe on 12th Street and Central Avenue, in the heart of black Los Angeles. In 1927 his band played at the Cotton Club in Culver City. They recorded for the Victor label such tunes as "The Ramble," "Stuff," "Quality Shout," and "Moonlight Blues" with Lionel Hampton on drums. The band played regularly at the Kentucky Club on Central Avenue but got a date and played at "Eddie Brandstatter's swank Montmartre on Hollywood Boulevard." The band recorded the tunes "California Swing," "Cuttin' Up," and "Harlem" before it broke up in the summer of 1930.[20] The Harlem and Hollywood connections meant the big time in entertainment, and individuals and groups more and more paid homage to them in name and song.

Louis Armstrong came to the Culver City Cotton Club to perform in July 1930. While there he made his first film, *Ex-Flame*, which starred Neal Hamilton, for the Liberty Film Company. He recorded with Les Hite, the Cotton Club house band, such songs as "Ding Dong Daddy," "I'm in the Market for You," "I'm Confessin'," and "Just a Gigolo," all of which were popular songs or were featured in current movies. Armstrong stayed in Los Angeles nine months because the Cotton Club was broadcast by radio from coast to coast, and Hollywood movie stars filled the club nightly. He and Vic Berton were arrested and jailed ten days for possession of marijuana. Earl Broady, a pianist and mailman who saw Armstrong during this period, recalled that Armstrong made marijuana popular among some musicians in Los Angeles. Armstrong returned in 1932 and remained for a three-month engagement at the Cotton Club because he was so impressed with Los Angeles and its emergence as a cultural capital.[21] Recording for Hollywood films and even playing "bit" parts became a regular feature of big name entertainers and their bands while traveling to Los Angeles.

Liquor and marijuana increasingly became part of the jazz and entertainment world, and for some blacks, it was a response to the Jim Crow system. In 1933, while on a ship to England, Louis Armstrong's white manager, Johnny Collins, called him a "nigger." John Hammond, the great jazz impresario, who was present, defended Armstrong's honor and, to Armstrong's dismay, knocked Collins down. Armstrong remained with his manager for another year. Armstrong had a reputation of smoking marijuana daily. He said, "It makes you feel good, man. It relaxes you. Makes you forget all the bad things that happen to a Negro. It makes you feel wanted, and when you're with another tea smoker it makes you feel a special kinship."[22] Many racists and critics used drug and alcohol abuse by musicians and cabaret culture to denounce jazz and its cultural recognition, cultural pluralism, and democracy.

Les Hite played with all the regular and big name Los Angeles musicians such as Curtis Mosby and Paul Howard. He played at Los Angeles City Hall in 1933. He played for Fats Waller in 1935 when Waller went to the Cotton Club in Culver City. One newspaper reported: "Les Hite and his famous Hollywood Orchestra is probably the most famous Negro band on the Pacific Coast!" Moreover, "Millions of movie fans have heard their music and seen the shadowy outline of their faces in cinema productions." Hite played on the air coast to coast from the Culver City Cotton Club on Sundays. He played the big Los Angeles theaters. "Now Playing at the Orpheum downtown is Les Hite and his orchestra in the Black and Tan Revue of 1938 starring Peg Leg Bates, Hattie Noel, Chocolate Brown Sisters and 16 Sweethearts. Two first run pictures are also on the bill." Hite disbanded his group in 1943 and died in 1962.[23] Among blacks, Hite and "Reb" Spikes made the most Hollywood films, at least sixty-five each, because they were first-rate band leaders, were organized, controlled large numbers of musicians through employment, and were based in the Los Angeles area. They were the mainstays and conduits for employment of black musicians in early Hollywood films.

Floyd Ray's Harlem Dictators went to Los Angeles in 1936 with a Miller and Slayter show that was organized in Scranton, Pennsylvania, in 1934. They became very popular at the Warner Brothers studio lot, where blacks often gave weekend dances. In 1936 Cab Calloway and his band went to Los Angeles. Eddie Barefield left that band to remain in Los Angeles because, in his view, there were so few first-rate bands in the city.[24] The opportunities were improving for work, especially in Hollywood, because it increasingly employed local talent as well as performers visiting the city.

Charlie Christian, the great black jazz guitar player, in August of 1939 left Oklahoma City for Los Angeles to play for Benny Goodman. Christian arrived wearing a "purple shirt and yellow shoes" and Goodman was dismayed. His apprehension was allayed after he told the band to play "Rose Room," a tune he thought Christian did not know. To his surprise Christian played so well that he not only inspired Goodman and the band, but the audience gave them the loudest applause ever for their performance at the Victor Hugo Restaurant in Beverly Hills.[25]

Thus blacks participated very early and at every level in the Hollywood and Los Angeles area entertainment culture. Moreover, they promoted cultural pluralism and integration of the races.

Increasingly, Los Angeles attracted blacks, especially those traveling to the city for work or pleasure. Many returned to stay. Black railroad workers often boasted across the country about the city and spread its reputation. Some brought family and girlfriends to the city to live. In 1933 about 100,000 blacks lived in Southern California, and 50,000 of these clustered around Central Avenue. Few black Pullman porters lived in Los Angeles, but many other transportation workers, like "red caps" and cooks, did. The Southern Pacific dining car employees had an "elaborate headquarters at Twelfth and Central" that was presided over by its president, Clarence Johnson. They were second in number in the work force to domestic workers. Many black domestics worked for whites in Hollywood's film industry, especially for the stars and moguls. Blacks working for the city and county of Los Angeles ranked third, "although the motion-picture industry sometimes leads" because of the large numbers of extras employed periodically in films. In 1932 blacks in films earned $35,000. The black community had "six motion picture theaters all conducted by its own people."[26] Thus Hollywood played a significant role in the social life and economy of black Los Angeles.

Local blacks in Los Angeles first got jobs in Hollywood. Hazel Augustine Washington, the wife of Roscoe Washington, a Los Angeles Police Department officer who was highly respected in the department and the black community, was one of the first black hairdressers and personal maids to white female Hollywood stars. She was a "licensed operator" (hairdresser) and a union member, and worked out of the union hall at a time when most unions excluded blacks. She first was an "aide" for Greta Garbo "when they had no Negroes around." "In the 1920s," Washington said, "Hollywood started hiring a lot of blacks." She later worked for years as a personal aide to actress Rosalind Russell. (As a pioneer "black Angeleno" and as the wife of a black policeman, which was high status in black Los Angeles, she never called herself a "servant" or allowed herself to be treated like one because she was a "licensed" and unionized "operator," unlike most other blacks in her field, who were at the mercy of the personal whims of their employers.) Russell helped her open a customized leather-goods store and even became a partner. In 1943 Hazel Washington was the hairdresser for the actors in *Stormy Weather* and *Cabin in the Sky,* and she became a close friend of Lena Horne.[27]

Hazel Washington's position was exceptional. Most blacks were traditional domestic servants and chauffeurs. For many blacks then it was a status symbol to work for prominent employers or Hollywood's film industry moguls or professionals.

Los Angeles had a small number of black males regularly employed (under contract) as actors and showmen in 1930. Out of a total of 4,451 actors, only 128 were black. Three blacks were among the 1,106 "directors, managers, and officials, motion picture production" in the 1930 census. Of 2,909 actresses and showwomen, only 85 were black. The census did not even list a category for female directors, managers, officials, and motion picture production workers.[28] In 1940 the United States Census listed the total number of actors in Los Angeles as 2,426, of whom 51 were black. Male dancers, showmen, and athletes were classed together for a total of 910, with 33 blacks. The total number of males seeking work as experienced actors in Los Angeles amounted to 1,271, with 42 blacks in this number. Similarly, male dancers, showmen, and athletes seeking work amounted to a total of 226, with 21 blacks. The total number of females employed in 1940 as actresses amounted to 743, with 15 blacks. No second category was listed.[29]

Clearly, only a small number of blacks were regularly employed in these fields at any given time. It is not clear if they were largely the same persons employed or different ones. A larger pool of blacks was employed from time to time as extras in Hollywood. Black workers in Los Angeles were largely unskilled and suffered frequent unemployment in the depression years. Hollywood often became a periodic employer for blacks unemployed and underemployed.

"When *King Kong* was filming at RKO in 1933, every out-of-work black musician, singer, actor, and dancer rushed to that lot for work on 'Skull Island'" as natives in the traditional stereotype "G-string" or "loin cloth" roles reserved for blacks from the Central Avenue community. Light-skinned blacks were not hired for these roles. Jazz trumpeter Buck Clayton was turned away from the *Kong* film for this reason. The best white musicians could get work in Hollywood studios, which paid good wages and where work was steady. Black musicians, however, had a rough time because of discrimination and because some lacked the musical literacy the studios demanded.[30]

In February of 1937, 1,500 blacks were hired in Hollywood as extras in *A Day at the Races* filmed by Metro-Goldwyn-Mayer and featuring the Marx Brothers. The song "All God's Chillun Got Rhythm" was to be used in the film. Harpo Marx insisted that black entertainers be used in the scene in which the song was used. Freita Shaw worked on the casting of blacks with the help of Ben Carter. Hundreds of juvenile dancers and bit players were signed as well. However, the weekly payroll amounted to only $800 since only a small percentage of the blacks were used at any one time. Duke Ellington and his band with Ivy Anderson, a singer and native Californian, were featured in the film. Other black acts were headlined, too.[31]

In the film *Slave Ship* 750 blacks were hired by 20th Century-Fox. This broke the record for the number of blacks ever hired by the studio. Blacks were jammed into a slave ship. "There were 400 men and 350 women, a larger number of colored players than has ever worked at one time in any picture in the history of Hollywood." The 350 women were cast in "bit" parts that paid them "$15 per day." Charles Butler played a key role in recruiting these blacks as the Central Casting Office's director for blacks. As usual, he recruited them from his Central Avenue office.[32] Many blacks looked more and more to employment and recognition from Hollywood.

The black press took a closer look at Hollywood's projection of the black image and sought more employment for black entertainers because of the possibility of earning fabulous fortunes. Also, recognition of the race could be won in this medium, and there were reasonable wages and work for blacks recruited for bit roles. Then, too, black pride had to be defended publicly, and Hollywood's projection of blacks in a favorable light was crucial. Also, substantial incomes often came with stardom. The Great Depression made employment a central concern of blacks. The economic crisis also made blacks more politically conscious as left-wing politics spread within the black urban communities.

The film *Green Pastures* (1936) resulted in the more socially and politically conscious New York blacks going to Hollywood to play lead roles. Among these were some old veteran Hollywood film actors such as Rex Ingram, who played the "De Lawd," George Randol as the "High Priest," and assistant director Hall Johnson and his Hall Johnson Choir, who provided the choral music arrangement. Johnson was also the conductor for the film. Ernest Whitman played "Pharaoh."

Los Angeles-based black actors resented the hegemony of New York blacks. When the Associated Negro Press theatrical correspondent, Fay M. Jackson, revealed that Rex Ingram was chosen to play the key role, her opinion was that Ingram was "to whom all the smokes [blacks] [in Hollywood] object." Moreover, she and Claude Barnett, president of the Associated Negro Press, attempted to use the film to advance the cause of black Hollywood actors by protesting the low pay scales and some scenes considered objectionable. Warner Brothers responded with a press release, "Fear 'Green Pastures' New Yorkers May Spoil Hollywood," which impressed some black critics, who felt Jackson's criticisms had been answered. The play and film of *Green Pastures* in Los Angeles resulted in some actors returning to stay in the city. It was such migrants who formed the nucleus of "Hollywood's Harlem" film colony that began "reproducing it [Harlem nightlife] in Hollywood and on Central Avenue," reported the *Chicago Defender*.[33] This influx of actors from New York overshadowed and threatened the black Los Angeles actors and promoters as second-rate imitators.

Blacks tended to resent plantation epics because of the negative connection of rural life with slavery, and especially the slander associated with *The Birth of a Nation* (1915). *Green Pastures* (1936) was generally well received because it had won fame as a play first. Broadway plays and Harlem cabaret shows of distinction would often later be reproduced as films in Hollywood. Marc Connelly's play, *Green Pastures* (1930), was well received by many blacks. It became a "sensational hit" on Broadway and dealt with black religious practices with respect. One critic, Sharon Kane, thought Connelly's play of black rural religious life and culture reflected "absolute originality." Moreover, "this extraordinary play" was a new "dimension" because Connelly had "produced a magnificently imaginative and absolutely new type of Race drama." Black actors were "coming into their own in the world of theater."[34] Another critic was impressed with *Green Pastures* because "the Negro is being taken seriously in drama in this epoch of ours—as a person, not as a caricature." Blacks and their religion were portrayed sympathetically. Nevertheless, Salem Tutt Whitney, presumably a black critic writing for the *Chicago Defender*, "the Harlem complex" (critical of and defensive toward racial slights and caricatures that offended Harlem blacks) "must be allowed to stalk a while" because *Green Pastures* had not completed "the work of exorcism" of prejudice and stereotyping of blacks.[35]

The ministry praised *Green Pastures* lavishly. Bishop Shipman, Bishop Wallace, Dr. W.A. Nichols, religious editor of the *New York Telegram*, and the Rev. Russell J. Clinchy of the Broadway Tabernacle Church attended the play at the Mansfield Theater and wrote raving reviews. Ministers attended every showing and were impressed. Bishops Shipman and Wallace came backstage to congratulate the performers. Dr. Nichols wrote in his column, "Instead of being shocked I was thrilled throughout." He confided, "I went there prepared to be shocked, I came away with the determination to be a better priest. And let it be added, no conscience need be violated by anyone seeing it during Lent, for it is a devotion in itself."[36] Rev. Clinchy said in the press, "May I commend to your readers the play which is now running at the Mansfield theater, entitled 'The Green Pastures,' because my interest in this is simply to aid in spreading news concerning one of the most significant dramas of modern times. . . ."[37] These ministers' approval was important in the reception of the play.

The National Association for the Advancement of Colored People (NAACP) honored Marc Connelly, the play's writer and director, as the guest of honor of the New York Men's Committee of the NAACP at a "smoker" in April 1930. Connelly was introduced by Heywood Broun, a columnist of the *New York Telegram* and Scripps-Howard newspapers. Connelly said he had used Roark Bradford's "Ol' Man Adam and His Chillun" to write his play and he had traveled to Louisiana to study black country life and religion, which were reflected in his play.[38] In 1931 Richard (Rex) Harrison won the NAACP's highest award, the Spingarn Medal, for his acting. Lieutenant Governor Herbert H. Lehman of New York presented Harrison with the medal on March 22, 1931, at the Mansfield Theater, where the play had been presented.[39] The play in 1930 and the film version in 1936 of *Green Pastures* were a relief and well received by most blacks and many whites. It became a standard by which they would judge other plantation epics.

Washington, D.C.'s black population was a proud and dignified group with many educated at Howard University as doctors, lawyers, teachers, dentists, and other professionals. Howard was the leading black college in the country. On February 26, 1933, the *Green Pastures* play was scheduled at the National Theatre for a two-week run. The National did not allow black patrons. Tickets had to be purchased in person to prevent blacks from buying by telephone or mail. Blacks mobilized rapidly to deal with their exclusion. The NAACP and a delegation of black ministers went to Baltimore, where the cast was then playing, to petition the cast not to play at the National Theatre unless blacks were allowed to freely buy tickets and attend the performance. Marc Connelly wrote a letter of protest against the Jim Crow policy, but only the Washington, D.C., *Daily News* published it. Others refused to do so, and the National stopped advertising in the *Daily News* as a protest against its liberalism. Black and white protesters were refused permits by the police to picket the play. A Jim Crow performance was arranged by the Black Elks who quickly had to renounce their role in the matter after an angry protest by key sectors of black leaders. A plot was hatched to kidnap Harrison in order to sabotage the play. Four or five hundred blacks, nevertheless, showed up for the performance and outraged those who had advocated a boycott.[40] Blacks demonstrated again that no broad consensus had been achieved within black society over protest and racial accommodations or how blacks should be portrayed and under what conditions they should perform.

The cast and Richard B. Harrison were under contract, wanted to work, received an income, and dared not refuse to play because their careers might be ruined. Many black and white civil rights activists were severely divided over the incident.[41] No consensus was ever reached among blacks and whites on this issue. Militant blacks, and some white allies, were sorely disappointed. They thought that many blacks by their passive accommodation to Jim Crow were, in effect, co-conspirators in their own oppression and degradation. W.E.B. Du Bois of New

York and Loren Miller of Los Angeles held this view.

Many blacks felt embarrassed by their rural past, which was often associated with slavery and passive accommodation to oppression. Migration to cities, especially in the North, brought greater freedom and job opportunities. Racial pride often increased along with a willingness to insist on public and media respect for the race. Harlem became the black urban capital because of its large black population and its racial militancy. As a result, the "Harlem complex" became well known throughout the country. Harlem as a black social and cultural capital was reflected in its pervasive influence and attempts at creating "little Harlems" across the country, and even back into history, which was evident with the film *Harlem on the Prairie* (1937) by prominent blacks of Los Angeles under the leadership of Maceo Sheffield.

A white film company under Jed Buell made *Harlem on the Prairie*, billed as "The first all-Negro musical Western." A reviewer noted, "The cast is an interesting cross-section of the upper crust of Los Angeles' South Central Avenue [Negro district]." Flournoy E. Miller, who played a key role in *Shuffle Along*, which ran on Broadway successfully for two years and opened up new artistic and cultural opportunities for blacks for generations, appeared in the film. *Harlem on the Prairie* merged a cowboy yarn with flashy Western dress outfits to reflect the Harlemites who adored fine dress along with dramatic acting and first-rate songs.[42] It was a radical departure from the highly resented plantation epics. Black Western films provided an alternative to Southern slavery epics that often portrayed negative "Uncle Tom" stereotypes with "dog-like devotion" to their slavemasters.

A reviewer of *Harlem on the Prairie* wrote, "It brings to life a cow-country as fabulous as the version of some Holy Roller prophet. In this apocalyptic land everybody—the prospectors and stagecoach drivers, the medicine men, outlaws, sheriff, the hero with the silver-plated stock saddle—is a gentlemen of color." Moreover, "it is in no sense a burlesque." It had a real plot that unfolded with dramatic acting. Its first-rate songs were written by a white man, Lew Porter. "Romance in the Rain," the Four Tones harmonizing "Albuquerque," and Herb Jeffries, who sang "The Old Folks at Home," were outstanding.[43]

Harlem on the Prairie was a jazzed-up black dude cowboy film with an urbane flavor designed to appeal to urbane blacks who resented Southern plantation films and caricatures. It romanticized the rural past that many black Harlemites felt ashamed of and were disturbed over—its poverty and peonage, which severely hampered blacks' social and economic mobility. Many blacks, as a result, eagerly sought to adopt a sophisticated urban culture as a means of seeking status and acceptance. Harlem had inaugurated the Harlem Renaissance to combat negative black stereotypes and usher in a "New Negro," an urban and sophisticated black, educated, talented, worldly, and able to secure his own status and social mobility by acquiring and skillfully applying sophisticated urban skills—often in the art and entertainment worlds.

The Club Alabam, run by Ralph Roberts, and later by Curtis Mosby, and the Dunbar Hotel located at 42nd Street and Central Avenue were the two main anchors of the nightlife on Central Avenue. Bill Robinson did a guest show in August of 1938 and the press noted, "Maxine Wows 'Em on L.A.'s Central Avenue: Bojangles Puts on One of His Famous Shows at Club Alabam— Sends Police Escort for Jeni LeGon's Shoes" so she could dance, too. Robinson was made an honorary "lieutenant of police" in Los Angeles (just as New York's Mayor La Guardia had honored him as "the Mayor of Harlem") which gave him petty special privileges. Earl Dancer served as master of ceremonies. Jeni LeGon came from Chicago but now, it was noted, "Jeni LeGon, the dancing darling of the films, carved her way into the hearts of Hollywood's Harlem" that centered on Central Avenue and served as a staging ground for blacks aspiring to get into Hollywood films as well as a showcase for those who had made it.[44]

Entertainers such as "Luther Thompson and Director Tom Jacobson, along with three pretties from his studio doing Hollywood's Harlem" were popular on Central Avenue.[45] Earl Dancer and Flournoy E. Miller had made it big, even if only briefly, in New York on Broadway and at the Apollo Theatre. They took Harlem entertainment culture to Los Angeles and became the founders and pacesetters of "Hollywood's Harlem" social and cultural movements. It represented class, style, and professional accomplishment. It became one of the elite black status groups in Los Angeles and on Central Avenue.

One contemporary observer noted in Los Angeles that Earl

Dancer "tried to impress people. He was a promoter, manager and director." He was a master of ceremonies at nightclubs and acted as an agent for entertainers, movie actors, and singers. He spent money lavishly. He talked confidently about breaking into the "big time" by getting into "the white time" entertainment world and money—that meant Hollywood films.[46] Dancer's big city talk, style, and goals impressed the local blacks who lacked the background, Broadway, and magical Harlem connections that he and Miller could boast about.

The *California Eagle* newspaper advertised in August 1938, "South East Harlem Aristocrat of Night Spots, Featuring T-Bone Walker, 11812 Parmalee Avenue, 2 blocks East of Central off Imperial Highway, JE-7434." Another read, "Dunbar Cocktail Lounge, Host Harry Spates, 4227 So. Central, Adams 4201." And visitors were solicited with "Summer Visitors! Los Angeles' 'Night Life' Is Found at the Club Alabam, Gala Opening July 9th, Fun-Freedom-Hilarity—Lavish Floor Show Produced by Mantan Moreland, For Reservations call Je-4569." In 1940 T-Bone Walker played at the popular Little Harlem nightclub located at 114th Street and Central Avenue. Also, a club named the Plantation was patronized and Harlem itself had a club called the Plantation.[47] The *California Eagle* ran a huge advertisement, saying "Hollywood Meets Harlem": "Grand Studio Ball & Movie Classics. Sponsored by Golden West Lodge No. 86, I.B.P.O.E.W. **Championship Big-Apple-Contest.** The Pick of Harlem–Harlem's Elect. **Sepia Bathing Beauty Parade.** California's Most Charming and Graceful Maidens. Directed by Clarence Muse. Warner Bros. Studio. Sunset Blvd. and Van Ness Ave., Hollywood. Thurs. Nite, July 21st, 1938, 9 P.M. Movie Stars, Radio Favorites, Famous Directors and Camera-men, the Baker, Butcher and Even the Ice Man will join hands when Hollywood Meets Harlem. Gen. Adm. $.75, Reserve Section $1.00, Boxes Seating six $7.00. For Reservations Call Room 200 Elks Bldg. Phone Adams 7578."[48] This ad was one of the most dramatic and lavish presentations of the social and cultural movement of "Hollywood Meets Harlem."

Other ads noted that Clarence Muse was the only male who met with the black women's Social Committee for the "Hollywood Meets Harlem" celebration at the Elks' Hall on Central Avenue. Still another ad noted: "Hollywood to Meet

Harlem" on Stage Six "in a gigantic movie ball." Muse said the winner among sixty black bathing beauty contestants would receive a movie contract. The "Hollywood Meets Harlem" celebration included a "Big Apple Swing Session" at this "movie jamboree." The *California Eagle* society editor, Helen F. Chappell, wrote a column called "Chatter and . . . Some News" in which she called Central Avenue "the Angel City Harlem."[49]

Los Angeles in Spanish means "the angels" and many commentators called it "The City of the Angels." The Angel City Harlem was the Central Avenue black entertainment colony. Blacks found many ways to express the Hollywood/Harlem connection, and Hollywood proper was often used very loosely to mean Central Avenue or just blacks in Hollywood films. In short, black Hollywood or "Harlem in Hollywood" most often meant blacks with the Harlem entertainment style working in Hollywood films or on Central Avenue.

Clarence Muse had good reason to promote dances at Hollywood movie lots. A reporter noted, "Mr. Muse says the only hope for young Negro actors is the loyal support of colored audiences. If they fail to come to the theatre the young Negro artist is doomed." He won success in New York at the Lafayette Theatre because blacks heavily patronized the shows. He believed that Earl Dancer "is one of America's best Negro theatre thinkers" in the country.[50] Such "Harlem in Hollywood" leaders as Dancer and Muse were cultivating their own black Los Angeles audiences to ensure their success in Hollywood films. Central Avenue played a key role in their efforts to cultivate a sophisticated black entertainment culture and they attempted to duplicate the black cabaret culture of Harlem there and in Hollywood.

The Elks Golden West Lodge No. 86, which sponsored the "Hollywood Meets Harlem" celebration, was a black fraternal organization that engaged in social and political activity. It was a significant institution in the emergence of the Harlem in Hollywood movement. Many of the black Los Angeles elite were members of the Elks or the Masons. The Elks had a huge hall at 40th Place and Central Avenue which was used for meetings, community affairs, ballroom dances, and jazz concerts. Many of the nightlifers and party-goers associated with the Elks because of the fun and social status at their huge and successful dances at the Elks' Auditorium, which often featured nationally renowned black entertainers and hosted black Hollywood stars.[51] The Elks promoted the glamour of urban life and cabaret culture. Its social and cultural activities helped rural blacks make the transition to urbane culture and sophistication.

Despite many blacks' misgivings about their rural past, they still reveled in the rural cabaret tradition, which they transferred to cities, where it reached new levels of cultivation. This was reflected in stage shows and parades. *Dixie Goes Hi-Hat* was an "all-colored musical comedy" produced by Charles K. Gordon. He and Flournoy E. Miller wrote the book, and the music and lyrics were by Otis and Leon Rene. Miller and black actor Mantan Moreland sponsored the show at the Wilshire Ebell Theatre—a prestigious white theater in Los Angeles off Wilshire Boulevard. Admission cost 50 cents, 75 cents, and 1 dollar.[52]

The Negro Division of the Screen Actors Guild participated in the 1938 Los Angeles Labor Day parade, for which F. Paul Sylas of Talisman Studios built a float. Jesse Graves was chair of the committee and Hattie McDaniel—a perennial film star in black mammy roles—and Theresa Harris helped finance the project. The committee members were Edward Boyd, Anna Mabry, Caldwell Clinton Rosamond, Clarence Muse, David Horton, and Mae Turner—all important community and Hollywood activists. The float had a rural cabin mounted upon it with Aunt Jemima flapping pancakes at the door and a few other black women in the front and rear.[53] The Cotton Club in New York had featured this scenario in *Cabin in the Cotton Club* in 1933 in which Ethel Waters starred. Its popularity resulted in a successful Broadway run in 1940, then a film in 1943.[54]

Dixie Goes Hi-Hat was a popular theme in black entertainment culture because it reflected the transition from rural crudeness to urbane sophistication. "Hi-Hat" meant high class, formality, and was derived from formal dress, the tuxedo and silk high hat. For many blacks, the shift from rural overalls dress to urbane fashions symbolized the release from rural poverty, shame, and white brutality to a new sense of race pride, energy, and joy fostered in big Northern or Western cities that offered better jobs. This, in turn, made possible a more vigorous, stimulating, and glamorous social and nightlife culture. Harlem in New York, Central Avenue in black Los Angeles, and "Harlem in Hollywood" culture were celebrations of this transition. What is more, fame and fabulous fortunes, at least by black standards of wealth at the time, could be won literally for a song and dance in Harlem and Hollywood. The Labor Day parade featuring a cabin with black mammies, however, indicated ambivalence and retention of rural customs and comedy. Indeed, the persistence of black stereotypes indicated their hold on both whites and blacks.

Blacks jubilantly celebrated their urbane sophistication. In September of 1938, the *California Eagle* reported that "Stars and Movie Fans Turn Out for Dedication of Bill Robinson Theatre" in the Central Avenue district "at 43rd and Central Avenue." The Tivoli Theatre was renamed the Bill Robinson Theatre. "All the glamour, crowds, confusion and grazed chins, typical of a Hollywood opening were present as the Tivoli—oops—Bill Robinson went to town." A new film, *The Duke Is Tops*, featuring Ralph Cooper and Lena Horne, was shown. The opening was attended "by the most outstanding of Legion big-wigs." What is more, the "most famous visitor of all was the Grand Duke of Dance, the Maharajah of Rhythm, His Highness of Tap—Bill 'Bojangles' Robinson." Nina Mae McKinney, Louise Beavers and Ralph Cooper, the Snowden Brothers (Al and Ruben), who owned the theater, and many others attended.[55] The new theater added prestige and helped institutionalize the "Harlem in Hollywood" movement in Los Angeles. An advertisement boasted: "Bill Robinson Theatre, 4319 So. Central, telephone AD-7367" and "(formerly Tivoli), **The Show Place of Holly-Harlem-Wood.**"[56] Another ad ran, "Savoy Theatre, 54th and Central" with Herbert Jeffries (who won a reputation as Duke Ellington's vocalist on the song "Flamingo") and Mantan Moreland in *Harlem on the Prairie*.[57] Its namesake was the famous Savoy Ballroom in Harlem.

Another Harlem Cotton Club luminary, Duke Ellington, went to Los Angeles and added to this movement. Ellington over the years had made trips to Los Angeles to play in Hollywood films and for musical performances. His was the main house band for years at the Cotton Club in Harlem. He performed live on radio from the Cotton Club. From 1929 to 1931 he recorded such tunes as "Wall Street Wail" (in recognition of the Wall Street stock market crash of 1929), "Cotton Club Stomp," "Runnin' Wild," "Mood Indigo" (a very popular hit and landmark tune), "Rockin' in Rhythm," and "Double Check Stomp." This resulted in his first film performance with the popular comics "Amos 'n' Andy" in the film *Check and Double Check* in 1930. He also recorded such tunes as "Harlem Speaks," "Caravan," "The Gal from Joe's," and many other songs in recognition of Harlem and its black culture.[58] Ellington epitomized success and sophistication within the highly competitive Harlem cabaret culture.

In 1940 Ellington went to perform at the Culver City Casa Mañana near the M-G-M film studios. He stayed at the Dunbar Hotel on 42nd and Central Avenue, in the heart of the black entertainment district. Segregation of the races prevented him from staying elsewhere. Sid Kuller, a Hollywood screenwriter who lived in Studio City, a Los Angeles suburb, saw Ellington and his band and was captivated. Kuller objected to the Jim Crow restrictions that kept Ellington out of the best white hotels. When Kuller saw the conditions of the Dunbar, where the walls were still cracked from the 1933 earthquake, he invited Ellington to stay at his home. They had nightly house parties while Ellington stayed there which were attended at various times by Tony Martin, Lana Turner, Jackie Cooper, Mickey Rooney, W.R. Burnett, John Garfield, Dan Daily, Bonita Granville, and many other Hollywood stars.[59] Thus some Hollywood whites practiced racial integration and democracy at a time when it was not popular and legally prohibited. Kuller, for the moment at least, played a role well established in New York by Carl Van Vechten of promoting interracial house parties as a means of breaking down race barriers with the hope that the pattern would spread throughout society. Another Harlem Renaissance tradition became part of Hollywood and the impact was obvious.

At one of these parties people pledged $20,000 toward a musical called *Jump for Joy* under Ellington's direction. Hal Borne, a Hollywood studio musician, and Ellington, as well as Mickey Rooney and Mercer Ellington, Duke's son, wrote sixteen songs for the show. Paul Francis Webster, a lyricist, and Hollywood sketch writer Hal Fimberg worked on the musical. Borne worked for the RKO film studio on dance and orchestra, and had arranged the Fred Astaire/Ginger Rogers masterpieces *Flying Down to Rio, The Gay Divorcee, Top Hat,* and *The Story of Vernon and Irene Castle*. In short, many of Hollywood's top artists supported and worked on *Jump for Joy*.[60]

The Hollywood film colony had always contained a group of radicals. They supported *Jump for Joy.* "Now you have to remember that all of them, including the Duke himself, wanted to do more than put together a jazz musical. They also wanted to make a social and political statement. They wanted to strike a blow for racial equality. And so, in various sketches and in some of the song lyrics, racial stereotypes were ridiculed and satirical broadsides were launched against the continuing injustices still being practiced against black people," Maurice Zolotow wrote.[61] One proposed sketch had an Uncle Tom on his deathbed with a chorus dancing about to send him on his way while Hollywood and Broadway producers desperately tried to pump adrenaline into his veins to keep him alive. It was a telling critique of Hollywood film stereotypes. Also featured was the number "I've Got a Passport from Georgia (and I'm Going to the USA)." Poet Langston Hughes also wrote for the musical. The final act featured "Uncle Tom's Cabin Is a Drive-in Now" with the verse: "There used to be a chicken shack in Caroline,/ But now they've moved it up to Hollywood and Vine;/They paid off the mortgage—nobody knows how/—And Uncle Tom's Cabin is a drive-in now!" The show lasted three months in 1941 and prepared for a new season in Chicago, then Broadway, but folded in Los Angeles. Ellington said the loss of personnel to the draft caused it to collapse, but others said it was too far ahead of its time, according to Almena Davis.[62]

Ellington, well respected in white and black circles, was not without critics, however. John Hammond, a famous talent scout and descendant of the Vanderbilt family, became enchanted with black jazz and jazzmen in New York in the 1920s. He charged that Duke Ellington had played only at the most exclusive white clubs and for white patrons in the 1920s and 1930s. Ellington's band was one of the first large black bands to perform on film— *Check and Double Check* (1930). "Duke had, I felt, an old-line point of view of the Negro's ability to survive in a white commercial world," said Hammond. He compromised to achieve success and recognition, charged Hammond, a fervent and chauvinistic supporter of black culture, especially jazz and spirituals, in the service of civil rights for blacks. Hammond also was a member of the board of directors of the NAACP and was well aware of the Harlem Renaissance faction which had sought to use arts for civil rights for blacks. Ellington had rejected Hammond's solicitation to create racially mixed bands. Hammond said Ellington gave him the impression, "why help the white bands by filling them with black players, thereby threatening the survival of the Negro bands?" Hammond rejected the notion that jazz was exclusively black. His view was: "I feel that jazz always has had a duty to promote racial understanding and interracial cooperation." He promoted the arts, as had Carl Van Vechten, in quest of cultural pluralism and racial democracy. On the other hand, "most Negro band leaders were discouraged, if not defeated, by the Depression," said Hammond.[63]

Hammond got involved with the NAACP and civil rights because "my dedication to their cause, growing out of my love for their music, made it seem essential to understand as much as I could about their problems, the solutions they proposed, and the men who were undertaking to lead American blacks in their long fight for equal justice."[64] He epitomized the Harlem Renaissance man who sought to use art for civil rights.

Hammond, however, partially represented the Du Boisian view that art should be used for propaganda. But he apparently did not agree that only black conservative images were valid while all others were suspect or stereotypes. Hammond tried to prod Ellington into a more direct propaganda role, which Ellington resisted. Hammond was quick to add, "None of this is to suggest that Duke was not proud of his own people. In his way he fought the battle for equal rights as effectively as any other Negro leader. Duke loved the highest of societies, white and black. He sought the best locations, both because he enjoyed mingling with the cream of any social circle and because the money was better."[65] Ellington replied to his critics: "All round the world I've had to answer questions about the race situation in my country, often hostile ones. People asking why Negro artists haven't done more for the cause, that kind of thing. It makes me very angry, and I say that people wouldn't ask questions like that if they knew what they were talking about. But then usually I cool down and tell them of the things since the 1930s, all the shows and concerts and benefits the band has done."[66] Ellington thought he had demonstrated his race pride and commitment.

A biographer of Ellington noted that he boasted with pride that he and his band did their own freedom marching in the

1930s throughout the South. "We went down in the South without federal troops." He recorded many famous black tunes such as "Black Beauty" and "Deep South Suite." He preferred to make his statements musically and rejected propaganda on stage: "Screaming about it onstage don't make a show."[67] Ellington epitomized the Harlem Renaissance man who thought that direct racial propaganda was harmful—a position with which many black and white Harlem Renaissance men and women agreed.

The Harlem Renaissance ideological battles brought the jazz world the same divisions between the art for propaganda faction and the pure art school which believed that subtlety and merit would break down racial stereotypes and thereby undermine Jim Crow. Ellington's appearance in Los Angeles must have electrified the local party-goers and the radicals struggling against Hollywood stereotypes. Apparently, they thought that due to Ellington's fame, the *Jump for Joy* musical was a vehicle for their radical ideas. Although the show was short-lived its impact was not necessarily negligible.

A series of Hollywood films in the early 1940s resulted in the continuation of the Harlem Renaissance controversy between those who differed over the nature of urban jive and rural simplicity of blacks as either negative stereotypes or worthy portrayals of black folk culture. The film *Tales of Manhattan* in 1942 caused ambivalence and controversy among blacks and some white critics. The blacks in the film were Ethel Waters, Paul Robeson, and Eddie Anderson.[68] The plot of the film was based around six episodes—five with an all-white cast with such stars as Ginger Rogers, Henry Fonda, and Charles Laughton, and the sixth with an all-black one—in which a coat brings bad or good luck to its owner according to his own character. In the fifth episode, a shootout aboard an airplane leads the owner to discard the coat, which falls to earth and winds up in the hands of Paul Robeson and Ethel Waters—two poor black sharecroppers.[69] Robeson and Waters and the Hall Choir singers find the coat with $50,000 in one pocket. They sing and praise the finding as manna from heaven. The coat finally winds up on the back of a scarecrow.

One reviewer said the sixth episode was "the most completely artificial" because of its stereotype" . . . with its comedy-relief treatment of Negroes." Another said the coat "is alternatively a jinx or joy to its successive owners, until it comes to rest as a raffish example of what the well-dressed scarecrow will wear in a Negro sharecropper's cotton field."[70] Another critic called the film "a socially conscious minstrel show in which Paul Robeson and Ethel Waters find $50,000 in the tail coat, and with the help of Jack Benny's Rochester (Eddie Anderson, who starred with Benny as his foil) divided it with the Hall Johnson Choir and other Hollywood sharecroppers." Moreover, he noted, "each actor was permitted to make changes in the script, but the only one who bothered much was Paul Robeson. He piously refused to have any religious words put in his mouth."[71]

Manny Farber, a constant critic of Hollywood's stereotypes of blacks, called *Tales of Manhattan* "the romantic distortion of Negro life" that "is a discrimination as old as Hollywood." He complained of the six Jim Crow episodes: "If the movies want to give a Negro front billing, it has to be an all-Negro picture or nothing." Moreover, "the segregation in 'Tales of Manhattan' is complete" because black and white performers were shown only in all-black or all-white casts in each episode. Farber added bitterly, "After segregating them, the movie shows the Negro his place in the social scale." The whites were professionals, and blacks were "either sharecroppers or nothing." Finally, noted Farber, "once the Negro recognizes his place in movies, he is treated with a great love."[72] These white critics did not approve of the stereotype roles assigned to blacks, and neither did some blacks.

Paul Robeson especially criticized the film and refused to act in any more Hollywood films as a result of *Tales of Manhattan*. As noted in a headline, he bitterly complained, "Hollywood's 'Old Plantation Tradition' Is Offensive to My People." He noted that Hollywood producers insisted on making the usual "plantation hallelujah shouters" and despite his objections and changes made in the film, "in the end it turned out to be the same old thing—the Negro solving his problems by singing his way to glory. This is very offensive to my people. It makes the Negro child-like and innocent and is in the old plantation tradition. But Hollywood says you can't make the Negro in any other role because it won't be box office in the South. The South wants its Negroes in the old style."[73] Robeson was determined to destroy these stereotypes which, in his view, injured the reputation of blacks and helped to justify Jim Crow practices.

Robeson called for a nationwide boycott of Hollywood films. The *Chicago Defender* endorsed the boycott. It added that Hollywood was "fascist-minded." It noted Robeson's views on Hollywood: "He has found it one of the foremost builders of a stereotype" that promoted a "'hat-in-hand,' 'me-too-boss' Negro." The *Defender* charged that "the presentation of Negro life on the screen is pure, unadulterated Hitlerism." Moreover, "it is un-American and subversive. It is treasonable." The *Defender* encouraged its readers to flood Hollywood with letters of protest and to send delegations to picket theaters showing films stereotyping blacks.[74]

Lawrence LaMar (or Lamar) disagreed with the criticism that *Tales of Manhattan* slandered blacks by portraying them as superstitious country bumpkins. He noted the "theatre management" and distributors arranged to show the Twentieth Century-Fox film at a "press preview" at the Lincoln Theatre (one of the Harlem in Hollywood institutions of film and entertainment for blacks) in the Central Avenue district of Los Angeles, where most blacks resided. They wanted to "feel out the public on some of the so-called objectionable scenes" because of black protest and threats of a boycott. Lamar said he had "failed to see anything in the film but good entertainment." He noted that in the scene featuring blacks they "are depicted as superstitiously religious."[75] Ethel Waters, who starred in the film, noted that "when Tales of Manhattan was released various Negro organizations picketed the theaters showing it. Their placards protested picturing us colored people as wretched, dirty, and poorly clad." She added, "I didn't understand that. These same organizations were forever complaining that we Negroes in America are under-privileged. So why did they object to anyone showing us that way on the screen?"[76] Black and white critics thought that black poverty and superstition were featured to ridicule black folk culture and promote contempt for blacks.

The film *Star Spangled Rhythm* epitomized the extreme of the black G.I. Jive movement. It was a wartime patriotic entertainment film capitalizing on the *Star-Spangled Banner*. It was designed to appeal to war fever and patriotism. A galaxy of Harlem and Hollywood black entertainers paraded across the screen. It featured "Slim" Gaillard and "Slam" Brown, who were masters of comedy, jazz, and Harlem Jive language; Katherine

Dunham, a scholar trained in African and Afro-Caribbean dances; Eddie "Rochester" Anderson, of Jack Benny fame; and dance director Danny Dare. Twenty-four top black male and female dancers from the Pacific Coast, largely black Los Angeles, were featured as well.

One tune from the movie "Belt in the Back" was written by Harold Arlen of Cotton Club fame and Johnny Mercer, a leading figure in the recording industry. Both built careers as well in Hollywood. Arlen had long been associated with the Cotton Club in Harlem. He was embraced by blacks as one of their own. He had mastered Harlem culture and wrote such torch tunes as "Harlem Holiday," "Pool Room Papa," "My Military Man," and "High Flyin' Man." He and Ted Koehler produced the Cotton Club shows called "Cotton Club Parades." Arlen was noted for his "inside look" at Harlem life which fascinated many white Americans and Europeans who came to the Cotton Club to revel in Harlem jazz and jive.[77]

Film critic Philip T. Hartung noted that *Star Spangled Rhythm* (1942) "is a sprightly film; it glitters almost as much as its name— but not quite." He noted that Paramount paraded its stars, who drifted in and out doing specialty dance and song numbers. "The two best numbers of this de luxe potpourri are: a song and dance item with Eddie 'Rochester' Anderson and Katherine Dunham (proving the advantages of a soldier's uniform over a Zoot suit); and Bing Crosby's singing the big patriotic finale: 'Old Glory.'"[78] *Time* magazine noted that the parade of top stars of Paramount Pictures made the film expensive: it cost $1,500,000, of which a third went for "its high-priced performers' salaries." *Time* added that Eddie "Rochester" Anderson "in a Zoot-suit," checkered, with a wide-brimmed white hat, and black-and-white spats" performed "with a strutting" wild jitterbug dance with Katherine Dunham to the song "Sharp as a Tack."[79] Hartung thought it simply harmless flashy high-priced entertainment. Anderson ended his routine by entering double doors in the background props in his Zoot suit and emerging in an Army khaki brown uniform to impress upon black Zooters who might view the film that it was cool to join the military.[80]

Hartung was impressed, but not so Manny Farber, who perpetually criticized what he judged to be stereotyped or all-black segregated films. He charged that there was a rush to produce segregated or all-black movies that were "obscene." He noted, "Now we are going to be democratic; it's the fashion. This is not in any way to say the movies have changed their attitude toward Negroes; there is just more of it." He charged in regard to *Star Spangled Rhythm*: "Witness the wholly objectionable caricature of Negro dress and dancing in the Zoot-suit number, in which Rochester and Katherine Dunham sing and dance something you could spend all your life in Harlem and never see the like of." He appreciated the Golden Gate Quartet in the film, but their "talent for rhythmic singing" was cancelled "by making the men clown."[81]

Farber was a diehard Du Boisian in his perspective that any depictions of blacks other than "normal" or middle-class were caricatures. Blacks should be integrated with whites rather than Jim Crowed into typical black stereotype menial and comedy relief roles. He believed that such roles helped to perpetuate the negative public opinion about blacks which undergirded the whole Jim Crow system of inequality. Billy Rowe and John T. McManus also followed this Du Boisian line.

Billy Rowe agreed with John T. McManus, writing for the newspaper *PM*, who charged that Hollywood had not kept its promise to NAACP president Walter White to halt stereotypes. *Star Spangled Rhythm*, in their view, reflected stereotypes. McManus noted that Hollywood films with more blacks were designed "simply to exploit more colossally than ever the reservoir of Negro talent." What is more, "no attempt has been made to purge films of the false but enduring Negro stereotypes—the eye-rollers, the Uncle Toms, the white ghost shiverers. To those have been added the Zoot-suits and the Afro-maniacs, as well as a variety of ingratiating new talents and faces, all ironically helping to perpetuate the concept that the Negro is still just a happy-go-lucky ward of democracy." McManus said *Star Spangled Rhythm*'s "Zoot-suit sequence proved that Negroes can be made their worst caricatures."[82] Black actors, he thought, should object to playing such roles and obviously thought Zoot suits were clownish and demeaning.

The black and white actors in the film, and many viewers, had a completely different perception of the roles they played. Many whites had starred in *Star Spangled Rhythm*, including Bing Crosby, Alan Ladd, Fred MacMurray, Vera Zorina, and Bob Hope, who was master of ceremonies. The film was a model "patriotic variety form" that became a norm for many similar films which soon followed, such as *Stormy Weather* (the film as a biography of Bill Robinson begins with a military parade of the New York 369th Regiment's return from Europe, a march down Broadway, and the grand party that followed) and *Stage Door Canteen*. These films merged jazz, jive, and jitterbug dancing into what became a popular and "patriotic" formula: G.I. Jive. Among performers, especially in Hollywood, where contributing to the war effort was a hot topic, it became hep to lift the morale of soldiers and war workers with highly entertaining musicals containing lively dance routines, flashy wardrobes—Zoot suit uniforms—and jive language and jazz.[83] Universal Studios signed Elyse Knox and Robert Paige to star in the romantic leads in the film *Oh, Say Can You Swing* to cash in on popular musicals which mixed escapism and patriotic fervor. It formerly had been titled *School for Jive!*[84]

In 1933 Ethel Waters performed in the Cotton Club "Stormy Weather Show" and was asked to do a dozen encores. It turned out to be one of the most successful shows in Cotton Club history. In the Cotton Club's "Stormy Weather Show" Waters sang "Cabin in the Cotton Club" while standing by a lamppost with a cabin in the background. Duke Ellington's band dramatized the show with musical sounds resembling a storm. In 1940 *Cabin in the Sky* was performed as a musical on Broadway, starring Ethel Waters with jazz pianist Eubie Blake.[85]

The film version was made in 1942 and played through the end of 1943. The plot was an allegory about good versus evil. Eddie "Rochester" Anderson played Little Joe Jackson, a gambler and hustler, whose wife Petunia (Ethel Waters) battles for his soul by pleading for his reform so they can go to heaven together. Meanwhile, Lucifer uses Georgia Brown (Lena Horne) to entice Little Joe back into his evil ways. In a dream, Little Joe and Petunia are shot and killed in a gunfight at Jim Henry's Cafe. Petunia pleads with the Lord to save Joe and let them go to heaven together. Her wish is granted. Little Joe Jackson wakes up from his dream and reforms himself. Louis Armstrong and Buck and Bubbles (Ford Washington and John Sublett), a dance team, and Duke Ellington and his band were featured in the nightclub scene. The Cotton Club's Harold Arlen and lyricist Yip Harburg produced the show and wrote the famous movie score, "Happiness Is Just a Thing Called Joe" sung by Ethel Waters.[86]

During the filming of *Cabin in the Sky*, Waters was bitterly resentful of Horne who kept her distance. Horne hurt her ankle while filming, and cast and crew rushed to Horne's side to assist her, offering a pillow to rest her ankle on. Waters blew up with jealousy and envy. They did not speak again.[87] Waters said during the film, "I objected violently to the way religion was being treated in the screen play." She felt the plea to save Little Joe undermined her role as a woman. She added, "I rejected the part because it seemed to me a man's play rather than a woman's. Petunia, in the original script, was no more than a punching bag for Little Joe." As a result of her protest, she noted, "some of the changes I demanded had been made [and] I accepted the role, largely because the music was so pretty." It was six years before she got another film role.[88]

Lena Horne had established a reputation as a "lady" and had joined with NAACP president Walter White to repudiate negative racial stereotypes. Ethel Waters often played stereotype roles, as in *Tales of Manhattan*, and she had protested pickets and critics of the film. Each actress symbolized a type in bitter contention for recognition and respectability. Apparently, it became very personal.

The critics, too, divided over the merits of *Cabin in the Sky*. *Time* magazine noted that despite their talent, blacks were portrayed "as picturesque, Sambo-style entertainers." It added, "This tendency, not confined to Hollywood, old in American life, is encouraged by a plot which has a flavoring of The Green Pastures fantasy. . . ." The dance routines were fantastic. "The best things in the picture are a rebuke to all kinds of pretentiousness."[89] Philip T. Hartung thought the black actors and the new songs by Harold Arlen and E. Yip Harburg of the Cotton Club were superb. He noted, "Since 'Cabin in the Sky' is a Negro fantasy, Hollywood might be excused for portraying Negroes as theatrical, crap-shootin', buck-and-wing darkies."[90]

Newsweek, too, was impressed with the black actors, music, and song and dance routines. *Cabin in the Sky* reflected the new policy worked out between Walter White and Wendell Willkie and the Hollywood moguls with the support given by the Office of War Information (OWI), which was concerned with building black morale in support of the country and the war. The OWI sought to undergird black G.I. Jive with its Harlem roots and traditions, and press it into the service of Uncle Sam. But the film fell short of those expectations. *Newsweek* noted that the understanding was a reaction to "plain-spoken hints last summer from Wendell Willkie, Lowell Mellett of the Office of War Information, and others, that now was the time to give the Negro his place as a dignified, responsible citizen." Marc Connelly, the author of *Green Pastures*, which was well received in earlier years, backed out of the film and refused to allow his name to be associated with it. He and *Newsweek* felt *Cabin in the Sky* perpetuated stereotypes and was not a New Deal for blacks.[91]

Manny Farber claimed that *Cabin in the Sky* was "Hollywood's latest example of segregation" and "is the usual religious-comic handout that is given the Negro by a white studio whose last thought is to make a movie that is actually about Negroes." He added that *Cabin in the Sky* was a Jim Crow [all-black] film that constructs "a niggertown—out of jimcrack architecture, stage grass and magnolia trees—to look like paradise." He lamented, "The tragic fact is that the Negro artists are in no position to bargain with Hollywood. . . ." He praised the black actors: "The one value of all-Negro films lies in giving Negro artists an outlet for their talents. And the one value of 'Cabin in the Sky' is the talent of Rochester, Lena Horne and Louis Armstrong, irrespective of anything in the movie script." The larger question, in Farber's view, and the damage of such a film was that "Hollywood, in its position of greatest public influence, solidifies racial prejudice to an enormous degree by its 'Cabin in the Sky,' which is an insidious way of showing the Negro his place."[92] Once again, Farber militantly restated the Du Boisian interpretation of what constituted stereotype characterizations.

The black press criticized *Cabin in the Sky*. Joseph D. Bibb suggested in his headline that "The Riff Raff: Unthinking Majority of Bad Actors Are Always in the Focus of Publicity." Bibb thought it was a "rancid movie." He bitterly charged that only "the riff raff of the colored American people" would patronize such a movie. Moreover, these black patrons were "the very characters, who in everyday life, are hanging like millstones around the necks of thirteen million dark people." This type was epitomized, in his view, by the film characters Domino Johnson, a "strutting, swaggering, amorous killer," and Mose Henry, "vice lord, gambler, cafe owner and evil spirit of the sordid community."[93] Bibb's bitter denunciation was a restatement of the Du Boisian attack on Carl Van Vechten's novel *Nigger Heaven* (1926), which, according to Du Bois, viewed black life in Harlem as one giant cabaret and vice orgy.

Los Angeles Sentinel editor Leon Washington objected to *Cabin in the Sky* because it was advertised with a drawing of a "Zoot-suited . . . couple doing a jitterbug dance while a long-headed, big, red lipped boy looks on grinningly." In Los Angeles, it was due to open in May of 1943 at Grauman's Chinese in Hollywood and Loew's State and the Rivoli on Western Avenue.[94] Leon Washington threatened to picket the theaters. The *New York Amsterdam News* noted a *Cabin in the Sky* appearance on Broadway at the Criterion Theatre. The film was the first big all-black movie since *Hallelujah* in 1929. The *News* thought that *Cabin in the Sky* was "an insult masking behind the label of folklore. It isn't folklore." What is more, "it pictures Negroes, heads tied up, with crap shooting inclinations and prayer meeting propensities at a time when Negroes are daily proving their heroic mettle in battle and defense plant. This is the sort of thing that keeps alive misconceptions of the Negro." It noted, however, the film was very popular and broke the house attendance record at the Criterion Theatre. The "excellent cast" was praised for its swell performance.[95]

Arthur Freed produced and Vincente Minnelli directed *Cabin in the Sky* and were very proud of it as the best black musical ever. Philip Carter, a native of Pasadena, California, who had been working in New York as a journalist for ten years, was hired by M-G-M and given an office on the company's lot to provide special publicity for the film to reduce the growing number of black critics.[96] Noble Sissle of Cotton Club and Broadway fame praised *Cabin in the Sky*. He said the film was "as powerful in fostering Americanism and tolerance as Harriet Beecher Stowe's 'Uncle Tom's Cabin.'" What is more, he said in defense of M-G-M, producing the film "promoted racial goodwill."[97] Many artists wanted to work and rejected the notion that jazz, jive, jitterbugging, all-black films, or certain roles were demeaning to blacks as a group.

Racists objected. A white mob in Mount Pleasant, Tennessee, raided a theater and halted the showing of *Cabin in the Sky* because of fear that the spread of black culture would break down the Jim Crow system as it was doing in New York and Harlem cabarets, on Broadway and in Hollywood films.[98] They did not want whites to patronize or appreciate black culture for fear whites would attempt to participate in local black entertainment and thereby integrate the races.

Sissle's defense of *Cabin in the Sky* was an understandable position from artist like himself, who had won fame and fortune in the highly prestigious Harlem cabarets, especially the Cotton Club, and Broadway entertainment culture. Moreover, he was part of the school of thought in the Harlem Renaissance that Carl Van Vechten, Langston Hughes, Claude McKay, Walter White, and many others were part of—they advocated cultural pluralism, even within black society and culture. They respected the black rural folk and urban jive cultures as exotic, beautiful, and unique. They had long ago rejected social Victorianism and the values and codes of conduct that placed their entertainment culture and behavior patterns out of bounds. Their success in Hollywood and at the box office had confirmed their views and behavior.

Amid the bitterness of Ethel Waters toward Lena Horne, who was hurt and distraught by the bickering among blacks and objections to her push for "better roles" for blacks, the filming of *Cabin in the Sky* almost came to a halt. During the filming Horne left for New York and jazz pianist Count Basie had to use some strong persuasion to get her to return. Lena told him, "I'm back where I belong. I'm never going to leave New York again." She felt comfortable in the Harlem and Broadway entertainment world, where Cotton Club culture was supreme. Harlem entertainment culture in Hollywood films resulted in bitter criticism of the films and, often in some quarters, the entertainers as well. Then, too, critics of black entertainers and some entertainers themselves were becoming bitterly divided over the images projected by the roles they played. Count Basie told Horne, "They chose you; we don't get the chance. You've got to go, and you've got to stay there, and you've got to be good, and you've got to be right and do whatever they want you to do and make us proud of you."[99] Blacks in the arts respected their own pioneers who opened doors and expanded the work, roles, and dignity of the race.

Lena Horne had become the symbol of genteel Harlem

Jive. Harlem entertainers looked to her to keep Hollywood open for them and to broaden the forum for their talents. Just as important, Noble Sissle, Lena Horne, and Walter White wanted to duplicate in Hollywood the Harlem entertainment cultural experience, by which black entertainers and their culture had broken down a substantial amount of Jim Crow practices and contempt of blacks because of the respect and appreciation they had achieved among white patrons who came from every quarter of the nation and the world to share the Harlem experience and culture. Moreover, Sissle insisted that *Cabin in the Sky* would boost blacks' standing during World War II just as Stowe's *Uncle Tom's Cabin* had helped to develop pro-black sentiment prior to the Civil War. He thought the film was a great black G.I. Jive movie that met the OWI standards.

Blacks were featured in the summer of 1943 in the film *This Is the Army*. Written by Irving Berlin during World War I, it was redone by him in the summer of 1942 on Broadway and was a huge success. The next summer it was made into a film.[100] Jack T. Warner pledged about fifty percent of the money raised by the film to the Army Emergency Relief Fund. Nearly $2 million was raised. The film was a G.I. Jive musical designed to raise "morale through putting on theatricals." It was a two-hour movie packed with first-rate entertainment. Irving Berlin provided four songs for the film: "This Is the Army, Mr. Jones," "I'm Getting Tired So I Can Sleep," "I Left My Heart at the Stage Door Canteen," and "Oh, How I Hate to Get up in the Morning." Other songs and acts were contemporary with World War II. Boxer Joe Louis led a group of black soldiers dressed in brown khaki in a skit to the song "What the Well Dressed Man in Harlem Will Wear," which critic Philip T. Hartung thought "almost steals the show—and this is something in a show that is full of outstanding entertainment."[101]

Joe Louis gave his now famous pro-war speech claiming America was "on God's side." Kate Smith performed her patriotic song, "God Bless America."[102] *Time* magazine noted that "the all-Negro 'What the Well-Dressed Man in Harlem Will Wear', vividly sung, scatted and danced, and abetted by some punching-bag polyrhythms from Sergeant Joe Louis and by his startling stage presence" was a work of art. The film stage had a large billboard backdrop with three huge black Harlem Zoot suiters in high step with bulging and surprised eyes, wide-brimmed flat topped hats and bow-ties and facial expressions suggesting that they were outdone by the black G.I. Jive routine of Sergeant Joe Louis and his soldiers dressed in khaki brown military uniforms with ties and wave hats. Both groups of men were sandwiched between buildings with one sign reading "Dixie's Beau Shoppe" and the other "Sporting Goods." Another read "Orchestra Club" and the street sign says "Lennox [sic] Avenue."[103] The unmistakable message intended for blacks in Harlem and throughout the nation was "Look at this black G.I. Jive" and if you really want to be hep, join the Army. Zoot suits must be exchanged for Army uniforms and jazz and jive must be pressed into service for the country's good in the war. The song, the dance routine, and Joe Louis's message epitomized the black G.I. Jive movement (well under way by 1943) which was undergirded by Harlem heroes and entertainers who were bringing the "Cotton Club Parades" cabaret culture into the civilian and military spheres to mobilize the nation—both its black and white citizens.

Another important G.I. Jive favorite was the film Sta*ge Door Canteen* of the summer of 1943. The American Theater Wing, which operated canteens in six cities, sponsored it. United Artists produced it and Sol Lesser directed. The film featured about 100 entertainers and "at least 48 are guaranteed, gilt-edged stars," noted one reviewer. It showed "six of jivedom's hottest swing bands" (Count Basie, Xavier Cugat, Benny Goodman, Kay Kyser, Guy Lombardo, and Freddy Martin). The picture "celebrates the well-known Forty-Fourth Street home-away-from-home for enlisted men" or the Manhattan Stage Door Canteen. Uniformed soldiers danced to the exciting swing music in the film.[104] It was an impressive musical.

Blacks performed in the film. Ethel Waters was "syncopating with Count Basie's Afric jazz band," noted *Time* magazine, and "the film's patriotism is as torrential as its talent." War songs like "Marching through Berlin" and "The Machine-Gun Song" were performed. Film critic James Agee thought it was an excellent period film because it "carries a saturation of the mannerisms of fourth-decade entertainment, patriotism, and sub-idealized lovemaking. . . ." He thought, however, that "the entertainment is best" in the film. Film critic Manny Farber agreed and predicted that "the jazz band will replace the movie player and the jazz singer the jazz band." Surprisingly, he had none of the usual objections to portrayals of blacks, apparently because they were integrated into the cast and performed classical jazz songs and music.[105]

Walter White was so impressed with *Stage Door Canteen* that he gave it the "unqualified endorsement of the National Association for the Advancement of Colored People" in appreciation of the integrated and dignified roles accorded blacks. Herman Hill wrote for the *Pittsburgh Courier*, "Stage Door Canteen is [a] Great Film." The film reflected the racial makeup of the United States and was clearly a response to black protest. It was made "for the soldiers of all the United States," including blacks.[106] These shows and films were Hollywood's and Broadway's salute to the armed forces and war workers. Their contributions were "a solid sender" (a jive language phrase used in the 1940s) to soldiers headed for overseas war theaters to face an uncertain and fearful destiny. *Stage Door Canteen* reflected an integration trend advocated by critics who rejected all-black movies as racist.

The film *Stormy Weather* (1943), an all-black musical, had its origins in the Cotton Club in 1933 as one of the shows written by Harold Arlen and Ted Koehler in the "Cotton Club Parades" series. The Cotton Club "Stormy Weather Show" featured Ethel Waters. "Singing 'Stormy Weather' proved a turning point in my life," said Waters, and it "became the talk of New York." She added, "Stormy Weather, which might have been the theme song of my life, was proving to be the first dramatic hit out of a night club."[107] *Stormy Weather* featured the who's who of the Cotton Club: Lena Horne, Bill "Bojangles" Robinson, Cab Calloway, Katherine Dunham and her dancers, Ada Brown, Zutty Singleton, Mae Johnston, Dooley Wilson, Harold and Fayard Nicholas, Flournoy Miller, and the comedian Nickademus.[108] M-G-M studios noted that musicals were more successful than heavy dramas because of the pressure to escape and be happy during the war. "This concentration upon musicals in particular, has meant a greater and more constant employment of Negro talent," reported the *Pittsburgh Courier*. As a result, M-G-M planned three more musicals. It produced *Girl Crazy* with Mickey Rooney, Judy Garland, and black dancers Buck and Bubbles, *I Dood It* with Red Skelton and Buck and Bubbles, and Kay Kyser and Lena Horne in *Right about Face*.[109]

The black press stirred up passionate interest in the new surge of blacks in film, especially *Stormy Weather* because it featured the best black talent in the country. Its filming resulted in an overflow crowd of observers. "Stormy Weather Gets Grandstand for Fans," noted the *Pittsburgh Courier*, because the "Galaxy of Stars Drew Such Hordes that Extra Seating Arrangements Were Supplied for the First Time in History." The crowds grew so large that the director put up "No Visitors Allowed" signs to halt the influx of onlookers.[110] Bill "Bojangles" Robinson was admired in Hollywood and thought blacks now had a bright future in films.[111] He and the other actors took time out and made trips to perform in California and nearby states.

Songs from *Stormy Weather* were played over the radio at home and abroad. At least four million people had heard or seen parts of *Stormy Weather* in personal performances or shortwave radio programming. Servicemen flooded the studio with fan mail: "A wave of fan mail from the servicemen has borne postmarks from Africa, Austria, Iceland and every military zone on the globe where U.S. men are stationed," reported the *Pittsburgh Courier*.[112] Lena Horne paid her own fare to Fort Huachuca, Arizona, to perform before the "Bronzed Yanks." The appreciative black troops dubbed her "Sergeant Lena Horne." Ernie Fields, also in *Stormy Weather*, and his orchestra performed at the Army Air Force Technical Training Base at Lincoln, Nebraska, to "boost servicemen's morale."[113] In the film he portrayed Lt. James Reese Europe, who led New York's 369th Regimental Marching Jazz Band to Europe and won international acclaim, and helped launch the jazz dance craze of the 1920s in association with Irene and Vernon Castle, who got Americans to dance to big bands. *Stormy Weather* opened with the New York 369th Colored Regimental Marching Jazz Band returning from Europe and parading through Harlem. This aspect of the film, contrary to the opinions of some film critics who considered it strictly an escapist film, put it in the musical and G.I. Jive genre of films designed to build morale among the soldiers and civilians.

The *Pittsburgh Courier* noted that *Stormy Weather* "Finish[ed] . . . Amid Fanfare, Color in Film Colony." The film featured impressive stage costumes and action "with Cab Calloway in a super 'Zoot suit.' It added, "many in Hollywood predict that 'Stormy Weather' will be one of the greatest box-office attractions of the year."[114] Billy Rowe, theatrical editor for the *Pittsburgh Courier*, campaigned to have black film stars "listed as essential" for building up morale at home in order to be excused from the draft. He noted that the Office of War Information (OWI) and a few other government agencies supported the view that actors and musicians could better serve at home by building up patriotism and participation in the war effort through entertainment. England and the Soviet Union deferred actors and musicians. In the United States only two blacks, boxer Joe Louis and John Kirby, were given any rank. Many whites, however, received officer rank in exchange for their services. Big band leader Kay Kyser had worked for the OWI's radio staff since the bombing of Pearl Harbor selling war bonds—$95 million worth. Nevertheless, he was classified as A-1 (immediately eligible for the draft).[115]

Kyser was drafted by his Rocky Mount, North Carolina, draft board, an action upheld by the Presidential Appeal Board despite the fact he was nearly 38, practically blind without his glasses and "stumbles from a trick knee," and had made 1,000 appearances in 300 camps to entertain the troops.[116] As a result, Rowe finally conceded that there was "little hope for listing of entertainers as essentials."[117] He saw *Stormy Weather* as a powerful G.I. Jive film which won acclaim from servicemen, white and black. He thought it a vehicle to promote black stars and entertainers, and win recognition for blacks in the war effort.

Critics had mixed reactions to *Stormy Weather*. Philip T. Hartung noted the fine black talent and performances but said the film was "such a fizzle." He added, "The film's weakness is its routine plot. . . ." The film's story line was based on the life of Bill "Bojangles" Robinson. He admitted that "Ain't Misbehavin'," "Diga, Diga Do," "I Can't Give You Anything but Love, Baby," and "Stormy Weather" "are first-rate songs." Moreover, "the film does not treat the Negroes as children even though it does little to boost their position as our most gifted entertainers."[118]

Newsweek thought *Stormy Weather* was an improvement for blacks. It noted, however, that *Casablanca* portrayed Dooley Wilson, the only black in the film, in a much better light.[119] Wilson met some critics' standards because he was portrayed as a normal human being and acted in an integrated setting. *Time* magazine best summarized the white magazines' views: "Stormy Weather is an all-Negro musical which packs enough talent and enough plain friendliness, if only they were used well to temper even the contemporary weather of U.S. race relations. Unfortunately, not much comes off as it might have."[120] Critics, black and white, had higher expectations for *Stormy Weather*.

Black critics had a mixed reaction to *Stormy Weather*. They praised the black actors but bitterly resented the showcasing of the Zoot suit in film. Billy Rowe complained to Twentieth Century-Fox officials "pointing out that the Zoot Suit isn't funny to clear-thinking theatre-goers, but is accepted as synonymous with crime and the illiterate . . ." and Rowe "asked Will Hays' office to start a vigorous censorship of such costumes on the screen."[121] Cab Calloway wore an all-white Zoot suit in the extreme of the fashion in *Stormy Weather*. He "parades" a new "take-off in the latest thing in Zoot Suits," noted the *Pittsburgh Courier*. Moreover, "The 'High Highness of Hi-De Ho' gets 'hep' and he's still 'groovy' in the 'Zooty' spell." Calloway added that his Zoot suit was "the Zoot Suit to end all Zoot Suits."[122] Malcolm Little (later known as Malcolm X) wore a Zoot suit during the war and was impressed by the film and Calloway's Zoot suit.

Herman Hill, writing for the *Pittsburgh Courier*, applauded the Zoot suit and Cab Calloway. He noted, "Cab Calloway, King of hi-de-ho, makes a spectacular entrance attired in a Zoot-Suit designed to end all Zoot-Suits."[123] Billy Rowe on the other hand thought Calloway's showcasing the Zoot suit was "An Ode to Crime." He noted that since the federal government and the police were then involved in "an extensive effort to suppress Zoot Suits, it's about time that the screen called a halt to its exploitation of the garb of the criminals." He thought that Cab Calloway, Eddie "Rochester" Anderson (who wore the suit in the film *Star Spangled Rhythm*), and other famous artists should stop wearing it. Rowe charged that film producers were "aiding an evil that will eventually destroy the minds of our youth. . . ."[124]

Harry Levette, a newspaper columnist, and Charles Butler, a black Hollywood talent recruiter, were disturbed because Levette revealed "Puzzled Hollywood Asks 'What Kind of Films [Do] Negroes Want?'" Militant letters were pouring into Hollywood film studios protesting black stereotypes despite a number of solid roles for blacks in recent films. Levette lamented, "in fact, they are wondering if when the script calls for a colored servant, if they should not make it Irish, Swedish, English, or any other nationality but Negro." He charged that the letters pouring in were uninformed and needed clarity. Butler feared that blacks were threatened with losing jobs and might get pushed out of Hollywood altogether.[125] Levette said Hollywood was discovering black skin color conflicts and "that there is a world of jealousy, and successful figures become the target for attacks for no other reason; that some will sell out the race for a 'mess of pottage.' . . ." What is more, blacks did not even support black film makers and some blacks threatened by their protest to ruin those blacks working in Hollywood. He concluded, "This new type of letters that are going to drive our famous established artists out of work, unless the complainants write again [and] explain themselves more clearly about the servant angle."[126] Levette was worried that blacks might get fewer jobs if they kept up what he obviously regarded as mixed signals to Hollywood producers based on petty critiques.

Lena Horne became the center of controversy among blacks and Hollywood producers over stereotyped roles. Walter White, executive secretary of the NAACP, courted and cultivated Horne. Both he and Horne feared that Hollywood "would force me [Horne] to play roles as a maid or maybe even as some jungle type." She felt that "it would be essential for me to try to establish a different kind of image for Negro women." She noted that Hollywood used white women in more respectable roles by using "Light Egyptian" skin cream in order not to use black women.[127] Other black actors met and protested Horne's and White's activities because blacks were threatened with losing their acting jobs and careers if so-called stereotype roles were reduced or cut out altogether. Horne recalled at a black protest meeting directed at her that "I was called 'an Eastern upstart' and a tool of the NAACP and I was forced to get up and try to explain that I was not trying to start a revolt or steal work from anyone and that the NAACP was not using me for any ulterior purpose." She lamented that "in a large part of the Hollywood Negro community I was never warmly received." She noted, however, that Eddie "Rochester" Anderson and Hattie McDaniel, two preeminent blacks who played so-called stereotype roles regularly, never attacked her and treated her with kindness.[128]

The old Harlem Renaissance ideological struggles reached a renewed intensity with the G.I. Jive films—especially *Stormy Weather* which included the best black actors and actresses of both schools of thought: those for roles of respectability and those for roles judged as stereotypes either for employment or who defended such roles as legitimate characterizations of blacks and art forms. Despite the internal bickering and hurt feelings among blacks, *Stormy Weather* was a superb G.I. Jive film which reached millions over the radio and screen or in live performances on military bases. It was part of a series of well-received films by both white and black G.I.'s and civilian jitterbuggers committed to jive and jazz.

New York blacks like Lena Horne, Cab Calloway, and Bill "Bojangles" Robinson were the star performers in *Stormy Weather* and they brought hallowed Cotton Club traditions in jazz, jive, and Harlem Zoot suit culture to Hollywood. The black New Yorkers often became the preeminent stars of black Hollywood. This generated resentment among some Los Angeles blacks. Black and white genteel factions that had emerged with the Harlem Renaissance had never achieved a consensus on how blacks should be portrayed in literature, in film, and on stage. The Harlem in Hollywood movement carried the seeds of the same conflicts which black and white Harlem Renaissance men and women had failed to resolve in the 1920s.

Notes

1. Quoted in Nathan I. Huggins, *Harlem Renaissance* (Oxford: Oxford University Press, 1973), p. 30.

2. Howard Swan, *Music in the Southwest* (New York: Da Capo Press, 1977), pp. 225–226.

3. *Ibid.*, pp. 225–226.

4. *Ibid.*, p. 231.

5. *Ibid.*, pp. 249, 254, 257–258.

6. *Ibid.*

7. *Ibid.*, pp. 258–260.

8. Judge Earl C. Broady Sr., Beverly Hills, California, telephone interview, 15 August 1988; Mrs. Mae Alice Harvey, Los Angeles,

telephone interview, 24 December 1988; "Death Takes Aunt of Earl Dancer," *California Eagle*, 11 August 1938, p. 2-A, col. 5.

9. "Hollywood Movie Colony Studios Resembles League of Nations: Cosmopolitan Air Vogue at Smart Film Colony; Race Actors Are Plentiful; 'Thunderbolt,' New Bancroft Vehicle Has 75 Colored Actors in Cast," *Pittsburgh Courier*, 15 June 1929, p. 3, sec. 2, col. 1.

10. Emory J. Tolbert, *The UNIA and Black Los Angeles* (Los Angeles: Center for Afro-American Studies, University of California, Los Angeles, 1980), pp. 66, 71–72.

11. "West Coast Jazz—Volume 1," Arcadia 2001, record album (n.d.), liner notes by Dick Raichelson; Judge Earl C. Broady, Beverly Hills, California, telephone interview, 16 August 1988.

12. Judge Broady telephone interview, 16 August 1988.

13. Ruby Berkley Goodwin, "From 'Blackbird' Chorine to 'Talkin' Star: At Last!" *Pittsburgh Courier*, 8 June 1929, sec. 1, p. 12, sec. 2, p. 7.

14. *Ibid.*

15. *Ibid.*; "'Hallelujah' at Regal for Entire Week of January 25," *Chicago Defender*, 25 January 1930, p. 10, col. 1.

16. "Many Find Steady Work in Hollywood," *Chicago Defender*, 22 March 1930, p. 11, col. 7.

17. "'Hallelujah' at Regal for Entire Week of January 25," *Chicago Defender*, p. 10, col. 1; Bruce M. Tyler's review of the film.

18. Judge Broady telephone interview, 16 August 1988; "West Coast Jazz—Volume 1," liner notes by Dick Raichelson; Frank Driggs and Harris Lewine, *Black Beauty, White Heat: A Pictorial History of Classic Jazz* (New York: William Morrow and Company, Inc., 1982), p. 186.

19. Driggs and Lewine, p. 175.

20. *Ibid.*, pp. 181, 184.

21. *Ibid.*, p. 187; Judge Earl C. Broady telephone interview, 16 August 1988; Louis Armstrong, *Swing That Music* (New York: Longmans, Green and Company, 1936), p. 95.

22. John Hammond with Irving Townsend, *John Hammond on Record: An Autobiography* (New York: Summit Books, Bridge Press, 1977), p. 106.

23. Driggs and Lewine, p. 189; "Les Hite's Famous Orchestra," *Pittsburgh Courier*, 1 May 1937, p. 18, col. 1; "Maestro Les Hite's Cuties Swing in Downtown Theatre," *California Eagle*, 11 August 1938, p. 3-B, col. 3.

24. Driggs and Lewine, p. 191.

25. *Ibid.*, p. 170.

26. Gardner Bradford, "Our Gay Black Way: Central Avenue," *Los Angeles Times*, Sunday Magazine, 18 June 1933, pp. 5, 10.

27. Hazel Augustine Washington, Los Angeles, telephone interview, 23 December 1988.

28. *Fifteenth Census of the United States, 1930, Population, Vol. IV,*

Occupation by States, Report by States Giving Statistics for Cities of 25,000 or More, United States Department of Commerce, Bureau of the Census, 1933, pp. 200–202.

29. *Sixteenth Census of the United States: 1940, Population, Vol. III, The Labor Force, Occupation, Industry, Employment, and Income, Part 2: Alabama–Indiana,* United States Department of Commerce, Bureau of the Census (Washington: United States Government Printing Office, 1943), pp. 244, 246, 248–249.

30. Driggs and Lewine, p. 180.

31. "1,500 Extras Auditioned," *Pittsburgh Courier,* 20 February 1937, p. 19, col. 8.

32. "Greatest Number Ever Used in One Day in Hollywood," *Pittsburgh Courier,* 20 March 1937, p. 13, col. 2.

33. Thomas Cripps, ed., *The Green Pastures* (Madison: The University of Wisconsin, 1979), pp. 204–205; Alfred LeGon, Los Angeles, telephone interview, 9 August 1988.

34. Sharon Kane, "'Green Pastures' Termed Biggest Hit of the Season," *Chicago Defender,* 22 March 1930, p. 11, col. 5.

35. "Green Pastures Renews Interest in Racial Dramatics," *Chicago Defender,* 10 May 1930, p. 11, col. 4.

36. Salem Tutt Whitney, "Timely Topics," *Chicago Defender,* 22 March 1930, p. 11, col. 4.

37. *Ibid.*

38. "Author of 'Green Pastures' Is Guest of N.A.A.C.P.," *Chicago Defender,* 19 April 1930, p. 11, col. 3.

39. "Harrison of 'The Green Pastures,'" *The Literary Digest,* 4 April 1931, p. 19.

40. Victor Daly, "Green Pastures and Black Washington," *The Crisis,* 30, No. 5 (May 1933), 106.

41. *Ibid.*

42. "The New Pictures: 'Harlem on the Prairie,'" *Time,* XXX, No. 24 (13 December 1937), 24.

43. *Ibid.*

44. Earl J. Morris, "Maxine Wows 'Em on L.A.'s Central Avenue; Bojangles Puts on One of His Famous Shoes at Club Alabam—Sends Police Escort for Jeni LeGon's Shoes," *Pittsburgh Courier,* 13 August 1938, p. 21, col. 4; Earl J. Morris, "Grandtown Day and Night: Happy New Year, Folks," *Pittsburgh Courier,* 31 December 1938, p. 17, col. 1.

45. Earl J. Morris, "Grandtown: Don't Kick a Guy When He Is Down—He May Get Up . . . and . . .," *Pittsburgh Courier,* 20 August 1938, p. 20, col. 1.

46. Roscoe Washington (retired L.A.P.D. officer), Los Angeles, telephone interview, 7 August 1988; Alfred LeGon telephone interview, 9 August 1988; Ethel Waters with Charles Samuels, *His Eye Is on the*

Sparrow: An Autobiography (Garden City: Doubleday & Company, Inc., 1951), p. 173.

47. "South East Harlem Aristocrat of Night Spots . . .," *California Eagle*, 25 August 1938, p. A-7, col. 5; "Dunbar Cocktail Lounge, Host Harry Spates . . .," *California Eagle*, 25 August 1938, p. 7-A, col. 4; "Summer Visitors!" *California Eagle*, 30 June 1938, p. 3-B, col. 5; Helen Oakley Dance, *Stormy Monday: The T-Bone Walker Story* (Baton Rouge: Louisiana State University Press, 1987), p. 50.

48. "Hollywood Meets Harlem," *California Eagle*, 14 July 1938, p. B-4, col. 5.

49. "Hollywood to Meet Harlem," *California Eagle*, 21 July 1938, p. 3-B, col. 7; "Complete Plans for Funfest at Warner Bros. Tonight," *California Eagle*, 21 July 1938, p. A-8, col. 6; Helen F. Chappell, "Society Editor": "Chatter and . . . Some News," *California Eagle*, 30 June 1938, p. 9-A, col. 1.

50. "Clarence Muse to Stage Gala Movie Ball at Warner's," *California Eagle*, 30 June 1938, p. 3-B, col. 2.

51. Ray Smith, Los Angeles, telephone interview, 23 December 1988.

52. "Dixie Goes Hi-Hat," *California Eagle*, 14 July 1938, p. 4-B, col. 1.

53. "As Thousands Cheered . . . The Winner!" *California Eagle*, 15 September 1938, p. 2-B, col. 3.

54. James Haskins, *The Cotton Club* (New York: Random House, 1977); Ethel Waters with Charles Samuels, pp. 254, 258.

55. "Stars and Movie Fans Turn Out for Dedication of Bill Robinson Theatre," *California Eagle*, 22 September 1938, p. 2-B, col. 4.

56. "Bill Robinson Theatre," *California Eagle*, 22 September 1938, p. 2-B, col. 7.

57. "Savoy Theatre," *California Eagle*, 22 September 1938, p. 2-B, col. 4.

58. Duke Ellington and the Jungle Band, "Duke Ellington 'Rockin' in Rhythm,'" Jazz Heritage Series, MCA Records, 2077 (formerly DL7-9247), Vol. 3 (1929–1931), notes by Stanley Dance, 1977; "Duke Ellington," Up Front Records, UPF-144 (no date given).

59. Maurice Zolotow, "The Duke's 'Forgotten' L.A. Musical," *Los Angeles*, 27, No. 2 (February 1982), 170–173, 223–224; Lena Horne and Richard Schickel, *Lena* (Garden City: Doubleday, 1965), pp. 122–124.

60. Zolotow, p. 172.

61. *Ibid.*, p. 173; Derek Jewell, *Duke: A Portrait of Duke Ellington* (New York: W.W. Norton & Co., Inc., 1977), p. 76.

62. Jewell, pp. 78–79; Zolotow, pp. 173, 223; Al Monroe, "Jump for Joy, Duke Ellington Will Stage the Show Here Soon," *Chicago Defender*, 22 August 1942, p. 11, col. 3; Almena Davis, "Jump for Joy Closes in L.A.," *Pittsburgh Courier*, 4 October 1941, p. 21, col. 2.

63. Hammond, pp. 136–137, 89, 91.

64. *Ibid.*, pp. 81, 158, 91.

65. *Ibid.*, p. 137.

66. Jewell, pp. 77–78.

67. *Ibid.*, pp. 77–78.

68. "Tales of Manhattan; Cast Has Many Stars: Ethel Waters, Paul Robeson and Eddie Anderson in Film," *Pittsburgh Courier,* 11 October 1941, p. 20, col. 1; "Screen News Here and in Hollywood," *New York Times,* 24 September 1942, p. 23, col. 17, col. 5 for ad.

69. David Lardner, "The Current Cinema: Actors Rampant," *The New Yorker,* 26 September 1942, pp. 53–54; "Make-Believe," *Commonweal,* XXVI, No. 22 (18 September 1942), 518.

70. "Make-Believe," p. 518; "'Tales of Manhattan' Is the Tricky Star-Studded Adventure of a Tailcoat,'" *Life,* 13, No. 4, (27 July 1942), 44 ff.; "Movies: Coat's Coterie," *Newsweek,* XX, No. 13 (9 September 1942), pp. 62–63.

71. "The New Pictures: 'Tales of Manhattan' (20th Century-Fox)," *Time,* XL, No. 12 (21 September 1942), p. 69.

72. Manny Farber, "Black Tails and White Lies," *The New Republic,* 107, No. 15 (12 October 1942), 466.

73. Philip S. Foner, ed., *Paul Robeson Speaks: Writings, Speeches, Interviews, 1918-1974* (New York: Brunner/Mazel Publishers, 1978), 142.

74. "Paul Robeson and Hollywood," *Chicago Defender,* 3 October 1942, p. 16, col. 2.

75. Lawrence F. LaMar (or Lamar), "Here's Tales of Manhattan; See If You Think It Objectionable," *Chicago Defender,* 31 October 1942, p. 14, col. 4.

76. Waters, p. 257.

77. "'Slim' and 'Slam' Join Rochester and Katherine Dunham in Picture," *Chicago Defender,* 4 July 1942, p. 12, col. 1; James Haskins, *The Cotton Club,* pp. 77–78; Richard Buckle, *Katherine Dunham: Her Dancers, Singers, Musicians* (London: Ballet Publications, Ltd., 1978), pp. vii–ix.

78. Philip T. Hartung, "Star Spangled Rhythm," *Commonweal,* XXXVII, No. 13 (15 January 1943), 328.

79. "'Star Spangled Rhythm,' by Paramount," *Time,* XLI, No. 3 (18 January 1943), 8.

80. This writer reviewed the film.

81. Manny Farber, "To What Base Uses," *The New Republic,* 108, No. 9 (1 March 1943), 283–284.

82. Billy Rowe, "Says Hollywood Made a Promise It Hasn't Kept," *Pittsburgh Courier,* 6 March 1943, p. 21, col. 4.

83. William Robert Faith, *Bob Hope: A Life in Comedy* (New York: G.P. Putnam's Sons, 1982), p. 170.

84. "Screen News Here and in Hollywood," *New York Times*, 18 February 1943, p. 19, col. 1.

85. James Haskins, *The Cotton Club*, pp. 84–89; Al Rose, *Eubie Blake* (New York: Schirmer Books, 1979), p. 121.

86. James Haskins and Kathleen Benson, *Lena: A Personal and Professional Biography of Lena Horne* (New York: Stein and Day Publishers, 1984), pp. 75–76.

87. *Ibid.*, p. 77.

88. Waters, pp. 254–255.

89. "Cabin in the Sky," *Time*, XLI, No. 15 (12 April 1943), 96.

90. Philip T. Hartung, "Lighter Side," *Commonweal*, XXXVIII, No. 9 (18 June 1943), 225–226.

91. "Hollywood Cabin," *Newsweek*, XXI, No. 17 (26 April 1943), 88.

92. Manny Farber, "The Great White Way," *The New Republic*, 109, No. 1 (5 July 1943), 20.

93. Joseph D. Bibb, "The Riff Raff: Unthinking Majority of Bad Actors Are Always in the Focus of Publicity," *Pittsburgh Courier*, 29 May 1943, p. 13, col. 1.

94. "Cabin Film Draws Fire," *Pittsburgh Courier*, 8 May 1943, p. 20, col. 5.

95. "Cabin Picture Called Insult: Despite Excellent Cast of 'Cabin in the Sky'; The Negro Is Belittled," *New York Amsterdam News*, 12 June 1943, p. 17, col. 2.

96. Haskins, *Lena*, pp. 73–74; "Scribe, In Film Job," *Chicago Defender*, 31 October 1942, p. 13, col. 2.

97. "Noble Sissle Previews 'Cabin in the Sky': Lauds Performance," *Pittsburgh Courier*, 23 January 1943, p. 21, col. 2.

98. Leonard Feather, *The Book of Jazz; From Then till Now* (New York: Horizon Press, 1965 [1957]), p. 39.

99. Haskins, *Lena*, p. 74.

100. "'This Is the Army': Sgt. Berlin and His Men Fight Battle of Broadway with Huge Success," *Newsweek*, XX, No. 2 (13 July 1942), 52, 54.

101. Philip T. Hartung, "The Screen: Is This the Army?," *Commonweal*, XXXVIII, No. 19 (27 August 1943), 466–467.

102. "Hollywood's Army," *Newsweek*, XXII, No. 6 (9 August 1943), 84.

103. "New Picture: This Is the Army," *Time*, XLII, No. 7 (16 August 1943), 93–94.

104. "Entertainment: Canteenful of Stars," *Newsweek*, XXI, No. 25 (21 June 1943), 100–101; David Lardner, "The Current Cinema," *The New Yorker*, XIX, No. 19 (26 June 1943), 43–44; Philip T. Hartung, "Three Ring Movie," *Commonweal*, XXXVIII, No. 11 (2 July 1943), 275–276.

105. "Cinema: New Picture," *Time*, XLI, No. 24 (14 June 1943), 94; James Agee, "Films," *The Nation*, 156, No. 24 (12 June 1943), 844; Manny Farber, "When the Pie Was Opened," *The New Republic*, 109, No. 4 (26 July 1943), 110.

106. Herman Hill, "Stage Door Canteen Is Great Film," *Pittsburgh Courier*, 26 January 1943, p. 20, col. 6

107. Waters, pp. 220–221; Cab Calloway and Bryant Rollins, *Of Minnie the Moocher & Me* (New York: Thomas Y. Crowell Company, 1976), p. 178.

108. Waters, p. 178; "Stormy Weather Features Kay Dunham-Dooley Wilson," *Pittsburgh Courier*, 6 February 1943, p. 21, col. 2.

109. "Metro-Goldwyn-Mayer Features Sepia Artists in Musicals," *Pittsburgh Courier*, 6 February 1943, p. 21, col. 2.

110. *Pittsburgh Courier*, 13 February 1943, p. 21, col. 2.

111. Herman Hill, "Hollywood Likes Clarence Robinson," *Pittsburgh Courier*, 13 March 1943, p. 20, col. 3.

112. "Servicemen Up on 'Stormy Weather,'" *Pittsburgh Courier*, 13 March 1943, p. 20, col. 4.

113. "Ernie Fields Boosts Servicemen's Morale," *Pittsburgh Courier*, 13 February 1943, p. 21, col. 4.

114. "Finish 'Stormy Weather' Amid Fanfare, Color in Film Colony," *Pittsburgh Courier*, 20 March 1943, p. 20, col. 2.

115. Billy Rowe, "Feels Performers Should Be Listed as Essentials," *Pittsburgh Courier*, 20 March 1943, p. 20, col. 4.

116. "The Draft: Nonessential Band Leader," *Time*, XLI, No. 14 (5 April 1943), 75.

117. Billy Rowe, "See Little Hope for Listing of Entertainers as Essentials," *Pittsburgh Courier*, 27 March 1943, p. 21, col. 1.

118. Philip T. Hartung, "The Screen: Rain! No Game!," *Commonweal*, XXXVIII, No. 14 (23 July 1943), 344–345.

119. "Hollywood Cabin," *Newsweek*, XXI, No. 17 (26 April 1943), 88.

120. "Stormy Weather," *Time*, XLII, No. 2 (12 July 1943), 94, 96.

121. Charlotte Charity, "Billy Rowe Told Film Producers Willing to Help," *Pittsburgh Courier*, 3 April 1943, p. 25, col. 5.

122. "Hollywood May Censor Screen 'Zoot Suits,'" *Pittsburgh Courier*, 3 April 1943, p. 25, col. 2.

123. Herman Hill, "Coast Fans Applaud Lena Horne at 'Stormy Weather' Opening," *Pittsburgh Courier*, 7 August 1943, p. 20, col. 1.

124. Charlotte Charity, p. 25, col. 5.

125. Harry Levette, "Puzzled Hollywood Asks 'What Kind of Films [Do] Negroes Want?'" *Pittsburgh Courier*, 1 May 1943, pp. 20–21.

126. *Ibid*.

127. Horne, *Lena*, pp. 120–121, 134, 136–137.

128. *Ibid.*, pp. 120–121, 134, 136.

THE USO AND JIM CROW

During World War II, a massive military entertainment and G.I. culture emerged under the auspices of the United Service Organizations, Incorporated (USO), to service the ten million members of the United States military and millions of Allied servicemen and women. Many civilian groups followed the USO pattern of entertaining the troops. Blacks played a leading role in this emergent G.I. entertainment culture, but on a segregated basis, and largely served the one million black G.I.'s. Black civilians and G.I.'s participated in patriotic entertainment—rather than take a revolutionary position of active or passive opposition to the war—while simultaneously protesting racial discrimination and segregation by an assertive participatory patriotism. Blacks rejected passive acceptance of military or civilian enforced Jim Crow.

White and black artists, especially jazz and swing band singers and musicians, increasingly demanded cultural and racial democracy. These artists shared the same entertainment culture, which drew them into a sort of alliance against social and cultural Victorians who opposed their art and lifestyles. In many ways, the Harlem Renaissance goal of using art to attack racial barriers was re-invigorated during World War II and became entrenched as never before.

Black G.I. Jive entertainers opened the fight against Jim Crow on the cultural front. This battle was just as intractable and hard fought as the ones on the political and military fronts. Blacks, with white allies, campaigned for the Double V program: They would fight for democracy abroad and racial democracy at home at the same time. The *Pittsburgh Courier* and black veterans from World War I in 1937 started the Double V campaign when they saw signs of war approaching in Europe. They wanted to correct the errors made in the First World War in which blacks fought without any pre-conditions or demands for racial democracy.

White civilians and military personnel dominated the USO.

Many of them took a position of promoting racial democracy within its operations. These whites, with their black allies, shared the jazz, jive, and entertainment culture which brought them together in their struggle to loosen, if not dismantle, a conservative and racist Victorian culture still powerful in large sections of society. The USO itself had a formal doctrine of separation of the races. A few powerful civilian and regular USO organizations dedicated to entertaining troops opposed and effectively dismantled Jim Crow practices in the New York, Hollywood, Washington, D.C., and Harlem canteens.

The USO was founded in February 1941 to serve the social, cultural, and religious needs of servicemen and women. It consisted of six organizations: the international Committee of Young Men's Christian Association (YMCA); the National Board of Young Women's Christian Association (YWCA); the National Catholic Community Service; the Salvation Army; the National Jewish Welfare Boards (JWB), and the national Travelers Aid Association. The first mass meeting was held in Washington, D.C., on April 17, 1941. In five years it attracted one million volunteers and raised $200 million. One billion people attended its shows and programs.[1]

In 1941 the War Department asked a citizens' committee to help supply entertainment at training camps and bases. A budget of $3,200,000 was allotted, and armed forces personnel were entertained by seven traveling shows on trucks borrowed from General Motors and specially outfitted for shows. The USO, the citizens' committee, and show-business representatives met in Washington and organized USO Camp Shows with the War and Navy departments for the armed forces as a whole. This body was designed as the "official entertainment" agency for the armed forces.[2] This civilian and military partnership organized and gave structure to the entertainment of the troops. It was essentially a civilian organization with military sanction to provide a service to the armed forces.

Musicians often were given special privileges, which caused some envy and resentment among some servicemen and women. Others thought it necessary to use musicians to entertain troops and build morale. Secretary of War Henry L. Stimson needed civilian specialists for the Army in a hurry. The War Department organized the Army Specialists Training Program Corps (ASTP) at the end of 1942 to get these civilian specialists. They were rewarded with military uniforms, often without basic training and frequently with military officer rank. The ASTP was designed to train college students as leaders and specialists, although the Army got most of its needed specialists from its own ranks. Stimson feared that the dignity of the combat uniform would be degraded by making concessions, but had little choice in the matter because of the war emergency.[3] Civilian specialists could demand higher wages in the civilian labor market. Only the draft or a reward of military uniforms and rank could entice them in significant numbers to join the Army. In April 1944 ASTP had 140,000 men who were needed as combat soldiers. The program was terminated, and they had to fight.[4]

Through the ASTP, many musicians and entertainers joined the armed forces, especially the Army—some with officer rank despite the lack of basic training. Frank Mathias became a bandsman in the Army through ASTP and served at Fort Benning, Georgia, and Camp Wheeler, Macon, Georgia. He played jazz. The non-ASTP soldiers and officers resented the ASTP as an institution that bestowed favoritism and special privilege on certain soldiers. Mathias said, "The regular Army men on the post had a low opinion of us. The best thing we were called was 'ASTPeewee.'" They were also "called WACC." (Apparently, this was a pejorative reference that equated them with the Women's Army Corps.) Mathias added, "They don't like us and call us dodgers [a pejorative term for draft dodgers or those seeking to avoid combat]."[5] Stimson had feared this sort of division and degradation of the combat uniform. More importantly, the ASTP recruiting of musicians and entertainers led regular soldiers to question these civilians' manhood and combat qualities as well as the special privileges shown them. They often received status and rank and frequently could operate outside the normal discipline and command structure.

The USO immediately encountered race problems and challenges. It provided all sorts of entertainers at various locations and situations. Some entertainers made the "Foxhole Circuit," which was the most famous and dangerous because it was at the battlefront. The first shows, sponsored by the USO in November 1941, made a 13,000-mile circuit through the Caribbean Islands. "American style" music and "American girls" were craved there as all over the world where American soldiers fought and were based. Shows and dances included formal, square dancing, classical music, and "Gay '90s."[6]

The United States recruited 50,000 troops, many black or mulatto, from Puerto Rico. The USO program was launched to deal with the entertainment and recreation needs of these and other troops from the Caribbean or Latin America. The Caribbean population called for multilingual troops, officers, staff, and program offerings.[7] Race and cultural tensions resulted.

In the United States race and sex were explosive mixtures not easily handled. The USO discovered that "the problem of recruiting and training appropriate Junior Hostesses throughout the Antilles Area was a challenging one. In British Guiana girls of various racial strains co-operated in club work: Chinese, Portuguese, East Indian, Negro, Dutch, and English."[8] This racial intermixture and integration was unique to the region, and not acceptable by American laws and traditions. But the United States was unable to undo centuries of race mixing and customs in Latin America.

The men in charge of entertainment in the South Pacific, however, established seventy-six clubs patterned after the USO, which operated only in the Western Hemisphere. Numerous cultural festivals and events were held to entertain the troops and Americans. Blacks held their own USO Victory Club event, the Pacific Jubilee.[9] Blacks and whites were segregated in the Pacific unlike the Caribbean, where free racial association was less restricted by law and custom.

The USO adopted the policy of separate but equal set in the 1896 *Plessy v. Ferguson* decision of the United States Supreme Court, which established legal segregation and discrimination based on race. The question of mixed racial dancing arose at USO clubs. Only very limited dancing between the races was allowed, to avoid altercations from whites who objected. The USO, as a rule, avoided and did not encourage mixing of the races.

The USO's official policy did not seek to break down segregation and followed the line "that if too much was demanded the whole program might be lost." Blacks were encouraged "to steer a middle course." They received USO clubs, staff, and funding where there had been none. To demand racial integration was self-defeating, since it was not going to be granted. The USO frankly told blacks that "such far-sighted and realistic facing of facts" allowed for gains where there would have been none.[10] A black female director of a segregated USO program, Mrs. Ellen Douglas, was simply called Ellen by white USO officials who observed the racial etiquette of not giving a title to blacks because of their inferior status.[11]

The USO recognized that the war emergency could be used to cross some racial barriers, but it would be temporary. The USO's main purpose was to be, as its slogan stated, "a home away from home." It depended upon volunteers and charity for its budget. To crusade against segregation or call for racial reforms was self-destructive. Moreover, each organization of the USO had its own race program and at least one-fourth of the states had segregation laws that made it illegal to engage in integrated activities. "In these states, if the USO was to render badly needed services to Negro servicemen, it had no choice but to operate under the law as it stood." On the other hand, the USO promoted its policy of separate but equal by attempting to convince blacks of the "joys" of a new, though segregated, club.[12]

The USO summed up its policy: "In some communities separate facilities are necessary. Sometimes this is required by law, either as separately operated clubs or as extensions from white clubs. However, when separate facilities are used, USO has been successful in its efforts to make the Negro facilities meet general USO standards in attractiveness, equipment and furnishings."[13] The USO essentially argued the win-the-war-first policy of the federal government. It adopted a pragmatic program of accommodation with the national separate-but-equal doctrine.

J. Saunders Redding, a black English teacher and author, was asked by the national USO board to survey black USO centers. He noted that a black USO "on the Eastern seaboard" had met with opposition, but black entertainers appeared and so did whites who wanted to be entertained. Community people came, and the center was integrated from then on. Black directors of the USO sought to win over whites to civil rights for blacks in the name of cooperation in the war effort. Redding discovered that in a few Southern towns black USOs were placed in the worst slums, where G.I. patrons were mugged. In Sacramento, California; Pittsburgh, Pennsylvania; Ayer, Massachusetts, and

other communities the USO centers were biracial. By August of
1944, there were 244 USO centers under black directors.[14] The
USO's branches adopted the local customs. Some were attractive
and others oppressive.

Ernie Pyle, the great American war correspondent, reported
on the American G.I.'s in war zones. He noted that G.I.'s had
an "impulse for kindness, generosity and affection." He added,
"Our boys couldn't resist the sad and emaciated little faces of
the children, and that was when they started giving away their
rations." Just as important, he noted that for every G.I. "the one
really profound goal" was to get home. "The American soldier
is a born housewife. . . . I'll bet there's not another Army in the
world that fixes itself a 'home away from home' as quickly as
ours does." He questioned thousands of G.I.'s and found that
their symbols for home were a "blueberry pie," "a blonde," books,
music, movies, and so on. "Home is where the good things are—
the generosity, the good pay, the comforts, the democracy, the
pie." Pyle concluded, "Home, not democracy or internationalism,
spurred the GI to fight." The G.I.'s sought to win the war as
quickly as possible to get home.[15] It was also true that "home"
was a Jim Crow society by constitutional law which many white
Americans did not want altered. They resurrected Jim Crow in
every war theater and base. They did not go to war to see it
dismantled at home. Americans, white and black, were born into
a constitutionally and socially racist society. Jim Crow was just
as American as "blueberry pie."

The Young Women's Christian Association said the USO
served "all involved in the war effort." About one million blacks
served in the war and were serviced by the USO's 294 national
service programs, 238 clubs and extensions, 14 war production
clubs, 19 military and war production clubs, 12 National Travelers
Aid Association (NTAA) service units, 11 troop and transit
lounges, 65 community conducted programs, and 57 clubs and
services. A total of 357 programs and services were established
to serve one million blacks, and most were segregated. Blacks
suffered from poor community services and programs, food,
restaurants, hotels, and other public accommodations. As a result,
the USO built new facilities or refurbished old ones. These
structures were left in the community after the war.[16]

The most racist region was in the South, Region VII

(Alabama, Florida, Georgia, Mississippi, South Carolina, Tennessee). The USO found it difficult to service blacks, even on a segregated basis. Blacks were often violently attacked as were USO personnel and establishments. Black USO women were harassed as prostitutes. The USO established interracial councils and meetings which racists opposed.[17] Many Southerners feared the USO's recognition of blacks and building of branches to service them. Apparently, it implied citizenship rights they opposed as contrary to their concept of the blacks' place in a rigid racial hierarchy supported in law.

Where no facilities existed on or off bases for black armed forces personnel, the USO often moved in to provide them. This service often stifled black protest for integrated facilities or was used to prevent it. In Arizona, 30,000 black troops were massed and one town panicked at the thought of these soldiers converging on the town until the USO stepped in.[18] USO facilities were used to contain blacks and keep the races segregated, and to prevent or redirect blacks' social and sexual urges away from the white community and its women. Black energy and aggression were absorbed by sports, games, education, dances, language classes, religious programs, clean-up projects, good food, hobbies, and crafts. Some white and black artists performed at white or black clubs, providing a limited measure of integration.

The segregation of the races kept the peace. Blacks who resented segregation were placated by such offerings as the USO's Negro People's Chorus, whose singing was called by some a "moving force for interracial understanding. Thus, even in a segregated program there is opportunity for creating new social insights and greater understanding."[19] The USO provided badly needed services even when it was unwilling and unable to attack Jim Crow.

The all-black 25th Infantry was stationed at Walla Walla, Washington, where it was denied public accommodations in accordance with state law. The regiment's white officers complied with the local custom of posting "off limits" signs denying blacks public accommodations. The War Department responded to the crisis by repeating the official policy of the federal government: "While many people sincerely believe that the force of the War Department should be used in advancing desirable reforms . . . nobody would wish to have the decisions as to just what reforms are . . . desirable made by anything less than a clear democratic majority."[20] The War Department recognized that white public opinion and social customs opposed integration and racial democracy. Racial authoritarianism was national policy and upheld by majority rule. The War Department would be insubordinate to national as well as state laws if it attempted to overthrow, by military fiat or force, Jim Crow. Regrettably, the War Department, from a legal point of view, was correct. Racial authoritarianism was a problem for the American people and government to solve, and neither was committed to the Double Victory—racial democracy at home and democracy abroad.

A few canteens patterned after the USO had an integration policy throughout the war—the New York Canteen, the Washington, D.C., Canteen sponsored by the Congress of Industrial Organizations, and the Hollywood Canteen. There was fear that the American Theatre Wing Stage Door Canteens would establish a segregated canteen in Harlem, which was denied. Isadora Bennett, director of publicity of the Theatre Wing War Services, Inc., rejected segregation as canteen policy. She said, "We have never at any time contemplated a special neighborhood canteen—in Harlem or anywhere else. It would be an absolute violation of basic policy. All of our canteens are open to all the servicemen of the Allied Nations. We would never single out a special group—even for special benefits. Certainly we would do nothing that would tend to segregate the negro serviceman."[21] Thus the canteens sponsored by the American Theatre Wing Stage Door Canteens were integrated across the nation.

At the large Stage Door Canteen in New York, "about six or eight per cent" of the servicemen who came were black. It was integrated during the four years of the war "and it worked." Its director, Margaret Halsey, said, "The canteen inadvertently became a sort of educational institution" in race relations. Northern whites who were outraged by Southern violence and rigor in race relations retaliated by attacking racism in the North, "where it is somewhat easier to do." Moreover, Halsey said, she and other whites believed in and practiced integration because "the wish of these Southerners to corrupt American democracy cannot be allowed to go unchallenged."[22] Halsey's New York Canteen preached and practiced racial democracy, but it was the exception and not the norm.

The hostesses in New York were forbidden to go out with servicemen for security reasons and by request of the military. All hostesses were required, however, to talk and dance with any serviceman as long as he was well behaved and not drunk. The canteen had about 1,000 hostesses, with a high turnover. Policy and race rules were constantly reiterated as a result. Some white hostesses complained to other whites that they were forced to dance with blacks. The New York Canteen asked those women to follow the policy or quit. Some whites tried to evade the rules by the tactic of "rescuing," or cutting in, on interracial conversations, and especially dancing. This was watched for to prevent it. "The canteen considered that a Negro serviceman who was good enough to die for a white girl was good enough to dance with her," said Halsey.[23] She thought that racism and segregation were a result of interracial attractions rather than repulsion. White men feared competition from black men for white women. White men assumed that black men were primitive and had a greater sexual drive. Industrial societal pressures, however, thwarted the sex drive of white men who had to focus on work and the competition for social mobility, unlike many blacks, who were restricted in the labor market and in social mobility by racial caste laws and practices.[24]

Some white men, however, sought out the black hostesses for fun and sex. Frequently, the approached hostess was asked, "Come on, take us up to Harlem, we know how to show you a good time." (This undoubtedly was a result of the 1920s and 1930s when Harlem was in vogue and whites went there when the cabaret owners catered to them. The war, race tensions, and the decline of Harlem in the depression made it less attractive.) Some even showed pictures of them having sex with native women, often blacks or mulattos, in Trinidad to prove that they were not racists.[25] These whites were motivated by stereotypes of blacks and of the exotic Harlem of the 1920s.

Margaret Halsey told white women hostesses there was no scientific evidence of superior and inferior races. Moreover, "you are given, in the canteen, a golden opportunity to come into contact with Negroes under the best possible circumstances and to find out what they are really like." She charged that their real fears were of getting pregnant by a black man and having to carry and have the child. She added, "The truth is, that while you are an extremely attractive group of young women, there isn't one single one of you who's that good." The machine age was forcing more contact between whites and non-European people and "you might as well get used to it here and now, on Sunday nights at the canteen."[26] She also offered a more practical political answer, "We need them in the war effort, so we've been forced to give them more equality than we were ever willing to concede before."[27] Halsey's modern views were very advanced for the times and Wendell Willkie and many other thoughtful Americans realized that international cooperation and good race relations were correct and good public policy.

Halsey's public letter and statements in the spring of 1943 drew condemnation from racists. Senator Theodore Bilbo of Mississippi bitterly complained that Halsey had "ordered" the white Junior Hostesses to dance with black soldiers and accept them as social equals. Moreover, a new canteen opened in Washington, D.C., by the Congress of Industrial Organizations (C.I.O.) in 1944 also allowed interracial dancing among 200 white and black patrons, Bilbo complained.[28] Representative Joseph R. Bryson of South Carolina protested on the floor of Congress that the Washington Canteen run by the C.I.O. allowed interracial dancing to the tune "Let Me Call You Sweetheart." He charged that such behavior by race mixers was "deliberately aggravating" race problems. Moreover, the C.I.O.'s constitution forbade discrimination because of sex, race, creed, or political affiliation. This disturbed the South.[29] Congressman McKenzie of Louisiana, too, objected to interracial dancing.[30] He feared that race mixing endangered white supremacy and might lead to a mongrel race.

Senator Bilbo charged that "mongrelization started in South America, and there was no power to stop it." He raved that as a result "half-breeds, cross-breeds, mix-breeds soon infested the land!" He argued that segregation and discrimination were the safeguards in the United States and provided "a permanent solution to our color problem."[31] He mourned the fact that eighteen states, including the District of Columbia, allowed interracial marriages. "The fact is a national shame, or should I say crime, against the white race of America. . . ."[32] He personally crusaded to prevent the establishment of a racial democracy in the United States by public denunciation of it and by political opposition to liberal race laws—and even by mob violence.

Margaret Halsey received hate mail because of her experiments with racial democracy at the Stage Door Canteen. One writer charged, "Your canteen is no doubt a Communist Front hangout and a cess pool of iniquity and degradation. . . ." Moreover, "You are a renegade white woman if you are a white woman and certainly no lady of refinement. There are many of your class in New York City. . . ." I "can only pray for the coming of the good Ku Klux Klan—then the like of you will be tarred and feathered as you deserve." He signed the letter, "A Real Pure White American."[33]

Halsey said the YWCA and Federal Council of Churches were for "racial democracy" and she defended this policy as standing on solid moral ground.[34] Bilbo and other unashamed racists recognized that some whites believed in racial democracy, publicly said so, and often practiced integration. G.A. Borgess, in "A Bedroom Approach to Racism" in *Negro Digest*, in December 1944, advocated racial democracy through interracial marriage and sex, which the racists violently opposed at all costs.[35] Whites who advocated such doctrines were called race traitors.

As the United States geared up for world war, there was an increasing concern for the health and welfare of the armed forces and the work force. Prostitution and venereal disease were seen as serious threats to their health and safety as well as the war effort. Jean Pinney, in a report issued in June 1942, said that prostitution "in times of national crisis like the present, unless firmly curbed, . . . may become like a raging torrent, damaging the health and morale of our armed forces and of workers in industry to an extent affecting the war's outcome."[36] The federal government moved to coordinate various agencies to deal with the problem. Legislation was reviewed. In 1910 the Mann Act had been passed to outlaw interstate and international traffic in women for prostitution. The Bennet Act was passed barring importation of aliens for prostitution. In July 1941 the May Act (H.R. 2475) was passed to prohibit prostitution near military bases. It overrode local and state laws not able to deal effectively with the problem.[37]

Secretary of War Henry L. Stimson reported that soldiers and workers stationed at Fort Benning, Georgia, were exploited financially and suffered from bad moral influences, and he wanted a national organization to deal with such problems near any

military base or where soldiers clustered. He said they needed
help in sanitation and health care. He asked for the help of local
law enforcement agencies to protect the health and morals of the
soldiers and war workers. His goal was to control "undesirable
persons and places" in or near military bases and personnel. He
wanted recreational facilities built to counter these negative
influences on the health and morals of soldiers and war workers.
He said that a neighboring town exploited soldiers "in all sorts
of ways," such as charging exorbitant prices for rents and liquor,
and enticed them and war workers into long hours in clubs with
loose women. Stimson asserted that "conditions of a moral
character in one of these towns are an even worse influence."
Many blacks were at Fort Benning and in some nearby towns,
and there was fear that the racial line might be crossed under
these immoral circumstances. Stimson instructed the Military
Police to intervene to protect soldiers and declare rowdy and
immoral places "out of bounds" for soldiers likely to be
exploited.[38]

Frank Mathias, a jazz musician, was stationed at Fort
Benning, Georgia. He played in a military jazz band there at the
main USO center, the Ralston Hotel, the Army-Navy YMCA near
Fort Benning, and over radio station WRBL. The announcer
introduced the jazz band: "From the main USO we bring you
Jerry Klausner and the ASTP Dance Band! Here they are now,
kicking off with 'GI Jive'!"[39] The military jazz bands and approved
centers of dance and recreation were organized by the USO and
the armed service to protect soldiers and war workers from
cabarets, night clubs, prostitutes, and red-light districts that
catered to soldiers and exploited them.

Problems of this sort existed near Camp Forrest, Tennessee,
where Stimson invoked the May Act, which prohibited
prostitution on or near military facilities, on May 20, shortly after
the law was passed in Congress.[40] Frank Mathias said of the
crusade against prostitution and venereal disease, "judging from
the material, the Army feared this stuff more than Japs or Nazis."[41]
Stimson had commended Dr. Thomas Parran of the Public Health
Service, whose book on red-light districts and military bases had
caused an outcry before the May Act had been invoked against
a local community.[42] Parran assured him that VD could be
detected at the induction stage of a recruit or soon afterward and

that eighty percent of the victims could be restored "to perfect health." Stimson noted that General Haskell of the 27th Division had taken the initiative and had "closed up some houses of ill fame in Anniston near the Division. . . ."[43]

In May of 1942 Stimson told a delegation of clergymen concerned with vice, morals, and crime near bases, along with Congressman May, who had sponsored the May Act, that he held commanders responsible for the venereal disease rate of their soldiers and appealed to the governors of the states to help protect soldiers and war workers by state laws rigorously enforced. He noted that the VD rates had declined.[44] Crusades against prostitution and venereal disease, which were associated with red-light entertainment districts, resulted in the formation of the USO to provide morally sound and healthy entertainment.

The USO entertainment shows ranged from formal dances to square dances, to listening to Bach to "Gay '90's" styles to jazz. Julia Carson noted that "in the simplest terms, [USO] Camp Shows' job is to bring Hollywood and Broadway to the servicemen" at the request of the Army and Navy.[45] Max Kaminsky, a noted jazzman, revealed the radical culture shared by many entertainers, especially jazz artists: "We were the pioneers rebelling against the Victorian-European music, as the writers of the twenties did in literature. We were ridiculed and called barbarians, too, as the boppers were in the forties. . . ."[46] These cultural rebels clashed with racist Victorians and a Jim Crow system.

The New York City Stage Door Canteen opened its doors on March 2, 1942, "under the auspices of the American Theatre Wing" in the basement of the Forty-fourth Street Theatre. It was integrated. It was not formally part of the USO or under its discipline. Sometimes a white racist Southerner was shocked to find black servicemen and hostesses there. The famous black poet Langston Hughes was an honored guest at a New York Stage Door Canteen dinner. Carl Van Vechten, writer and patron of the Harlem Renaissance and blacks, wrote "An Ode to the [New York] Stage Door Canteen" because "the place is absolutely democratic in its organization and social behavior, perhaps one of the few democratic institutions in existence anywhere: English soldiers, sailors and RAF men dance beside, mingle and eat with Chinese airmen, Americans from every branch of the service, including Negroes and Indians, Canadians, Austrians, South Africans, Dutch and French sailors (how pleasant it is to listen to the 'Bon Soirs' which greet them every side of the room when they enter), occasionally Russians: all are a part of the Stage Door Canteen. Hostesses and busboys are an equally heterogeneous lot." He thought this experiment so grand that "a new kind of spirit has developed which might be utilized profitably in another field in the post-war era." That is, he hoped, like other Harlem Renaissance artists, that the arts and interracial entertainment could be used to break down Jim Crow.[47]

Carl Van Vechten had long dreamed of and promoted cabaret culture as a means to break down Jim Crow because of his observations of its effectiveness in Harlem for many years. He thought that the New York Stage Door Canteen provided a unique opportunity to demonstrate it as a viable model for the rest of the nation to follow.[48]

Harlem was still patronized by many whites during the boom years during World War II. The Andrews Sisters, a popular white group, performed at the Savoy Ballroom in Harlem in October 1942. The dance was sponsored by the United States Treasury Department. Such white and black bands as Stan Kenton, Will Osborne, Cootie Williams, Eddie Durham's All-Girl band, the Savoy Sultans, and Al Sears Renaissance Band were performed for $2 in war stamps.[49] Black and white patrons came to dance and enjoy the bands there. The Savoy had an international reputation for excellent entertainment, dancers, interracial dancing, and dating.

The Andrews Sisters had sung "Don't Sit under the Apple Tree" ("with anyone else but me") in Seattle, Washington, "when a whole shipload of troops went out." And "we stood there on the deck and [there were] all those young men up there waving and yelling and screaming." They were joined in the song by sweethearts, mothers, and sisters as the ships sailed off. The women were promising through song to be sexually abstinent and loyal to their loved ones. Many men, obviously, felt threatened by their separation from family, sweethearts, and wives. The song served as a warning to girls and women to be loyal to their soldier husbands and boyfriends. This message endeared the Andrews Sisters to many soldiers.

The Andrews Sisters sang on the USO circuit and overseas. They also made popular "Boogie Woogie Bugle Boy," which became a G.I. Jive favorite. The sisters "always" visited the hospitals.[50] They tried their best to cheer up the men and pacify their fears by glamorizing the soldier and his life.

The Hollywood Canteen was started by John Garfield and Bette Davis with the help of forty-two unions and guilds of the motion picture industry. It opened in October 1942 on Sunset Boulevard in Hollywood. The Hollywood Canteen Foundation ran it. Bette Davis was voted its president. Soldiers dined with such Hollywood stars as Betty Grable, Harry James and band, Hedy Lamarr, Marlene Dietrich, Eddie Cantor, Fred MacMurray, Bing Crosby, Fred Astaire, Ginger Rogers, Frank Sinatra, Humphrey Bogart, Jimmy Cagney, Joan Crawford, Linda Darnell, Rita Hayworth, Errol Flynn, Spencer Tracy, Boris Karloff, and many others. It had a paid staff of nine, with 6,000 volunteers. A crew of 100 worked every night. Two work shifts on average served 3,000 men, attended by 3,500 volunteer dancing hostesses.[51]

The Hollywood Canteen had 100 black female dance hostesses. The lack of black soldiers resulted at first in their being "wallflowers." Soon white soldiers started dancing with them because of the shortage of white female hostesses. Some white women started complaining to other whites as the competition with black women escalated. Black men danced with white women, too. A pattern developed of "stagging" (whites kept dancing or talking with one another to prevent a black from asking to dance or talk to them) and "cutting in" on one another to break up mixed racial dancing. Once discovered, these practices were forbidden. Bette Davis refused to allow any sort of racism or segregation patterns to develop and persist. The Hollywood Victory Committee's policy was to let black hostesses and white soldiers dance. The committee responded to inquiries about its policy with "Let them dance if they want to." The black press praised its policy of racial democracy.[52]

Davis insisted on an open policy. She noted that "each night in the Canteen there were many G.I.'s who came from the South. As president, I refused to have the black G.I.'s put in one section of the Canteen. They were free to mingle with the rest. Why not? The blacks got the same bullets the whites did and therefore should have the same treatment." There was fear of trouble. The band was "instructed to play 'The Star Spangled Banner'" if trouble occurred. The song would snap most men to attention and give the staff time to intervene and stop any fights. Only twice did it have to be used. Racial democracy remained in force until the Hollywood Canteen closed on VJ Day in 1945.[53]

The Hollywood Victory Committee was headed by George Murphy, who asked comedian Bob Hope to help organize it in late 1942. During World War II, it arranged more than 86,000 variety shows all over the world.[54] Hope started what became a tradition of entertaining American troops overseas. He went to North Africa where G.I.'s constructed a nightclub "made out of boxes that fragmentation bombs came in." The clubs were named after famous New York clubs such as "Stork Club," "21," "El Morocco," and "Copacabana." Liquor came from Cairo. Jack Benny performed in Cairo. Joe E. Brown and Al Jolson were loved by the soldiers on the Hollywood Victory Committee's circuit. Hope entertained black troops overseas and in England.[55] Lanny Ross produced a radio show called "Camel Caravan" which featured live entertainment. He took his show on the circuit to New Guinea and Guadalcanal. His black entertainers were well received by the white troops.[56]

Ingrid Bergman volunteered for the USO circuit and was asked, "Would you go to Alaska because no one ever wants to go there? They all want to go to the South Pacific." She agreed to go and arrived in Alaska in December of 1943. At the USO Show she and "a boy from Palladium, Hollywood danced the jitterbug in the middle of the Service Club with 500 boys around looking." On her tour she signed 5,000 pictures. One said: "To see a woman like you makes you want to live again."[57]

In Hollywood, who was in the military and was not, and why, was a hot topic. The most famous Hollywood stars joined the military circuit called the "Hollywood Victory Caravan" or the "Hollywood Caravan of Stars" that went on tour for the Army and Navy Relief Fund. Bob Hope entertained all over California and then went abroad. He was in the vanguard of Hollywood actors for the war effort. Hope said he got started in May of 1941 because his "producer had a brother who was in the service, and so, the next Tuesday, I was on a bus with Jerry Colonna and Francis Langford and the audience was . . . so sensational, we said, 'Where have these guys been?' and we went for five straight years." They toured nearly every section of the country. The Hollywood Victory Caravan wound up in

Washington, D.C., where Eleanor Roosevelt received the troupe on the White House lawn. Hollywood raised nearly one million dollars for the entertainment of troops through the War Activities Committee and more than $2 million for the Army and Navy Relief Fund. In an attempt to raise a billion dollars Hollywood sent out films and seven troupes of stars to 5,000 theaters in 300 cities in the United States. Moreover, by 1943 there were 27,677 film workers in military uniform.[58] Needless to say, Hollywood stars and films had a tremendous impact on Americans and the mobilization for war.

During the war, a large influx of blacks from the deep South flooded Los Angeles seeking war work and freedoms denied them in the South. Black soldiers also were in the area in large numbers. The NAACP and black leaders in 1942 started an "interracial program in USO clubs on the West Coast." This program was established for camp dances and at the YWCA and on a college campus. The Interracial Committee established a training program for black female hostesses. "A professional dress designer" gave a talk on "The Language of Clothes" to correct girls who dressed in poor taste.[59] Apparently, the Interracial Committee wanted to avoid the embarrassment experienced at Radio City Music Hall in New York, where black female Lindy Hop dancers performed without panties, which was noticed when they were thrown into the air in dance routines. A loud protest by the older white patrons brought the practice to a halt.[60] The Los Angeles program had its greatest impact at the Hollywood Canteen, where Bette Davis and others were receptive to a program of racial democracy.

Hollywood film star Carol Landis performed three days at Camp Bowie, San Antonio, Texas, in August 1942. She objected to the Jim Crow arrangements in force at the camp. She defended black soldiers' right to equal treatment. Blacks were excluded from seeing her show. She protested by spending an entire evening the next day with black troops in their service club singing and playing ping pong. She told the press, which refused to print anything about her protest activities there, that "Bette Davis showed how she felt about it recently, by appearing in California camps with Hattie McDaniel, Ethel Waters, and the rest of an all-colored cast. Maybe by the time the war is over, we will have acquired some of the tolerance we are fighting for."[61] Bette Davis set a standard that many Hollywood stars followed either quietly with little or no incident or with public protest, as in the case of Landis. In either case, Hollywood's cultural rebels undermined Jim Crow wherever they went.

A friend in the Air Force wrote Frank Mathias from Maxwell Field, Alabama, that women could be bought for as little as a quarter! At Creighton University Air Force Cadet School Mathias's friend noted with glee: "There are 15 women to one man here in Omaha. Our air force cadet uniform really attracts women. Believe me when I say that there are so many pretty women out here that you feel guilty to stay with one more than a half hour. You'll walk into a bar with the most beautiful blonde on your arm that you could ever want, and then at a table are 3 beautiful redheads or brunettes just begging you to sit down with then, but you already have the blonde so you make an excuse to the blonde and forget where you left her. No kidding it's really that pitiful—no stuff."[62] The attraction of women in such numbers worried officials because it endangered the G.I.'s morals and health because venereal disease might result. The USO was to provide healthy and controlled relations designed to avoid sexual encounters. Hostesses were warned against sex as a matter of USO policy.

Many soldiers ordered to the South Pacific theater were disappointed and bitter because Europe was regarded as the area of the "glamorous war" and the South Pacific was the least desirable, with its pests, diseases, and hated Asians. Melanesians and black Americans were referred to as "fuzzy wuzzies" for their thick woolly hair and dark skin color. Black Americans deeply resented being taunted as "fuzzy wuzzies," and it often led to fights and riots.[63] Mathias recalled that when he was shipped to the South Pacific, "as we loaded, the usual taunts reserved for unlucky G.I.'s headed for the Pacific jungle were shouted at us: 'Have fun with the fuzzy wuzzies!'" And they were chided with: "We won't see you in gay Paree!" Some added, "Commit hara-kiri now!" or "Tokyo Rose eats shit!" Others said, "Say hello to a yellow-bellow!"[64] Every war theater ranked below being at home or in the European theater. The USO (and the Red Cross, which handled USO entertainment abroad) tried to counter this and build morale by being "a home away from home."

Antipathy toward blacks, in uniform or not, led to fights and riots everywhere. Walter White of the NAACP was asked to investigate race riots and low morale of blacks in the South Pacific. He was instructed to report to Navy Public Relations. The Lieutenant Commander, Joe Magee, a white Texan, told White upon his arrival: "We've been expecting you for weeks to do something about the trouble Southerners have been causing out here."[65] He wondered what had held White up. Admiral Chester W. Nimitz of the Pacific fleet had experimented with integration of black and white Navy men as a matter of principle and as a means of reducing racial clashes, fostered by group plotting and grievances nursed undetected under segregation. He permitted black officers to exercise authority over whites to build morale among blacks and reduce racial chauvinism among whites.[66]

Lieutenant General Robert C. Richardson Jr. in Hawaii, however, was a racist who thought that any conflict was instigated by blacks. He used the Military Police (MPs) to intimidate and violently repress any black protest against injustices or racial indignities. Blacks who objected to unfair treatment were judged "bad actors." Racist whites threatened and demanded of Hawaiians that blacks be excluded and segregated in public accommodations or face riots and destruction of their property.[67]

The Hawaiian press supported these demands. Hawaiians sought statehood and thought it best to comply with mainland practices. Racists objected to blacks dating native women. One native woman told a black who wanted his picture taken with her in the traditional welcome ceremony, "The American whites tell us that you are inferior and that you have tails." This state of affairs, harsh Jim Crow regulations, slurs, and indignities heaped upon blacks, resulted in numerous race riots in which white G.I.'s threw live hand grenades and smoke bombs into the Jim Crow bases where blacks were isolated. Whites taunted blacks by calling them "fuzzy wuzzies." Trash with racial epithets written on it was thrown into the blacks' base area. Racist Marines beat and ran blacks out of the town of Agana because they resented their dating native women. MPs violently repressed blacks, and the military criminal justice system court-martialed many blacks for simply objecting to racial slurs and indignities.[68]

The USO Camp Shows, under the auspices of the Red Cross, had sent 266 entertainers in forty-five units overseas by April 1943. It had staged more than 4,000 shows in Hawaii in twelve months.[69] This was the last fling for many soldiers before going

into combat. Also, many veterans returned from combat through
Hawaii. A significant number of soldiers in Hawaii, whether going
or returning from the South Pacific war, were embittered about
their assignment in the least desirable war theater. Their
traditional racial and sexual hatreds against blacks and non-
whites, now inflamed by race war in the South Pacific, fears of
an uncertain fate, detachment from loved ones, and sexual
competition with black soldiers, Asians, and Hawaiians, caused
them to turn on black soldiers with a vengeance. Racists
intimidated Hawaiians into compliance with mainland Jim Crow
patterns.

The USO was not the only agency that provided armed
forces personnel with recreation and entertainment. The various
branches of the armed forces had well-established military bands.
These bands played traditional martial music and marches.
Musicians entering the armed forces brought with them their
jazz and swing band music. They disliked playing traditional
martial music and marches. They wanted to play the popular
music of the day—jazz and swing music. Many musicians also
insisted on jazzing traditional martial music. Military and civilian
traditionalists resented the transformation of martial music to
jazz and swing styles. A struggle for cultural and musical
democracy developed in the armed services and the modernist
musicians won a stunning victory.

During World War II, many musicians joined the armed
forces or were drafted. Many bands were left in disarray as a
result. Many jazz fans were scattered throughout the world in
war theaters. A different type of audience emerged at home.
Men rejected by the draft, or who evaded it, showed up in jazz
audiences. They were "4-F, jivey characters in Zoot suits to match
the frantic screaming tenor saxes which were the precursors of
bop," said musician Max Kaminsky.[70] Many whites and some
blacks resented Zoot suiters, who were perceived as dodgers,
criminals, or women chasers threatening the security of others
by their behavior.

In December 1941 Artie Shaw, a big band leader, was
drafted and his band broke up. In early 1942 Eddie Condon and
Ernie Anderson staged jazz concerts at Town Hall in New York.
These drew only about thirty people or so until the war
enthusiasm and war songs caused jazz to explode into greater

popularity. The Town Hall concerts became so big that police had to come in force to keep order. Songs like "The White Cliffs of Dover," "The Last Time I Saw Paris," and "When the Lights Go on Again All over the World" became very popular because they evoked an emotional response.[71]

Artie Shaw formed a Navy band and recruited Max Kaminsky and many New York musicians. Shaw enlisted some physically unfit musicians who could not meet military standards. The standards were waived or ignored to organize jazz bands. Many regular soldiers deeply resented this as special privilege. Shaw's band played such popular war tunes as "Stars and Stripes Forever," "Under the Double Eagle," "Anchors Aweigh," and "The Washington Post March" at Pier 92 in New York when soldiers sailed to the European war theater. The band was transferred to California and then to Honolulu, Waikiki, Treasure Island, and Pearl Harbor.[72]

Admiral Nimitz loved jazz and asked Claude Thornhill to organize a band for his command.[73] Thornhill performed aboard ship as they sailed for New Caledonia on the *Saratoga*. The band staged a famous "Saratoga Concert," in which the bandsmen ascended on the ship's elevator to the deck. The doors opened as the band played, with the men "wildly cheering." The band played "Sail On" and "St. Louis Blues" to homesick men, and all "three thousand went stark, raving crazy." Despite appreciative audiences, some jazz musicians chased a lot of women and "a lot of friction started." Artie Shaw had serious problems avoiding officers' wives who pursued him.[74] Musicians' reputations suffered from their womanizing.

Jazz musician George Simon noted that "those who escaped the draft had themselves a field-day. Many acted like spoiled brats." Some jazzmen demanded high salaries. Some left band after band because they could command a higher salary. Others blamed servicemen for the problems they encountered traveling to military camps and for having to play early morning sessions to accommodate soldiers. A musicians' strike in 1942 hurt the big bands because it resulted in the rise of vocalists such as Frank Sinatra. The swing bands declined soon after the war, and singers became popular. Hollywood used many jazz bands in films during the war. This boosted their popularity and that of singers.[75]

Max Kaminsky noted: "There was always a lot of resentment against the band on the part of other Navy men.

. . . We were in the Navy as regular sailors, and not in the Special Service, but we hadn't even gone through boot training, and in the eyes of the regular servicemen we weren't one of them, which was true, and they thought we received extra privileges, such as extra pay, which was not true." When sailors got drunk and tore up a club, they blamed the band.[76] On the other hand, added Kaminsky, "our troops all over the world were clamoring for jazz bands, jazz records, and jazz broadcasts, and eventually even the top brass were becoming aware of the morale value of jazz." In 1943 Duke Ellington started an annual jazz concert from Carnegie Hall in New York that was played over the air and became very popular. As a result, "the Jazz V-discs and the weekly WRCS Jazz broadcasts" started by Eddie Condon were broadcast to military bases over the world by short-wave radio.[77]

By 1943, many of Stan Kenton's popular West Coast bandsmen had been drafted. Some were drafted before their uniforms or "victory pants" were paid for. Bandsmen left for higher pay elsewhere. Kenton was drafted while he was in Miami, Florida, but he snatched his papers, called Hollywood to protest, and while in Detroit he was reclassified 2-A. Kenton was accused by jazz critic Leonard Feather of racial discrimination because he refused to hire black musicians, and his "music was Wasp music. . . ." Kenton hired Jessie Price, a black musician, but Bob Ahern, a white member of the Kenton band, made life so miserable for him that he quit. Nevertheless, during the war years Kenton recorded such tunes as "Harlem Folk Dance," Duke Ellington's "Do Nothing till You Hear from Me," "Old Black Joe," "A Little Jive Is Good for You," "Flamingo" (made famous by Ellington's band with Herb Jeffries, whom Kenton's vocalist, Red Dorris, imitated), and the popular West Coast dance tune "Balboa Bash." Some of these tunes were made famous by Harlem's black jazz musicians. Kenton modeled his band after Earl "Fatha" Hines, Benny Carter, Louis Armstrong, and George Gershwin.[78] No matter what Kenton's views were on race relations and blacks, he could not afford to ignore Harlem jazz and jive.

Big bandsmen and jazz musicians elicited strong ambivalence because of their personal behavior and the impact they had on some patrons. Frank Sinatra's promoter, George Evans, taught him to caress the microphone as if he'd fall over and to twist his hips in a very sexually suggestive manner that caused young girls to shout, shriek, and faint and pandemonium to break out at his concerts. New York City's education commissioner said Sinatra's concerts resulted in mass truancy. Further, "we can't tolerate young people making a public display of losing control of their emotions." One Congressman charged that Sinatra was "the prime instigator of juvenile delinquency in America." The New York Police Department blamed him for runaway girls. A New York psychiatrist said Sinatra caused "hysteria to the point of swooning [which] is definitely harmful." A sociologist noted that Sinatra's singing style induced "mass frustrated love without direction." Sinatra was dubbed "Swoonatra" and "The Voice."[79] For some these were pejorative terms and Sinatra was viewed by some as an unhealthy and anti-social influence on youth.

Sinatra fought two soldiers in a night club for calling him a "Wop." It was bad publicity during a time of fervent war fever. What is more, he was classified 4-F because of a hole in his left eardrum. This added fuel to his critics' distaste for him. In October of 1943, he auctioned off his clothes and raised more than $12,000 for the war. Nevertheless, writer William Manchester said, "I think Frank Sinatra was the most hated man of World War II, much more than Hitler . . . because we in the Pacific had seen no women at all for two years, and there were photographs of Sinatra being surrounded by all of these enthusiastic girls." He made a number of war musicals and films. He sang in August 1943 at the Hollywood Bowl before 5,000 howling teenagers. The Hollywood Bowl featured classical as well as jazz music on its programs. On October 12, 1944, Sinatra sang to a sellout crowd of teenagers, about 30,000 and mainly girls, at Times Square in New York. One seventeen-year-old girl said, "Our folks would rather have us following Sinatra than chasing sailors and soldiers." Sinatra publicly and repeatedly denounced racism at a time when it was very popular and Jim Crow was part of the constitutional system.[80] Many racists resented Sinatra because he was an Italian and for his support of racial democracy. They often said so with no apology.

Betty Hutton was dubbed "Hollywood's newest musical comedy star" by age twenty-two and was awarded the title of 'America's No. 1 Jitterbug. . . .'" And, it was noted, she "uses more than her voice to put over a song. She mugs and grimaces, socks herself in the jaw, battles with imaginary adversaries, and at times looks more like an acrobat than a singer." She performed in Cole Porter's show, *Panama Hattie*, and the Hollywood film *Happy Go Lucky*. She also starred in the movie, *"Murder," He Says*. She sang jive words and phrases such as: "He says, 'Murder,' He says, 'Solid,' 'Takes me in his arms,' 'Meaning all my charms,' 'Zoot are we livin',' 'Now he can talk plainer than that!,' 'Shoot the snoot to me,' He says, 'Woof, woof.'"[81] This jive and jazz style was typical Harlem culture shared by black and white hepsters.

Jive, jitterbug dancing, and jazz dance and concert bands became very popular in the 1930s and reached a watershed of popularity during the war years. Cab Calloway led the way with his "Harlemese" language, or jive talk spoken by "Harlemites." He published *The Cab Calloway Hepster's Dictionary* and another book called *Professor Cab Calloway's Swingformation Bureau* between 1938 and 1944. Dan Burley, a black newspaper columnist for the *People's Voice*, wrote a jive column on the new language. He published *Dan Burley's Original Handbook of Harlem Jive* (illustrated by Melvin Tapley). Jive became the language of the entertainment world—both black and white—but especially of jazz bandsmen and women. Calloway called the language "Negro slang, the super-hip language of the times."[82] This language helped to cement friendships between black and white entertainers and set them apart from racists and conservative social and cultural Victorians. It became, too, the language of G.I. Jivers during the war years.

Johnny Mercer, born in Savannah, Georgia, in 1909, contributed mightily to the G.I. Jive culture during the war. He wrote the lyrics for the film *Star Spangled Rhythm*. He wrote and recorded the witty and popular lyrics to the war hit "G.I. Jive." The song epitomized jive and jazz, and was critical of military life. The music was a mixture of jazz with a boogie woogie opening. A few of the opening lyrics were: "This is the G.I. Jive; Man alive! It starts with the bugler blowing reveille over your bed when you arrive; Jack, that's the G.I. Jive; Rootalee Toot; Jump in your suit; Make a salute. . . ."[83] The jive lyrics of the song interpreted military life in "Jive culture" terminology, and, perhaps, helped Zoot suiters and jitterbugs to cope by trivializing basic military routine—that one can master the routine without the same enthusiasm as one invested in "pure jive culture" in civilian life.

Glenn Miller, a popular big band jazzman, epitomized the dilemma of the white G.I. Jive musician. He promoted jazz and jive and found a solution to neutralize his critics, those opposed to the vigorous emergence of the G.I. Jive military cultural movement. Miller was playing in the Sunset Serenade room of the Cafe Rouge in the Hotel Pennsylvania on October 4, 1941, and allowed kids to pay with United States savings bonds which he donated to the USO. Keenly disturbed by the war in Europe, he registered for the draft despite the fact he was thirty-seven years old and married.[84] He wrote a letter on August 12, 1942, to Brigadier General Charles D. Young which said in part that military men had written him "expressing their appreciation of our various Army camp appearances and our USO broadcasts." Moreover, these letters indicated these boys wanted the kind of modern, popular music his band played. Miller played at the Hollywood Bowl on April 15, 1942, for a "Military Ball" to benefit a local Army hospital, and raised $7,300. The same month, he recorded the popular tune "American Patrol," that was "complete with its flag-waving sounds."[85]

On June 20, 1942, Miller applied to the Commandant of the Ninth Naval District for a commission in the United States Naval Reserve. Initially he was rejected, but he pleaded his case and was accepted.[86] He was inducted in New York City and assigned to the Army Specialist Corps on October 7, 1942. Disgusted with the old martial music, he constantly complained to his friends about it. He was transferred to the Army Air Corps and to Maxwell Field, Alabama, because an officer recognized him and aided him in getting transferred to that branch of service. He wrote musician Jerry Gray to join him and help transform the old-style martial music into modern jazz and swing music. "We have the authorization for a 14-man arranging staff to provide music for the Army Air Forces Technical Training Command, and it is my plan to place you in charge of this when you get one of Uncle's Zoot suits," boasted Miller to Gray. Military officers who opposed jazz and jive music in the military ruined Miller's plan and had him assigned to Atlantic City, New Jersey.[87]

Miller was assigned to Yale University, which the military practically took over. He was still frustrated because of opposition to modern music by top brass at headquarters and by cadet training officers who opposed any modernization of such traditional military music as John Philip Sousa's march arrangements. Cadets, however, appreciated the "most swinging marching band" Miller was trying to create. George T. Simon, a musician and Miller biographer, noted, "Glenn and his arrangers had instilled some swinging syncopations into the trite old marches."[88]

Ray McKinley and Perry Burgett suggested that they jazz up "St. Louis Blues" into a military march jazz tune. Miller and Jerry Gray made a full arrangement of it. "The idea of creating swinging march arrangements of jazz tunes knocked us all out— Glenn included—and soon we were playing jumping martial versions of 'Blues in the Night' and 'Jersey Bounce.'" As a result of these experiments, "the Cadets' grins grew wider and wider, their strides more bouncing than ever," said Simon, a member of Miller's band. "But some of those officers dedicated to reliving their good old West Point marching days rebelled against breaking with the Sousa tradition." They resented Miller and his band and attacked Miller and others as "instant captains."[89]

The commandant of the cadets hated Miller and loved Sousa. He told Miller: "Look, Captain Miller, we played those Sousa marches straight in the last war and we did all right, didn't we?" Miller replied, "You certainly did Major. But tell me one thing: Are you still flying the same planes you flew in the last war, too?" Miller continued to play his blues marches. He tried to protect himself against the well-known excesses of some musicians, in and out of the service, by ordering his bandsmen to shave and cut their mustaches. Many were upset over the order. Bernie Privin, a trumpeter, complained: "The only explanation that he ever gave us was that he thought we looked too much like gangsters!" Johnny Desmond joined the band as the replacement singer for Tony Martin and wore an Army crew-cut hairstyle. Miller had him cut it short three times. He told Desmond that "the band had to act and look more disciplined than any other outfit because we were musicians and all those officers were just looking for something, like hair that was too long, to pin on him and on us."[90] Miller adopted social Victorian codes of dress and conduct to promote jazz styles into martial music.

Miller's group was a full orchestra, including strings and singers "with dramatic episodes glamorizing the activities of the Army Air Forces Technical Training Command. Its purpose: to entice volunteers into that branch of the service," said Simon. The Army Air Force Command relieved Miller of his duties of training the band so he could conduct a radio show. He was glad to go because of harassment by those who opposed swing jazz and the special treatment accorded some musicians in the armed forces. He complained, "I don't understand why so many people want to make it so difficult." Miller plowed ahead. At a July 28, 1943, Yale Bowl performance he presented for "a giant war-bond rally" his "modernized military band"—two jeeps filled with musicians. "The sight and sound electrified the large crowd. Cheers went up as the swinging band marched by. The cadets strutted as never before. Military music in general, and the Sousa marches in particular, had never had it so good."[91] Miller thought it a major victory. His critics thought otherwise and a public debate ensued over the appropriateness of the infusion of jazz into martial music.

Time magazine complained of this grand, jazzed-up martial presentation of Glenn Miller's Army Air Force Technical Training Command Band. It noted under the heading "Sousa with a Floy Floy": "Oldtime, long-haired U.S. Army bandmasters had the horrors last week. A U.S. Army band (the 418th Army Air Forces Band from the Technical School at Yale) had suddenly, and disconcertingly, got rhythm. When it swung down the line blaring such hallowed items as John Philip Sousa's Stars & Stripes Forever in jive tempo, sober listeners began to wonder what U.S. brass-band music was coming to. Obviously, there was an Afro-Saxon in the woodpile."[92] This was a swipe at Miller and his use of jazz in martial music. *Time* called the performance "this military rug cutting" of Captain Glenn Miller, the "recruit from the swank hotel ballrooms and broadcasting studios." He was now "embarking on an earnest crusade to put swing on the U.S. parade ground. . . ." Miller defended his performance. "There hasn't been a successful Army band in the country, and if someone doesn't get after band music and streamline it, Army music will be extinct in another couple of years. We've got to keep pace with the soldiers. They want up-to-date music. Why, there's no question about it—anybody can improve on Sousa."[93]

Edwin Franko Goldman, a old-style concert band leader and Sousa's successor, was outraged. "Personally I think it's a disgrace! There isn't any excuse for it. Perhaps they think they can add more dash and appeal. But no one can improve on a Sousa march. . . . My God!" Others, too, said *Time*, were "fearful that Captain Miller's crusade would leave the U.S. Army swinging its hips instead of its feet."[94] One person complained in a letter to *Time* that he had read "with complete disgust . . . that Captain Glenn Miller has begun to 'swing' the age-old, magnificent marches of John Philip Sousa. . . ." He added, "When Sousa wrote them he left no room for improvement." Lee Tyler wrote, "Captain Glenn Miller has the right idea swinging those Sousa marches." Edwin Franko Goldman was so embittered that he too wrote a letter to *Time* to register another protest. "No! Sousa marches do not need 'streamlining'—but probably a few of the 'bandmasters' who advocate the 'swinging' of his music do." What is more, said Goldman, "personally, I feel that the question of swinging military marches is a question for commanding officers to settle. Do they want their armies to march with military bearing, to fine inspiring rhythm—or do they prefer to 'jitterbug' their way along?"[95]

The outcry compelled Miller to modify his statement and say that civilian bands did not know how to play marches anymore. Marshall Bartholomew, director of the Yale Glee Club, supported Miller. In a letter to *Time* he complained that "the trouble lies in Washington, not in New Haven." He praised Miller's patriotism and music, his personal sacrifices, and for changing a dull music to one with dash. Miller had "such energy, enthusiasm, and skill as to quicken the pulse and lighten the heart of everyone within hearing distance."[96] Miller's enemies, however, limited his recordings to arrest the spread of his style of jazz marches. Miller complained, "This seems to me like a hell of a good way to win the war." Other officers joined the fray and aided Miller and his band because they wanted the new music incorporated into the armed forces. As a result, Miller went on to greater success and acceptance despite his critics.[97]

Overseas, Miller's band triumphed in the battle against the old guard, and its name was changed to "Captain Glenn Miller and his American Band of the Supreme Allied Command" to reflect its new status. In England, a 17-piece dance band led by

Ray McKinley from the Miller group was called the "Swing Shift." Miller's shows had such names as "A Soldier and a Song" and "Strings with Wings." General Dwight D. Eisenhower, a Miller fan, shook his hand and congratulated him for his contribution to the soldiers' morale. The Army recorded "Victory Discs" of jazz bands and sent them free to soldiers around the world. A *Metronome* article claimed that Miller's band was the most popular among the G.I.'s. He performed a "Jazz Jamboree" at Stall Theatre in London. Miller's band played at more than 800 separate events, 500 radio broadcasts, and 300 live performances to a total of 600,000 people during the war. He recorded "Stormy Weather," which had been sung by Lena Horne in the 1943 film of the same name. Johnny Desmond sang a recorded version of it with Miller. Miller recorded the "St. Louis Blues March," a popular rendition of that tune, as jazzed blues. On December 15, 1944, he took off from England in General Goodrich's private plane for Paris and was never heard from again. He was promoted to Colonel in absentia and awarded a Bronze Star.[98]

Glenn Miller and his band brought the G.I. Jive movement to its highest peak of success during World War II. He adopted a conservative code of dress and conduct to disarm his enemies. He won over the top brass to the necessity of making modern martial music appeal to the new American soldiers. His strategic location at Yale University thrust him into the center of the elite officer corps, where the battle was joined at the highest level, and brought the issue to a head and was recognized by the press, which alerted the public to a fundamental shift in the martial music tradition. Miller made jazz and jive more acceptable, and thereby increased cultural pluralism and social democracy because blacks were recognized as leaders and participants in jazz and jive.

The USO's Jim Crow policy was not enforced uniformly across the nation. The USO itself was not disposed to enforce it where either the community or leadership was opposed to it. The USO policy of bringing Hollywood and Broadway to the troops opened the door to blacks, jazz, and jive because blacks had already won a place in Hollywood and on Broadway. Then, too, black jazzmen and Zoot suiters had won widespread recognition as hepsters and jitterbuggers. Many whites had adopted this culture too. Black and white jazzmen and jitterbuggers either joined or were drafted into the armed forces; they took their culture with them and demanded and won its recognition. Their demand for cultural pluralism and modernity severely undermined social and cultural rigidity in both civilian and military life, and thereby increased the social and cultural freedom of blacks and whites who shared one another's culture and social styles. This had been the original intent of the Harlem Renaissance writers, editors, and publishers.

The Harlem Renaissance idealists had not envisioned a military angle to their plan of using the arts, especially by blacks and their allies, to break down Jim Crow. They were aware of the influence of James Reese Europe's jazz band in Europe during World War I. Their literary movement had emerged between the wars and had formally collapsed by the early 1930s. Nevertheless, the seeds they had planted sprouted in the performing arts during the war on the USO circuit, in the armed forces, and, most notably, in the Hollywood, Washington, D.C., and New York City canteens. Carl Van Vechten clearly recognized what was happening and paid homage to the new phenomenon in his "An Ode to the [New York] Stage Door Canteen" as a cabaret with a racially democratic culture he prized and had written about in his 1926 novel, *Nigger Heaven*. He was overjoyed at its fruition at the New York Stage Door Canteen. During the war, a significant measure of ethnic cultural and social democracy was carved out by new institutions within a society and government still committed to a formal Jim Crow system of law, culture, music, and social life.

Notes

1. Julia M.H. Carson (historian for the USO), *Home Away from Home: The Story of the USO* (New York: Harper & Brothers, 1946), pp. xi–xii; Eileen Southern, *The Music of Black Americans: A History* (New York: W.W. Norton Company, Inc., 1971), pp. 488–489; Laurence Jolidon, "USO Show Goes On and Over There," *USA Today*, 27 November 1987, p. 1-A, col. 3, p. 2-A, col. 1.

2. Carson, p. 110.

The USO and Jim Crow 167

3. Henry L. Stimson and McGeorge Bundy, *On Active Service in Peace and War* (New York: Harper & Brothers, 1947, 1948), pp. 455–456.

4. *Ibid.*, p. 458.

5. Frank F. Mathias, *G.I. Jive: An Army Bandsman in World War II* (Lexington: University Press of Kentucky, 1982), pp. 1–4, 10.

6. Carson, pp. 111–115.

7. *Ibid.*, p. 142.

8. *Ibid.*

9. *Ibid.*, pp. 149–150.

10. *Ibid.*, pp. 185–186.

11. *Ibid.*, p. 190.

12. *Ibid.*, pp. 193–199.

13. U.S. National Board U.S.O. Division, *Experiments in Democracy* (New York: Young Women's Christian Association [n.d.]), pp. 5–6, 7–8 (hereafter cited as YWCA).

14. J. Saunders Redding, "Here's a New Thing Altogether," *Survey Graphic*, XXXIII, No. 8 (August 1944), pp. 358–359, 366–367.

15. John M. Blum, "The G.I. in the Culture of the Second World War," *Ventures*, 7 (Spring 1968), 52, 54–55.

16. YWCA, pp. 46–47.

17. *Ibid.*, pp. 8–9.

18. *Ibid.*, p. 59.

19. *Ibid.*, pp. 24–26, 29.

20. John Morton Blum, *V Was for Victory: Politics and American Culture during World War II* (New York: Harcourt Brace Jovanovich, 1976), p. 190.

21. "No Segregated Harlem Stage Door Canteen," *Pittsburgh Courier*, 7 August 1943, p. 21, col. 3.

22. Margaret Halsey, *Color Blind* (New York: Simon and Schuster, 1946), pp. 68, 11–12, 144–145, 47.

23. *Ibid.*, pp. 19, 24, 26, 29, 69.

24. *Ibid.*, pp. 103–104, 110–117.

25. *Ibid.*, p. 100.

26. *Ibid.*, pp. 54–55, 57.

27. *Ibid.*, p. 58.

28. Theodore G. Bilbo, *Take Your Choice: Separation or Mongrelization* (Poplarville: Dream House Publishing, Co., 1947), pp. 176–177.

29. Congressman Joseph R. Bryan, South Carolina, *Congressional Record, 78th Congress, 2nd Sess., 1944*, Vol. 90, Part 2, 8 March 1944, p. 2396; Charles S. Johnson, *To Stem This Tide: A Survey of Racial Tension Areas in the United States* (Boston: The Pilgrim Press, 1943), p. 67.

30. Bilbo, pp. 177–178.

31. *Ibid.*, pp. 52–53.

32. *Ibid.*, p. 103.

33. Halsey, pp. 62–63.

34. *Ibid.*, p. 151.

35. Bilbo, pp. 179–184.

36. Jean Pinney, "How Fares the Battle Against Prostitution?," *The Social Service Review*, XVI, No. 2 (June 1942), 224.

37. *Ibid.*, pp. 237–238, 226–227.

38. "Claim Exploitation of Fort Benning Soldiers. 'subjected to Bad Moral Influence,' Sec'y of War Says," *Pittsburgh Courier*, 4 January 1941, p. 5, col. 2.

39. Matthias, p. 45.

40. Pinney, pp. 237–238.

41. Mahias, p. 11.

42. The Henry Lewis Stimson Diaries in the Yale University Library. Microscripts and Archives, Yale University Library, New Haven, 1973, entry for 18 November 1941, p. 33, and entry for 22 June 1943, p. 133.

43. *Ibid.*, entry for 12 May 1942, p. 7.

44. *Ibid.*

45. Carson, pp. 10–11, 113, 115, 131.

46. Max Kaminsky with V.E. Hughes, *My Life in Jazz* (New York: Harper & Row, Publishers, 1963), p. 172.

47. Walter White, *A Rising Wind* (Garden City: Doubleday, Doran, Co., Inc., 1945), pp. 36–37; YWCA, pp. 40, 46.

48. Carl Van Vechten, "An Ode to the Stage Door Canteen," *Theatre Arts*, XXII, No. 4 (April 1943), 229–231.

49. "Andrew Sisters Head Savoy Talent Stars at War Bond Dance Set for October 21," *People's Voice*, 17 October 1942, p. 28, col. 1.

50. Studs Terkel, *The Good War: An Oral History of World War Two* (New York: Pantheon Books, 1984), pp. 294–297.

51. Bette Davis, *This 'N That* (New York: G.P. Putnam's Sons, 1987), pp. 121–126.

52. *Ibid.*, p. 128; A.A. Hoehling, *Home Front, U.S.A.* (New York: Thomas Y. Crowell Company, 1966), pp. 128–129.

53. "Bette Davis Overrules Objection to Mixed Couples At Hollywood Canteen," *Pittsburgh Courier*, 16 January 1943, p. 21, col. 3.

54. Charles Thompson, *Bob Hope: Portrait of a Superstar* (New York: St. Martin's Press, 1981), p. 64.

55. Bob Hope, *I Never Left Home* (New York: Simon & Schuster, 1944), pp. 120, 112–113, 47.

56. Hoehling, p. 130.

57. Ingrid Bergman and Alan Burgess, *Ingrid Bergman: My Story* (New York: Delacorte Press, 1980), pp. 127–128.

58. William Robert Faith, *Bob Hope: A Life in Comedy* (New York: G.P. Putnam's Sons, 1982), pp. 159–161, 149–150, 170–171, 164; Laurence Jolidon, pp. 1-A, 2-A.

59. YWCA, pp. 29–30.

60. Kaminsky, p. 90.

61. "Carol Landis Attacks Army's Jim Crow Show," *Chicago Defender*, 22 August 1942, p. 12, col. 1.

62. Mathias, p. 25.

63. *Ibid.*, pp. 68, 75.

64. *Ibid.*, p. 54.

65. Walter White, *A Man Called White: The Autobiography of Walter White* (Bloomington: Indiana University Press, 1970 [1948]), p. 271.

66. *Ibid.*, pp. 272–273.

67. *Ibid.*, pp. 272–274, 277–280.

68. *Ibid.*

69. "USO Shows Carry Entertainment to American Troops Abroad," *Victory*, 4, No. 15 (14 April 1943), 424.

70. Kaminsky, pp. 121–124; George T. Simon, *The Big Bands* (New York: Schirmer Books, 1981), pp. 29–31.

71. Kaminksy, pp. 127–129.

72. *Ibid.*, pp. 131–135.

73. *Ibid.*, pp. 135–138.

74. *Ibid.*, pp. 139–143.

75. Simon, *Big Band*, pp. 31, 66–69.

76. Kaminsky, pp. 143–144, 138–139, 151.

77. *Ibid.*, p. 157, 167.

78. Carole Easton, *Straight Ahead: The Story of Stan Kenton* (New York: William Morrow & Co., 1973), pp. 79, 90–92, 86, 60, 37; "Stan Kenton and His Orchestra, 1941," Hindsight Records, Inc., HSR 118, 1978, liner notes by Chris Pirie and Dave Dexter Jr.

79. Kitty Kelly, *His Way: The Unauthorized Biography of Frank Sinatra* (New York: Bantam Books, 1986), pp. 66–73.

80. *Ibid.*, pp. 75–76, 83, 94–95, 515, 101–110.

81. "Betty Hutton: Jitterbug Girl Sings and Acts in 'Happy Go Lucky,'" *Life*, 22 March 1943, pp. 64–65.

82. Cab Calloway and Bryant Rollins, *Of Minnie the Moocher & Me* (New York: Thomas Y. Crowell Co., 1976), pp. 114, 178–182; Frank Driggs and Harris Lewis, *Black Beauty, White Heat: A Pictorial History of Classical Jazz 1920–1950* (New York: William Morrow and Company, Inc., 1982), p. 132.

83. "Johnny Mercer/Mercer Sings Mercer," Capitol Records, Hollywood, California, M-11637 (no date given) liner notes by Randall Davis.

84. George T. Simon, *Glenn Miller: And His Orchestra* (New York: Thomas Y. Crowell Company, 1974), pp. 283, 275.

85. *Ibid.*, pp. 311, 300.

86. *Ibid.*, pp. 302, 309.

87. *Ibid.*, pp. 321–324, 334, 332.

88. *Ibid.*, pp. 326, 332–333, 335, 337.

89. *Ibid.*, pp. 337–338.

90. *Ibid.*, pp. 339–340, 343.

91. *Ibid.*, pp. 344, 348–349.

92. "Music: Sousa with a Floy Floy," *Time*, 6 September 1943, pp. 48–49.

93. *Ibid.* (and see Simon's account, *Glenn Miller*, pp. 349–350).

94. *Ibid.*

95. "Sousa Swung," *Time*, 27 September 1943, p. 4.

96. Simon, *Glenn Miller*, pp. 350–351.

97. *Ibid.*, p. 352.

98. *Ibid.*, pp. 361, 367–380, 389, 423; "Glenn Miller & His Orchestra, 1940–1944," a record album, RCA, NL 45116, 1982, liner notes.

BLACK G.I. JIVE

The struggle for cultural and racial democracy intensified during World War II. During the war, however, black artists fighting for the Double V on the cultural and artistic fronts remained divided between the original cultural theories and methods of the Harlem Renaissance. Nevertheless, a consensus emerged among a faction of thoughtful blacks, Jews, and liberal whites that a powerful weapon against white racists and authoritarians was cultural pluralism and social equality. They felt this had to be promoted during the war under the cover of patriotism and with participation of every ethnic and religious group within the nation to protect its national security and international interests.

The war hysteria and the formal United States policy maintaining a segregated military resulted in racial violence as more blacks joined and were drafted into the armed forces. Sammy Davis Jr. came from a family of entertainers and had danced with his father. Shortly after the Japanese bombed Pearl Harbor, he tried to join the Army Air Force but was rejected as too young. He was drafted not long afterward. His father told him, "We always had the name of the best-dressed colored act in show business. Can't let 'em think different about us in the Army. Now, Poppa, you're goin' in a boy but you'll come out a man."[1] He was inducted at the Presidio of Monterey for the San Francisco area.

Davis asked a white enlisted man for directions at Fort Francis E. Warren in Cheyenne, Wyoming, and was told, "I didn't join no nigger Army." Shocked, he walked on. Davis danced and performed at the Air Force Service Club and after a show sought to go into the club for a drink. His black companion warned him it would result in trouble. Davis replied, "Trouble? I just entertained them for an hour. They cheered me." An impressed white G.I. invited Davis to join him in an act which was accepted and they performed regularly at the club. A group of racist whites who had been building up resentment finally cornered Davis, humiliated him, and beat him without mercy. They covered part of his body with white paint. One painted "I'm a nigger" on his chest and something on his back. He crawled and stumbled about. His tormentors demanded that he dance and shouted, "So, come on, Sambo, you be a good little coon and give us a dance. Dance, Sambo. That's better, Sambo. Keep it going. And a little faster. . . ." Davis was forced to dance for thirty minutes while he was hit and kicked. One of his tormentors said, "Well, guess we can't be mad 'cause you don't dance good. Anyway we gotta get back to your education."[2] He told Davis:

> Now, we figure you've got the idea you're the same as white 'cause you're in a uniform like us and 'cause you dance at the shows and you go in and sit down with white men and because you think you got manners like a white man with your flowers and candy you give our women. So we gotta explain to you how you're not white and you ain't never gonna be white no matter how hard you try. No matter what you do or think you can't change what you are, and what you are is black and you better get it outta your head to mess around with white women.[3]

Davis mournfully recalled, "Then I was alone. I looked at myself in one of the mirrors. I wanted to crawl into the walls and die. I sat down on the floor and cried."[4] Davis had been humiliated but not defeated by his tormentors.

Davis's experience epitomized the dilemma of the black G.I. entertainers who sought dignity and acceptance, who were often cheered by some whites, but had to face violent racist whites who resented them and their influence on others. Racists wanted to be sure blacks remained the Sambo. They rejected cultural pluralism and social equality that might lead to racial and sexual acceptance of blacks as equals. They feared that white supremacy and the whole system of racial segregation and discrimination would crumble.

The United Service Organizations (USO) Camp Shows sponsored entertainment programs for G.I.'s that were inherently threatening to the racial status quo. Hollywood and New York's Broadway theatrical districts were heavily influenced by jazz and blacks—even if by stereotypes whether performed by blacks or whites black style, like Eddie Cantor and Al Jolson. Also, Broadway and Hollywood were heavily influenced by Jews, whom racists often resented as much as blacks because Jews, as well as Italians, often sponsored black entertainers and jazzmen and ran clubs that catered to them.[5] Julia Carson of the USO said, "In the simplest terms, Camp Shows' job is to bring Hollywood and Broadway to the servicemen."[6] Hollywood and Broadway were eager to participate in packaging shows for the troops.

Maurice Zolotow reported in September 1942, "Uncle Sam Brings Vaudeville Back: Broadway Does Its Entertaining Bit." It sent off a group that played seventy-three camps for four months. The show featured lots of girls and legs. It played one night stands for the USO Camp Shows. Girls from the Roxy were billed as the Sixteen Dancing Darlings. The Broadway troupe played "The Three Sailors," "Roy Smeck," and numbers by banjo and guitar virtuosos. The seventy girls, however, were not allowed to date the soldiers.[7]

Hollywood and Broadway were on the cutting edge of social and cultural pluralism and interracial mixing and intimacy. Entertainment personalities integrated the New York and Hollywood Stage Door Canteens during the war while practically all others across the country were strictly segregated except for a few black and white entertainers who were allowed to perform before segregated troops and audiences. Since the 1920s, blacks had influenced Broadway and Hollywood. Therefore, black influence and styles continued and affected the USO Camp Shows whether white or black entertainers performed because some black patterns had been adopted by white entertainers.

In the 1920s Harlem, the largest black community in the Western world, became the Mecca of entertainment for the West. People from all over the world came to Harlem for its nightlife and gaiety. Often booze, drugs, sex, gambling, and other illicit activities abounded in and around the cabarets, salons, supper clubs, and jazz haunts. At the center of these activities was the Cotton Club in black Harlem. Harlem had more booze and jazz than any other section of New York. Entertainer Cab Calloway boasted that in the 1920s and 1930s:

> Attending that Cotton Club show were our number one celebrity, Mayor Jimmy Walker, and Betty Compton; New Yorker cartoonist Peter Arno and actress Sally O'Neill; Harry Richman and Clara Bow; Edmund Lowe and the beautiful

Lylyan Tashman; Dutch Schultz, the gangster, who put two
bottles of Scotch on Jimmy's table before he sat down at his
own; Morton Downey, Bea Lillie, Irving Berlin, George White,
Earl Carroll, Fannie Brice, Jack Donahue, James Barton, Jack
Dempsey, Jock Whitney and his Liz, Warden Lawes of Sing
Sing, Will Rogers, Corinne Griffith, and dozens out of the social
register. And Bing Crosby.[8]

He added that Tom Wolfe, Leonard Lyons, and Orson Welles
also came. Huey Long of Louisiana was bounced because he
tried to join the chorus line. William Saroyan, Gene Kelly, Benny
Goodman, Artie Shaw, Glenn Miller, and the Dorsey brothers,
Jimmy and Tommy, came. Mayor Fiorello La Guardia had his
aides escort dignitaries to the Cotton Club but stayed away
himself.[9]

England's Lady Mountbatten visited the Cotton Club one
evening and called it "The Aristocrat of Harlem." That became
its nickname.[10] Although the club was segregated, whites and
blacks did establish contact, especially between the entertainers
and gangsters who ran the club and the celebrities who invited
them to parties and their homes. Cotton Club music and shows
were often imitated on Broadway and in Hollywood films. And,
in turn, many stage shows and clubs across the country followed
Broadway and Hollywood trends.

Such black newspapers as the *Pittsburgh Courier* and the
New York Amsterdam News regularly carried columns on
"Theatrical News" and "Hollywood" or "Harlem-Broadway-
Hollywood," respectively, in prominent print and headlines with
plenty of pictures of Hollywood and Broadway black
personalities. Black entertainers who broke down racial barriers
were especially esteemed.[11] The *Courier* on January 4, 1941, ran
the headline, "Duke [Ellington] Opens in L.A. Nitery." Jimmy
Lunceford had been the first black to play at Casa Mañana. They
broke down the racial barriers with their appearances.[12]

At the same time Lena Horne became the "Third Race Girl
to Be Used by White Band." The black press reported that "Charlie
Barnet, the white orchestra leader whose brand of swing is similar
to that of the best colored bands in the country, signed Lena
Horne, the ex-sepia darling of the world-famous Cotton Club,
to become a part of his orchestra." Barnet, however, refused to
take Horne on his Southern tours because he feared racial

objections and violence. She was, however, kept on the payroll and understood the difficult circumstances her presence would have caused the whole band under the established pattern of accommodation to Southern customs.[13] Barnet feared he would have to defend Horne's honor and that would be a losing situation for all concerned.

Newsweek took note of the major impact black entertainers were having on formerly segregated entertainment institutions. Lena Horne especially impressed the media and whites. "Now, she is the first Negro entertainer ever to be featured at the fashionable Savoy-Plaza." She broke all attendance records. The Savoy Plaza remained segregated and black guests were unwelcome. Horne became ill one evening and fainted. A shamed management offered her a room to stay over night. She rejected the offer because the management had refused her room service earlier. She called a cab and left for the Theresa Hotel in Harlem. Her movie career was booming and she was scheduled to star in the Hollywood film *Cabin in the Sky*.[14]

Walter White of the NAACP was especially interested in Lena Horne's career because he believed she could serve the Civil Rights movement by breaking down race barriers, prejudice, and stereotype roles. She refused to play traditional, demeaning black stereotype roles. She rejected the star role in Countee Cullen and Arna Bontemp's *St. Louis Woman* because of its stereotype casting. At the beginning of World War II Lena Horne, Duke Ellington, Paul Robeson, Lillian Hellman, Groucho Marx, Edward G. Robinson, Orson Welles, Erskine Caldwell, and many other luminaries organized The Emergency Committee of the Entertainment Industry for the United States in order to draft a code to reject racial stereotypes in Hollywood films, but lack of money and staff caused it to collapse.[15] Blacks and their white allies, however, especially key Hollywood and New York Broadway social and entertainment stars, maintained their principles and pushed for racial dignity and pluralism.

Pittsburgh Courier headlines in March 1943 blazed, "Noble Sissle Brings Harlem to Hollywood, So Say Coast Scribes." He was praised for taking his "Harlem in Hollywood" show to the popular Hollywood Casino. "The spirit of Harlem exudes from every skit." The show opened with a patriotic salute. Such stars of Harlem and Cotton Club fame as the Nicholas Brothers, who tap danced; Ada Brown, a famous Cotton Club torch singer; Bill Robinson, tap dancer and featured co-star with Shirley Temple in a series of films; Lena Horne and Joe Louis were featured. Most of these stars were making *Stormy Weather* while in Hollywood.[16] It became a G.I. Jive favorite.

Not all black entertainers were accepted into formerly all-white clubs as musicians or patrons. In October 1942 W.C. Handy, a blues writer and musician, Sammy Stewart, and Wilbur Sweatman were rebuffed at Mitchell Field, Louisiana, when they and sixteen white musicians entered to perform for the soldiers. The Song-Writers Protective Association had arranged the program for the troops. White officers separated blacks and whites, but a protest by the musicians caused the authorities to back off. One officer commented, "I'm sorry, but we do not want to offend the Southern officers at the field who do not want to eat with colored people."[17]

At Camp Livingston, Louisiana, in October of 1942, black Lieutenant Preston C. Lloyd of the Army Medical Corps was ordered out of the officers' section and into the black segregated section for a performance of *Keep Shufflin'*, an "all-Negro show at Negro Theatre No. 2," for black troops of the 46th Field Artillery Brigade. Brigadier General G.H. Paine ordered Lloyd to move to the rear, which was reserved for blacks. Lloyd refused and later was barred from the theater while charges against him were pending. He had been involved in a similar incident in July 1941.[18] It was common that blacks were not allowed front-row seats even in shows featuring all-black entertainers if whites wanted to see the same show, which they often did. Blacks often protested, but success was not frequent.

In October 1942 the War Department sponsored Irving Berlin's *This Is the Army* at the National Theatre, which refused to sell blacks tickets until a protest swelled and forced a reversal of the policy. Several years earlier, when *The Hot Mikado* was presented with Bill "Bojangles" Robinson playing, blacks had been refused tickets. Their outrage finally boiled over in the war years. Blacks called off their boycott when Robinson used his awesome prestige to plead that whites were paying him a huge sum of money for the show, and he insisted it must go on. The film *Green Pastures* (which many blacks thought portrayed them with dignity) was shown and a special matinee was held, but blacks still boycotted the segregated show.[19]

As more blacks entered the military and as civilians demanded equal treatment, the USO responded by planning more work and USO shows for black entertainers and audiences. A $4 million, seventy-show program was organized from New York, Chicago, and Hollywood revues. It was to start in mid-November 1942 for the soldier circuit, featuring such popular shows as *Bubbling Over, Pleasure Bound, Keep Shuffling Along, Shuffle Along from New York, Chicago Revues on the Fun Parade,* and *Hats Off.* The Hollywood program was unnamed.[20] Harlem-style entertainment was featured.

Some blacks were not satisfied with the pace of change. Paul Robeson, the militant black concert singer, film and stage actor, and orator, told a San Francisco reporter that he was tired of Hollywood stereotypes of blacks. He threatened to quit films until Hollywood took a more realistic approach to blacks. Robeson charged that Hollywood insisted on making the usual "plantation hallelujah shouters." He resented *Tales of Manhattan,* with its all-black sequence about poor, superstitious black sharecroppers. The solution for his people and him in the film "turned out to be the same old thing—the Negro solving his problem by singing his way to glory." He complained that "this is very offensive to my people. It makes the Negro child-like and innocent and is in the old plantation tradition. But Hollywood says you can't make the Negro in any other role because it won't be box office in the South. The South wants its Negroes in the old style." He asked why not have a "Hardy family" for blacks or a Negro girl-meets-boy romance of the Ginger Rogers and Jimmie Stewart kind.[21] He wanted a more stable or middle-class image for blacks rather than the hustler/prostitute images Hollywood fostered. Robeson did not think the Harlem Renaissance theory of promoting racial democracy and integration through the arts could occur without some major breakthrough or political action.

Robeson, who had the reputation as "democracy's greatest voice," refused to sing before segregated audiences, which was a trend among some black entertainers who also protested stereotype roles in film and on the stage. He canceled a singing engagement in Wilmington, Delaware, because the audience was segregated. He had appeared four or five times in the South in the concert season in 1943, and had refused to sing before segregated audiences. "I wouldn't sing to segregated audiences, so I sang in Negro schools and white people came." Moreover, Robeson had said as early as 1937 in reference to the Spanish Civil War that "the artist must take sides. He must elect to fight for freedom or slavery. I have made my choice." What is more, he challenged both white and black critics by insisting that in regard to World War II, "This is every man's war; this is not a white man's war nor a white man's victory, nor a colored man's war nor a colored man's victory. Let us make sure that the victory that follows will be one that assures full freedom for all people in this world regardless of race or color."[22]

Black stereotype film roles such as coons, toms, mulattoes, mammies, bucks, pimps, and prostitutes undermined the drive for black dignity and social and cultural pluralism. Robeson and Lena Horne led the fight for the Double V campaign by direct and personal protest. Horne was not as radical as Robeson, who admired the Soviet Union and its ideals for racial democracies. He wanted a more effective coordination of cultural and political action. He also followed the racial cultural theory of Du Bois. In 1944 Robeson was awarded the NAACP Spingarn Medal for his work for "freedom for all men." A year earlier Morehouse College in Atlanta awarded him an honorary degree for his efforts.[23]

Earl Dancer of Hollywood wrote "An Open Letter to Paul Robeson and Walter White," complaining that the Hollywood film industry held back blacks and kept them in a low status through negative stereotype characterizations of blacks in films. Bill Robinson, Hattie McDaniel, Mantan Moreland, Louise Beavers, Ben Carter, Clarence Muse, and Ernest Whitman disagreed (some of these actors were masters at the stereotype roles that Robeson and Horne detested) and wrote a letter to counter Dancer's critique. Their letter stated that an "honest attempt to lift the status of the race in Hollywood" was being made. Another group complained that his criticisms "implicate the Jewish race when we, too, are fighting so hard against the forces fostering racial hatred." The *Pittsburgh Courier's* theatrical editor, Billy Rowe, who covered the story, surveyed Hollywood people and believed that more were in favor of racial democracy than opposed to it. Moreover, they were committed "to bring democracy into the picture."[24]

Black film historian Donald Bogle argues that some black

actors named above portrayed stereotypes with such skill that they became real personalities and transformed black stereotypes into a serious and skilled art form that transcended negative and degraded characterizations.[25] Clearly, some blacks wanted to work and others disagreed over what constituted demeaning roles. The artists and the black community, then as now, were divided over the Hollywood image of blacks.

Billy Holiday, "Lady Day," the famous jazz singer whose drug-addiction problems became a public scandal, sang "Strange Fruit," about a lynching of a black man. It became her theme song. The song was shocking to many people. Holiday declared, "I'm a race woman." She was the featured singer who opened the Cafe Society West club in October of 1941. The Los Angeles club was integrated at Holiday's opening. Jerry Colonna was a part owner and a musician. He was a racial democracy man. Holiday sang at the Boogie Woogie club in Cleveland, Ohio, which was integrated during the war years.[26] In May of 1942, she opened at the Trouville Club in West Hollywood, mixed with the patrons, and integrated that club. Bette Davis, Lana Turner, Orson Welles, and Merle Oberon attended, and Holiday sat with them. Billy Berg, who opened his own club as an avid jazz fan and promoter of racial democracy, insisted on integrated clubs, and had gotten Holiday hired at the Trouville.[27] These cultural and racial rebels defied the Jim Crow rules observed and supported by most whites.

In the old Harlem Cotton Club, black entertainers were not allowed to mix with patrons. This was true for most clubs with all-white patrons and black entertainers, who as a rule had to enter the club through the back door or the service elevator. Holiday recorded "Travellin' Light" in Los Angeles in 1942 in part as a protest against the lack of public accommodations for blacks. In May of 1942, in New York's Golden Gate Auditorium, she sang for an event sponsored by the Associated Communist Clubs of Harlem.[28]

Lena Horne worked and performed at the Hollywood Canteen. She toured for the USO Camp Shows. She christened a liberty ship the "George Washington Carver," named for a black scientist from Tuskegee Institute. The studios used her work for publicity to build her career and their income.[29] "I was always expected to entertain the white soldiers first, then the Negroes—

and often under the most degrading conditions for both the soldiers and me. I was getting full—up to here—with the whole situation, but I wasn't about to quit USO work, for I was genuinely lovingly received by the men of both races and I wanted to be with them."[30] She sang at Fort Riley, Kansas, for an all-white group and soldiers who sat in the front. The second day she sang for blacks but asked that they be allowed to sit in the front. Instead, German prisoners of war sat in front of the black American troops. Horne protested, to no avail, but sang, cried, and left bitterly disappointed.[31] It was a degrading and humiliating experience for her and the black troops.

At Fort Dix, New Jersey, "the German prisoners would be in the mess line with black troops and you'd have a separate line for white troops. Lena entertained the blacks and the German prisoners and then she left." She got the opportunity to entertain them before the whites and left as a protest and rebuke against white supremacy.[32] This tactic demonstrated her commitment to the Double V and black troops, and that she would perform, if necessary, under segregated conditions rather than deny black troops entertainment and recreation. Black troops responded warmly and appreciated her commitment under trying circumstances. Rather than give in to the intimidation of USO sponsors not committed to the Double V, she paid her own way to perform before the troops at these camps.[33] Horne performed at the Great Lakes Naval Training Station before thousands of black G.I.'s. "I'll never forget the scream that went up when they saw me." With Navy escorts, "I made a movie star entrance."[34] Such receptions kept up her morale and will to perform before the troops.

She performed for black soldiers—just before they left for war overseas—at the segregated black Theresa Hotel in Harlem. In Hollywood she praised Mike Romanoff for allowing black G.I.'s to eat in his restaurant. G.I.'s developed a tradition of having pin-up girls, pictures they carried or pinned to their lockers. White officers forbade black G.I.'s from having white pin-up girls. Horne's performances before the black soldiers and her championing of their cause, the Double V, resulted in her becoming their No. 1 pin-up girl. Horne performed two days at segregated Fort Huachuca, Arizona, where the black troops affectionately dubbed her "Sergeant Lena Horne." The cast from the recently released film *Stormy Weather* performed with her and a group with Pearl Bailey as the lead vocalist.[35] Horne was beautiful, sexy, a singer, dancer, "race woman," and a model practitioner of the Harlem Renaissance cultural theory of using the arts for civil rights for blacks. During the war, she was the preeminent female leader of the black Double Victory campaign.

Cab Calloway, of Cotton Club fame, made a Southern tour in 1931 and compared his reception with that to which he was accustomed in New York. The segregation, discrimination, insults, and near riots shocked him. "We weren't used to that kind of treatment. In the Cotton Club we were the cream of the crop, and we were used to being celebrities. In New York we were the toast of the town with big cars and sharp clothes and broads all over the place."[36] He added, "And talk about integration: Hell, when the band and I got out to Hollywood, we were treated like pure royalty." He performed in *The Swinging Kid* with Al Jolson, who had starred and sang in the first talking movie, *The Jazz Singer*.[37] Calloway was exempted from service during the war "because he had an enlarged heart." He played the USO circuit on Army bases, in bond drives, and more.

Calloway played in all of the major defense plants, giving six or seven shows a day to accommodate all shifts.[38] "We played the armed forces installations in different parts of the country, and we got a heck of a reception from the servicemen." In St. Louis, Benny Payne, a former sideman then in the Army, came in and sat in on a session. "He got a standing ovation. The war spirit was high everywhere and they just loved the idea of this guy in an Army uniform playing with us." Calloway, like many other band leaders, lost a number of musicians to the draft.[39] His publicity manager sent out a false release that he had "jazzed up" the "Star-Spangled Banner." As a result, he was briefly banned from the air.[40] Traditional martial music was still highly regarded, and many wanted it kept distinct from jazz. Calloway and Duke Ellington refused to play at the Great Lakes Naval Training Station unless they were allowed to perform for the 8,000 black trainees there, even if separately from whites.[41]

Eubie Blake, then sixty years of age, a black pioneer artist of early Harlem and Broadway fame (Blake and Noble Sissle wrote and starred in the all-black musical *Shuffle Along* in May 1921 which started a vogue that made black musicals popular

on Broadway), played one-night USO stands from Savannah to
Seattle. He had new lyrics written for the show, which included
many chorus-line girls. Blake played many military hospitals to
cheer up the wounded. "Those kids are the greatest audience in
the world. They really appreciate a show. That was a thrill. It
made me feel so good I didn't even care if I got paid—but I took
the money."⁴²

Blake took many of his Harlem and Broadway styles into
the military camps, where both white and black troops approved
of his offerings. Noble Sissle presented his *Harlem on Parade* show
at Camp Robinson, Little Rock, Arkansas, for three days in May
of 1942. Clarence Robinson, who had produced many of the
Cotton Club's shows, staged the show. In June of 1942 the
eighteen-week tour came to Fort Knox, Kentucky, and performed
four days. "No admission was charged and house was packed.
Patronage was about 50-50 white and colored. Colored soldiers
were seated in the centre section of the lower floor, while the
whites were in side sections, and officers, their wives and families
were in the rear section, an elevation of the floor." The "Copper
Colored Chorus, 12 shapely, dusky hoofers, and the lads in
uniform gave 'em a reception that figuratively made the rafters
ring." In late 1942, Sissle produced *Keep Shufflin'*, an all-black
musical staged by Clarence (Bill) Robinson with forty performers,
Eubie Blake's nine-piece orchestra, twelve high-stepping chorines,
comedians, and other entertainers, to be performed at Camp
Robinson.⁴³

The Office of Defense Transportation (ODT) started putting
restraints on transportation in order to reserve vehicles, gas, and
rubber for the military. Musicians—even those entertaining the
troops—found it increasingly difficult to obtain adequate
transportation. The ODT limited black bands touring the South
to five buses between October 1 and December 31 of 1942. John
Hammond, a promoter; Judge Hubert Delany, who presided over
the New York Domestic Relations Court; and representatives of
black bands met on September 12 at NAACP headquarters in
New York to work out a schedule that would allow forty-five
bands to tour ten days each. Cab Calloway and Walter White
got authorization from the ODT for "buses for three months."
In June of 1943, the ODT refused to allow buses for black bands
touring the South because the "gas and rubber shortage made

it inadvisable."⁴⁴ Blacks were not happy with this outcome.

In early 1943 Louis Armstrong went on a 15,000-mile tour with his band "stopping off at every Army camp" to help build morale for the war. In Texas he played at Duncan Field for the 304th Aviation Squadron. He played "both days and nights with little time to rest, but," he said, "I don't mind it because those boys fighting out there aren't resting. Just as long as they are willing to carry a gun, I will be willing to blow my trumpet, day and night, for them."⁴⁵ Armstrong, like most other famous artists, did his part for the entertainment and recreation of the troops.

Joe Louis, black heavyweight boxing champion, became an early symbol of the struggle for the Double V and cultural pluralism. In 1936 he fought and lost to German boxer Max Schmeling, who boasted about his Aryan race superiority. The fight was held in New York. Jewish Americans passed out fliers to boycott the fight because Schmeling "represented" Nazi Germany. Louis and Schmeling met again on June 22, 1939. Louis said, "We were hearing more and more about the concentration camps for the Jews. A lot of Americans had family in Europe and they were afraid for their people's lives. Schmeling represented everything that Americans disliked, and they wanted him beat and beat good." Ironically, said Louis, "Now here I was, a black man. I had the burden of representing all America. They tell me I was responsible for a lot of change in race relations in America" for the better. Strangely, said Louis, "white Americans—even while some of them still were lynching black people in the South—were depending on me to K.O. Germany."⁴⁶

President Roosevelt invited Louis for dinner and sent a special car for him. Roosevelt felt Louis's arm muscles and told him, "Joe, we're depending on those muscles for America." Louis's manager, Mike Jacobs, was under strong pressure from Jews to cancel the fight. Some threatened to ruin Jacobs's career. He convinced the committee that the fight had to occur; Louis would win and destroy the myth of Aryan superiority, that his victory would stand as a rebuke to the murderous anti-Jewish program of Hitler and Schmeling who believed in Hitler and his race views. Louis beat Schmeling to a pulp in the first round and the country went wild with delight. Harlem blacks threw bottles and cans from rooftops until police had to be called in.⁴⁷ The tumult and pride were overwhelming. Black and White

Americans, especially Jews, shared the cause for racial democracy abroad and repudiated Hitler's brand of racial authoritarianism. Most white Americans, however, remained committed to their own brand of white authoritarianism.

Joe Louis reacted to the Japanese bombing of Pearl Harbor with a fighting spirit. "I was mad, I was furious, you name it. Hell, this is my country. Don't come around sneaking up and attacking it." He joined the Army and at Fort Riley, Kansas, and met Jackie Robinson, a University of California, Los Angeles (UCLA) football and baseball star who wanted to play ball and go to Officers Candidate School (OCS). Robinson was rejected because of his race. Louis protested to Brigadier General Donald Robinson, who got Jackie Robinson on the Fort Riley team which subsequently won baseball and football championships. Robinson graduated from OCS a lieutenant. The Army opened up sports for blacks. As a result, they played even in Virginia and Georgia. Louis was promoted to sergeant but "I told the Army I wouldn't appear anywhere to segregated Army audiences." The Army agreed to this condition. At Camp Sibert, Alabama, Louis and Sugar Ray Robinson, another black boxer, were ordered by an MP to sit in the colored section. They refused and were arrested. Louis complained to the provost marshal, "Listen, I'm an American, I'm fighting in this war like anybody else, and I expect to be treated like anybody else." He agreed to abide by the Jim Crow laws in the towns but insisted that military buses desegregate. Soon all military buses on the bases were integrated. Louis reflected on the matter, "But you know, if I was just an average black G.I., I would have wound up in the stockade." He traveled over 70,000 miles, performed before nearly five million people, had ninety-six exhibition bouts, and received the Legion of Merit medal "for exceptional meritorious conduct."[48] Joe Louis was a "race man" who fought for the Double V as both a civilian and soldier.

Louis took special pleasure in entertaining and talking with black troops. He had been sensitized to the plight of European Jews as a result of his championship fights with Max Schmeling. He especially feared for Jews in Nazi Germany and thought that black Americans best understood Jews' bitter and violent subjugation under Nazism. Their plight was similar to that of blacks in the United States. Louis remarked, "Then there was the common enemy—Nazi Germany. Wasn't a black man there who didn't understand what the Jews were going through. Somehow they could place their own lives into what was happening over there, and a lot of them, for real, wanted to get to Hitler."[49] On the other hand, said Louis, "then you turn the coin over. Here are all these 'niggers' ready and willing to go out and try to kill Hitler, and maybe get themselves killed, but they can't sleep in the same barracks with the white guys or go to the same movies or hardly get in officers' training. Made me start thinking."[50]

Louis became a conscious and diligent promoter of the Double V. He, like many blacks and Jews, had a deep personal dislike for Hitler and Nazi Germany because of Nazi opposition to the Double V and genocidal assault on Jews. Many blacks and Jews fought racial authoritarianism at home as well as abroad.

Frank Mathias, a white jazzman in the Army in Phenix City near Columbus, Georgia, was fascinated by a $1 steamboat ride and show where "numerous whores plied their trade as a seven-piece Negro jazz band thumped away on such numbers as South, Basin Street and Perdido."[51] Mathias and a buddy went to a nearby USO Club where the white matron questioned them at the door: "And you, sir, where are you from?" Mathias said Kentucky. She replied, "Why boys, come right on in—you're one of us!" Mathias said she hated white Yankees and blacks. "For her the Civil War was far from over."[52] Mathias observed black servants in white officers clubs where he played. They often made requests for the band to play jazz tunes. All the clubs he played in were strictly segregated.[53]

The National YWCA made a survey and reported that "the extent of integration in these clubs ranges from practically no contact and complete separation, to complete integration, except social dancing." Few had mixed staffs. Those that did have some integration were called "Experiments in Democracy."[54] These experiments occurred only where a racial democracy consensus held firm or strong-willed individuals were successful in implementing integration. These cases were highly exceptional.

Hollywood film star Carole Landis performed at Camp Bowie in San Antonio, Texas, and attacked the segregated USO club. She defended black soldiers' rights to equal treatment during her three-day stay at the USO club, where they were excluded. She performed the next evening entirely for blacks, singing and playing ping pong as a rebuke to Jim Crow. She told the press, "Maybe by the time the war is over, we will have acquired some of the tolerance we are fighting for."[55]

Many whites took a stand against Jim Crow during the war years. Jewish Americans had long been involved in the struggle for racial and religious democracy in America. They fought discrimination against the foreign born and the negative stereotypes fostered against Jews. Indeed, Jewish artists had long been leaders of the movement in their own right. Jewish scientists had produced a body of science against racism. In Philadelphia in January 1942 Jews awarded the great black contralto concert and opera singer, Marian Anderson, the "B'rith Sholom Citizen Award for Musical Achievement and Devotion to Interracial Goodwill" in "recognition of outstanding achievements in the field of music and devotion to the cause of interracial equality and democratic ideals."[56] This was a rebuke to the Daughters of the American Revolution (D.A.R.) who had refused to allow Anderson to sing in Constitution Hall in Washington in 1939.

Howard University had invited Anderson to sing in Washington, D.C. Frank Ballou refused to allow her to sing at the all-white Central High School's 2,000-seat auditorium. After an uproar and embarrassment, he agreed to allow a one-time use only. Howard rejected the humiliating offer and asked the D.A.R. for Constitution Hall. The D.A.R. refused, choosing to follow local Jim Crow custom. Harold Ickes, Roosevelt's Secretary of the Interior and former NAACP president in Chicago, proposed that Anderson sing on the steps of the Lincoln Memorial. Howard accepted. Franklin and Eleanor Roosevelt supported this, too. Eleanor resigned from the D.A.R. in protest. Violinist Jascha Heifez announced from the stage of Constitution Hall that he was personally shamed by the denial. Anderson wanted to avoid controversy, but said, "I could see that my significance as an individual was small in this affair. I had become, whether I liked it or not, a symbol, representing my people. I had to appear." *The Nation* magazine editorialized: "Because she is famous Miss Anderson can perform a unique function. She can, for a moment, crystallize and bring clear before our eyes the social indecencies that permeate race relations in this country. This is an important service to democracy."[57]

Many Congressmen and their wives, cabinet members, Mayor La Guardia of New York City, dignitaries, and society people went to hear Anderson and lend their support. Walter White, Eleanor Roosevelt, John L. Lewis of the United Mine Workers, and Katharine Hepburn attended. More than 75,000 people were there. Blacks wore their Sunday-best clothes, and it was a religious experience for many who had never seen or heard an opera singer before. She sang "America the Beautiful" and many cried when she sang "And crown thy good with brotherhood, from sea to shining sea." She concluded with the spiritual, "Nobody Knows the Trouble I've Seen." Later, some musicians refused to appear at Constitution Hall as a protest. Ickes had a mural painted in celebration of her appearance and hung it in the Department of the Interior.[58]

The D.A.R. refused a second request by Anderson to sing for War Relief because she insisted on integrated audiences. Overwhelming public sentiment supported Anderson's demand for a racially unrestricted concert at Constitution Hall. She sang in January 1943 for China Relief before 3,800 people, raising $7,777. The house was packed and integrated. "It was difficult to tell whether the colored or the whites had the greater representation and the peasant and the noble, regardless of color, sat where he chose." Eleanor Roosevelt was applauded by the crowd when she sat in her box. Henry Morgenthau Jr., Justice Hugo Black, Attorney General Francis Biddle, Secretary of the Interior Harold L. Ickes, Secretary of Agriculture Claude Wicker, and their wives, along with many other Washington public officials and dignitaries heard Anderson sing.[59] It was a symbolic victory of sorts for the Double V, social equality, cultural pluralism, and racial integration programs. Some whites traditionally attended and enjoyed black entertainment, but that did not mean they were committed to political and racial democracy for blacks.

In November of 1942, Eleanor Roosevelt had returned from a tour in Britain and reported to Secretary of War Henry L. Stimson that General John Lee was doing great work among blacks to keep down racial riots. She said the troops were lonely and needed entertainment at least three times a week. Stimson said that "she mentioned [Paul] Robeson" as an entertainer who would do some good there.[60] With Robeson's radical reputation and Eleanor's recommendation to Stimson, her level of commitment to cultural pluralism and racial democracy on the social and entertainment fronts was unquestioned.

The NAACP board of directors publicly announced in March of 1943 its outrage at the treatment of Jews at home and abroad and supported their struggle by pledging in a letter sent to the conference committees of national Jewish women's organizations "unqualified and unlimited effort in behalf of the persecuted Jews of the world which includes anti-Semitism in the U.S. as well as mass slaughter in Poland." Further, "civilized human beings throughout the world of every race, creed and color, stand appalled at the cold-blooded campaign of extermination of the Jews inaugurated by Adolf Hitler." It was not enough merely to denounce Hitler, but "the most effective means of ending this slaughter is the extermination of Hitler and Hitlerism wherever they exist. To the attainment of this goal we pledge our unqualified aid."[61]

The highly visible public challenges and announcements of the Double V coalition groups outraged many whites. Mississippi Congressman John R. Rankin denounced the Double V coalition of blacks, Jews, and alleged Communists. He charged that they had tried to integrate the House of Representatives restaurant, brought on the Detroit race riot, and caused the conflict between the races to escalate. Rankin deeply resented Jews, integrationist whites, and Communists, and blamed them for instigating conflict between the races. "It is dawning on the American people who is creating and promoting this race trouble and these race riots throughout the country." He bitterly charged: "When those Communistic Jews—of who the decent Jews are ashamed—go around here and hug and kiss these Negroes, dance with them, intermarry with them, and try to force their way into white restaurants, white hotels and white picture shows, they are not deceiving any red-blooded American, and above all, they are not deceiving the men in our armed forces—as to who is at the bottom of all this race trouble."[62]

Senator Theodore Bilbo of Mississippi also denounced integration and the Double V as a Communist plot. He charged, "The Communists in this country have secretly and openly tried to indoctrinate the Negroes with the idea of social equality with the white race for their own purposes and are part of their plan to overthrow the American dual system of Constitutional government."[63] He denounced the Jews, especially intellectuals like Dr. Franz Boas, Ruth Benedict, and Gene Weltfish, for denying, in their book *The Races of Mankind* (1943) that racial differences existed. These Columbia University professors argued that there was no scientific evidence of inferior and superior races. They rejected segregation of blood plasma by blood banks in the United States because there were no differences in human blood types, no proof of superior brains in any one group, and they attacked Adolf Hitler's use of Aryan race concepts, slander and murder of Jews, and his violent racism. Nevertheless, on April 27, 1944, the Military Affairs Subcommittee of the House of Representatives, taking a racist position, denounced the work as untrue.[64] Bilbo blasted whites and Jews who wrote books in favor of racial equality and democracy as "Quislings of the white race."[65]

The black newspapers and Jewish and black intellectuals were engaged in a massive campaign against Jim Crow. Bilbo denounced Dr. Rayford Logan's book, *What the Negro Wants* (1944), with its numerous essays by such black intellectuals as Logan, Langston Hughes, Roy Wilkins, Edwin R. Embree, Walter White, Doxie Wilkerson, and others dealing with every aspect of racial authoritarianism in need of attack and correction. He lamented that during the war, "only five or six books have been written in the interest and in the defense of white America." On the other hand, black, white, and Jewish intellectuals were publishing massive amounts of material (such as Wendell Willkie's *One World* [1943], Pearl Buck's *American Unity and Asia* [1942], and Clayton Wheat's *The Democratic Tradition in America* [1943]), in quest of racial democracy at home and abroad. "These demands are clearly evidenced and openly stated in the 200 or more books which have been written in the past four years by Negroes and Quislings of the white race," Bilbo raved.[66]

In his own book, Bilbo attacked what he called, "False Interpretations of American Democracy," "False Concepts of the Christian Religion," "The Campaign for Complete Equality," and "The Demands of the Negro Leaders." He charged, "They have used every conceivable argument in an attempt to support their appeal for full equality which to them means social equality." He used pseudo-scientific race theories and history to justify Jim Crow and to counter black, white, and Jewish intellectuals whose arguments were "merely smokescreens which cannot and will not stand any sane, sound, and logical analysis."[67] Bilbo refused to recognize any legitimacy in social equality in theory or practice. Racial democracy meant racial suicide for whites, he reasoned.

Bilbo charged that Doxey A. Wilkerson, black editor of *The People's Voice* newspaper in New York, was a member of the "National Committee of the Communist Political Association." Wilkerson supported the Double V and exposed racial repression, and with William Z. Foster had taken over the Communist Party from Earl Browder, Bilbo noted. "They have been leading the Negroes to believe that through the Communist Party they will soon seize the deep South, drive out the native whites, and convert the land of Dixie into a Soviet Republic owned, controlled, and dominated alone by the American Negro."[68] The Negro Soviet Republic idea in the South was part of the Communist Party's "right of self-determination of the Negroes in the Black Belt" thesis developed from Joseph Stalin's writings.[69] Bilbo made it clear no such plan would ever take place in the South.

Bilbo charged that New York Communists founded the Southern Conference for Human Welfare and sent its members from "Harlem, New York, to the heart of Dixie." He blasted Harlem. "In the ungodly, immoral, sin-soaked sections of Harlem, New York" came these Communists to spread their doctrines and create trouble. He said their headquarters was in Nashville, Tennessee.[70] By implication, he charged that only immoral "Quisling whites" and deluded blacks and Jews who were immoral would advocate the destruction of Jim Crow, because it protected all races with any self-respect, from "mongrelization," so the racist argument went. Just as important to Bilbo, Harlem, Nashville, Hollywood, and New York's Broadway were on the cutting edge of entertainment, race music, jazz, intimate race contacts, and cultural collaboration and pluralism.

During the war, Malcolm X operated as a hustler, pimp, and dope dealer in New York's Harlem and Roxbury, Michigan. He observed that "no Negroes in the world were more white-woman-crazy in those days than most of those musicians. People in show business, of course, were less inhibited by social and racial taboos."[71] In other words, artistic and cultural integration, along with increasing public performances by integrated groups, endangered Jim Crow and white racial purity.

Racists feared that blacks and whites might get carried away in their lust and emotions and engage in interracial sex or marriage or both. Easy social and cultural mixing disturbed racists such as Bilbo and the soldiers who attacked Sammy Davis Jr. They feared that racial pluralism and mixing were being exported to the South from New York, especially Harlem.

Racist politicians like Bilbo and Rankin identified blacks, Jews, renegade whites, and Communists and their influence in the entertainment centers of the United States as the source of racial democracy that threatened the old order of racial authoritarianism. They understood the political thrust of the Double V as well as the nature of G.I. Jive, and the influence that Hollywood, Harlem, Nashville, and Broadway were having within the armed forces and society. They rejected racial democracy in politics, war, and culture. They fought the Double V in all its aspects. Bilbo protested, "If we sit with Negroes at our tables, if we attend social functions with them as our social equals, if we disregard segregation in all other relations, is it then possible that we maintain it fixedly in the marriage of the South's Saxon sons and daughters? The answer must be 'no.' Whenever the mingling of the races on terms of social equality is permitted, then the possibility of intermarriage must be admitted." It then becomes a "personal preference," something he abhorred because it endangered white racial purity and supremacy.[72]

Eugene "Bull" Connor, Birmingham's chief of police, wrote President Roosevelt a letter dated August 7, 1942, in which he said, "There is no doubt that federal agencies have adopted policies to break down and destroy the segregation laws of . . . the entire South." He expected the rise of the Ku Klux Klan to counter these policies. He objected to the U.S. Employment Service, National Youth Administration, and the Federal Fair Employment Practices Commission's policies as the source of trouble. He feared race war. "Don't you think one war in the South . . . is enough?" He pleaded, "Help us before it is too late."[73] It was obvious to many racists that to allow the New Deal, the war emergency, or the Harlem Renaissance artistic strategy to win civil rights for blacks or for G.I. Jive to integrate Americans socially and culturally would destroy white supremacy and the separation of the races. Racial democracy undoubtedly would result in a certain percentage of intimate contacts and marriages. Racial authoritarians mobilized to block racial democrats from overturning Jim Crow.

Langston Hughes said the Harlem Renaissance brought blacks into vogue, "but some Harlemites thought the millennium had come. They thought the race problem had been solved through art plus Gladys Bently [a popular entertainer]. They were sure the new Negro would lead a new life from then on in green pastures of tolerance created by Countee Cullen, Ethel Waters, Claude McKay, Duke Ellington, Bojangles [Bill Robinson], and Alain Locke."[74] He criticized those black artists who tried to be white and denied their racial heritage through assimilation. He charged that it was bound to fail. "Nordic manners, Nordic faces, Nordic hair, Nordic art (if any), and an Episcopal heaven. A very high mountain indeed for the would-be racial artist to climb in order to discover himself and his people."[75] Hughes fought for racial pluralism and cultural democracy so blacks could maintain their identity and dignity.

In an essay, "My America," in Rayford Logan's book, Hughes said, "I would suggest an immediate and intensive government-directed program of pro-democratic education, to be put into the schools of the South from the first grades of the grammar schools to the universities, as part of the war effort, this is urgently needed." What is more, said Hughes, "I would suggest that the government draft all the leading Negro intellectuals, sociologists, writers, and concert singers from Alain Locke of Oxford and W.E.B. Du Bois of Harvard to Dorothy Maynor and Paul Robeson of Carnegie Hall and send them into the South to appear before white audiences, carrying messages of culture and democracy, thus off-setting the old stereotypes of the Southern mind and the Hollywood movie, and explaining to the people without dialect what the war aims are about."[76]

Hughes also proposed sending Southern white liberals and Army troops to protect them while they carried out this mission.[77] This sort of program was precisely what the Jim Crow Southerners feared. They had witnessed too many accommodations to black demands by the armed forces and President Roosevelt. Moreover, many Southerners believed that Northern black troops stationed in the South, and even some whites, were actually implementing such a policy by denouncing, challenging, and disrupting Southern racial segregation customs and laws. Moreover, many believed that President Roosevelt, his New Deal program, and certainly Eleanor Roosevelt, were actually assaulting Jim Crow in the South and throughout the nation.

Bilbo violently objected to Logan's book and the articles that appeared in it. He took Hughes to task and rejected any government program or invasion of the South for any such purposes. "Although Langston Hughes is a fair writer and poetically inclined, the Negro race and intelligentsia cannot get much consolation out of his literary progress because three of his great grandfathers were white men." Bilbo added, "Let me say to Langston Hughes that the American Republic is still white, and our civilization is still safe because it is white. The mongrelization of the nation, as Hughes seems so much to desire, would be far worse than an atomic bomb dropped upon every township of American soil."[78]

Bilbo especially feared mulattoes such as Hughes, W.E.B. Du Bois, and Walter White, who easily passed for white, because they seemed the most committed to integration and intermarriage. He charged that "while the mulatto is inferior to the white man, it is often true that those generally recognized as leaders of the Negro race have some degree of white blood in their veins. It is also true that this is the group which leads the campaign for racial equality in the United States. The supersensitive mongrels are constantly agitating the race question and clamoring for the destruction of all racial lines in this country."[79] Bilbo believed that these mulattoes, white Quislings, Communists, and Jews misled the black masses into demanding integration they did not really want.

During the war, the South Carolina House of Representatives objected to the Double V and interference with Jim Crow in the South. This body declared, "We reaffirm our belief in our allegiance to established white supremacy as now prevailing in the South and we solemnly pledge our lives and our sacred honor to maintain it." Moreover, they said, "insofar as race relations are concerned, we firmly and unequivocally demand that henceforth the damned agitators of the North leave the South alone."[80] Racist politicians, civilians, and armed forces officers, as well as many white soldiers, opposed the Double V and racial democracy. Theodore Bilbo and many racists associated racial democracy with racial intermarriage that would result in a mulatto population and destroy white civilization. They were determined not to allow the war emergency and reforms to destroy white supremacy or the war slogans and their goal to

save European democracies to mean racial democracy at home.
On the other hand, minorities in the United States were
determined to promote racial and ethnic democracy and give
substance to the world war as a crusade for freedom for all and
the dismantling of white supremacy at home and abroad. Racial
totalitarianism, they argued, was contrary to the democratic creed.

Black G.I. Jive was a continuation of the Harlem Renaissance
social protest and civil rights program. It was a strategy that
Charles S. Johnson and James Weldon Johnson believed would
be more immediately effective and less rancorous if devoid of
obvious racial propaganda and would have more enduring
consequences than the political gains blacks made during
Reconstruction, then lost as a result of a white political backlash.
They believed that blacks had lost their rights because whites
did not think they were their social or cultural equals. By
promoting social and cultural pluralism, they could build the
foundation for black political and economic rights.

Their program followed the reasoning of William Graham
Sumner in his book *Folkways* (1906), in which he argued that
people's mores and culture, not laws, determined how they
behaved. He rejected civil rights laws as a solution to the race
problem. Black G.I. Jive, by using the Harlem Renaissance theory
of protest, sought to change the mores of whites at the social and
cultural base. Then political and economic rights would follow
as a natural consequence. The struggle for social and cultural
pluralism, nevertheless, resulted in racial confrontations and
political action to modify racist restrictions because of national,
governmental, and racist white resistance.

Notes

1. Sammy Davis Jr. and Jane and Burt Boyar, *Yes I Can: The Story
of Sammy Davis Jr.* (New York: A Payset Cardinal Edition 1966 [pbk.],
[1965 hardcover]), p. 45.

2. *Ibid.*, pp. 45, 47, 53, 61–62, 65–66.

3. *Ibid.*, pp. 65–66.

4. *Ibid.*

5. See Norman Zierold, *The Moguls* (New York: Coward-McCann, 1969); see David L. Lewis, *When Harlem Was in Vogue* (New York: Vintage Books, 1981); Stanley Coben, "The Assault on Victorianism in the Twentieth Century," in Daniel Walker Howe, ed., *Victorian America* (Philadelphia: University of Pennsylvania Press, 1976), pp. 160–181.

6. Julia M.H. Carson, *Home Away from Home: The Story of the USO* (New York: Harper & Brothers, 1946), p. 131.

7. Maurice Zolotow, "Uncle Sam Brings Vaudeville Back: Broadway Does Its Entertaining Bit," *Saturday Evening Post*, 213, No. 11 (12 September 1942), 20–21, 69, 70.

8. Cab Calloway and Bryant Rollins, *Of Minnie the Moocher & Me* (New York: Thomas Y. Crowell Co., 1976), pp. 98–99, 10–11; see Winthrop D. Lane, "Ambushed in the City: The Grim Side of Harlem," *Survey*, 53, No. 11 (1 March 1925), 692–694, 713–715; see James Haskins, *The Cotton Club* (New York: Random House, 1977).

9. Calloway, p. 90.

10. *Ibid.*, p. 103.

11. "Theatrical News," *Pittsburgh Courier*, 4 January 1941, p. 21, col. 2; Harry Levette, "Hollywood," *New York Amsterdam News*, October 1940; "Harlem-Broadway-Hollywood," *New York Amsterdam News*, 5 June 1943, p. 16, col. 4.

12. "Duke Opens in L.A. Nitery," *Pittsburgh Courier*, 14 January 1941, p. 18, col. 1.

13. "Lena Horne Signed by Charlie Barnet," *Pittsburgh Courier*, 4 January 1941, p. 20, col. 2; "Lena Takes Time off as Charlie Barnet and Band Go South," *Pittsburgh Courier*, 3 February 1941, p. 21, col. 5.

14. "Music: Song Seller," *Newsweek*, XXI, No. 1 (4 January 1943), 65; James Haskins and Kathleen Benson, *Lena: A Personal and Professional Biography of Lena Horne* (New York: Stein and Day Publishers, 1984), pp. 81–82.

15. Walter White, *A Man Called White: The Autobiography of Walter White* (Bloomington: Indiana University Press, 1970 [1948]), pp. 337–339, 232; Lena Horne and Richard Schickel, *Lena* (Garden City: Doubleday & Co., Inc., 1965), pp. 120–121.

16. "Noble Sissle Brings Harlem to Hollywood, So Say Coast Scribes," *Pittsburgh Courier*, 27 March 1943, p. 21, col. 4.

17. "Handy and Others Rebuffed Jimcrow," *The People's Voice*, 17 October 1942, p. 7, col. 2.

18. "Officers Slot Reserved, But Not for Army Negro," *The People's Voice*, 17 October 1942, p. 70, col. 2.

19. "Call off Jimcrow for Berlin Show," *The People's Voice*, 17 October 1942, p. 26, col. 2.

20. "More Sepia Revues for Soldiers under New USO Camp Show Plan," *The People's Voice*, 17 October 1942, p. 26, col. 1.

21. Ted Taylor, "Why Not a Negro 'Hardy' Family? Or Some Honest-to-Gosh Folks?" *The People's Voice*, 17 October 1942, p. 24, col. 2; "Hollywood's 'Old Plantation Tradition' Is 'Offensive to My People,'" (*The New York Times*, 24 September 1942), in Philip S. Foner, ed., *Paul Robeson Speaks: Writings, Speeches, Interviews, 1918–1974* (New York: Brunner/Mazel Publishers, 1978), p. 142.

22. Paul Robeson, *Here I Stand* (Boston: Beacon Press, 1977 [1958]), pp. 31–32, 52; "Paul Robeson Cancels Concert; Protests Bias," *Pittsburgh Courier*, 6 February 1943, p. 21, col. 2; "Democracy's Voice Speaks," *The People's Voice* (New York), 22 May 1943 in Foner, ed., pp. 143–144; Paul Robeson, "The Artist Must Take Sides" (speech 24 June 1937 in London), in Foner, ed., pp. 118–119; Paul Robeson, "A Victorious War Must Free All" (remarks at Free People's Dinner in Honor of Paul Robeson in Berkeley, California, 20 July 1943, *The People's Voice*, 4 August 1943), in Foner, ed., pp. 144–145.

23. Robeson, *Here I Stand*, pp. 29–30.

24. Jack Schiffman, *Uptown: The Story of Harlem's Apollo Theatre* (New York: Cowles Book Co., Inc., 1971), p. 146; Billy Rowe, theatrical editor, "Artists Assail Dancer's Article as Thoughtless," *Pittsburgh Courier*, 30 January 1943, p. 20, col. 3.

25. Donald Bogle, *Toms, Coons, Mulattoes, Mammies, & Bucks: An Interpretive History of Blacks in American Film* (New York: Bantam Books, 1974 [pbk.]).

26. John Chilton, *Billie's Blues: Billie Holiday's Story, 1933–1959* (New York: Stein and Day Publishing, 1975), pp. 68–69, 78–79.

27. *Ibid.*, pp. 79, 80–82.

28. *Ibid.*, pp. 82–83.

29. Horne, p. 155.

30. *Ibid.*, p. 173.

31. *Ibid.*, pp. 174–175.

32. Studs Turkel, *The Good War: An Oral History of World War Two* (New York: Pantheon Books, 1984), p. 369.

33. Horne, pp. 176–177; "Nazi Prisoners Allowed to See USO Show, So Lena Horne Walks in Huff," *Variety*, 10 June 1945.

34. Horne, pp. 185–186, 6.

35. *Ibid.*, pp. 148, 228, 172; "Lena Horne Big Hit with Men in Service," *Pittsburgh Courier*, 20 March 1943, p. 20; Pearl Bailey, *The Raw Pearl* (New York: Pocket Books, 1969 [orig. pub. by Harcourt, Brace & World, 1968]).

36. Calloway, pp. 122–130, 125.

37. *Ibid.*, p. 131.

38. *Ibid.*, pp. 198, 163.

39. *Ibid.*, pp. 163, 173.

40. *Ibid.*, p. 248.

41. See *Variety*, 5 June 1944.

42. Al Rose, *Eubie Blake* (New York: Schirmer Books, 1979), pp. 118–119; Eileen Southern, *The Music of Black Americans: A History* (New York: W.W. Norton & Co., Inc., 1971), pp. 438–440.

43. *Camp Robinson News*, 27 February 1942 and 2 October 1942; "Keep Shufflin'," *Variety*, 17 June 1942. Dr. Nancy D. Baird, professor of Library Special Collections, Western Kentucky University brought this material to my attention.

44. "Standing Up in Trains Hard on Musicians," *Variety*, 29 June 1942; "Mapping Negro Bands' 3-Mo. Bus Sked," *Variety*, 2 September 1942, and see *Variety*, 13 June 1943.

45. "Trumpet King Plays at Duncan Air Field," *Pittsburgh Courier*, 9 January 1943, p. 20, col. 20; "Famous Trumpet King Builds Morale at Army Camps with His Infectious Swing," *Pittsburgh Courier*, 9 January 1943, p. 22, col. 3.

46. Joe Louis with Edna and Art Rust Jr., *Joe Louis: My Life* (New York: Harcourt Brace Jovanovich, 1978), pp. 85—86, 89, 137.

47. *Ibid.*, pp. 137, 139–140, 142–143.

48. *Ibid.*, pp. 169, 177–179, 184–185, 189, 190.

49. *Ibid.*, p. 175.

50. *Ibid.*, p. 175.

51. Frank F. Mathias, *G.I. Jive: An Army Bandsman in World War II* (Lexington: University Press of Kentucky, 1982), p. 19.

52. *Ibid.*, p. 18.

53. *Ibid.*, p. 46.

54. U.S. National Board U.S.O. Division, *Experiments in Democracy* (New York: Young Women's Christian Association [n.d.]), p. 7.

55. "Carole Landis Attacks Army's Jim Crow Show," *Chicago Defender*, 22 August 1942, p. 12, col. 1.

56. "Marian Anderson Gets Jewish Award," *Pittsburgh Courier*, 9 January 1943, p. 1, p. 4, col. 2.

57. "The Refusal of the D.A.R. to Allow . . .," *The Nation*, 148, No. 10 (4 March 1939), 251; White, *A Man . . .*, pp. 180–185; Marian Anderson, *My Lord, What a Morning: An Autobiography* (New York: Avon Publications, Inc., 1956 [pbk.]), pp. 154, 156–161; David Brinkley, *Washington Goes to War* (New York: Alfred A. Knopf, 1988), pp. 20–22.

58. Brinkley, pp. 20–22; White, *A Man . . .*, pp. 180–185; Anderson, *My Lord, What a Morning*, pp. 154, 156–161.

59. "Marian Gets Jewish Award," *Pittsburgh Courier*, 16 January 1943, p. 9, col. 2; "Marian Thrills 3,800; Also Adds $7,777 to China Relief," *Pittsburgh Courier*, 16 January 1943, p. 11, col. 3.

60. Henry Lewis Stimson Diaries in The Yale University Library, Manuscript and Archives, Microfilm, New Haven, Connecticut, 1973, 20 November 1942, p. 55.

61. "NAACP Board Hits Treatment of Jews," *Pittsburgh Courier*, 6 March 1943, p. 12, col. 4.

62. Congressman John F. Rankin, House of Representatives, Mississippi, "Communistic Influence on Racial Disorders," *Congressional Record, 78th Congress, 1st Sess. 1943*, 1 July 1943, Vol. 89, Part II, p. A3371.

63. Theodore G. Bilbo, *Take Your Choice: Separation or Mongrelization* (Poplarville: Dream House Publishing Co., 1947), p. 6.

64. *Ibid.*, pp. 164–169; Ruth Benedict and Gene Weltfish, *The Races of Mankind* (New York: Public Affairs Committee, Pamphlet, No. 85, 1943), pp. 7–8, 10–13.

65. Bilbo, p. 122.

66. *Ibid.*, pp. 67, 122–123.

67. *Ibid.*, Ch. VII, p. 94 ff., Ch. VIII, p. 105 ff., Ch. IX, p. 117 ff., Ch. V, pp. 60 ff., 79.

68. *Ibid.*, pp. 69–70.

69. See Theodore Draper, *The Rediscovery of Black Nationalism* (New York: The Viking Press), 1970.

70. Bilbo, pp. 139–140.

71. Malcolm X (Little) with Alex Haley, *The Autobiography of Malcolm X* (New York: Grove Press, Inc., 1984 [pbk.]), p. 93.

72. Bilbo, pp. 55–66.

73. John Morton Blum, *V Was for Victory: Politics and American Culture during World War II* (New York: Harcourt Brace Jovanovich, 1976), pp. 193–194.

74. Langston Hughes, *The Big Sea: An Autobiography* (New York: Hill and Wang, 1977 [1940]), p. 228.

75. Langston Hughes, "The Negro Artist and the Racial Mountain," *The Nation*, 122, No. 3181 (23 June 1926), 692–693.

76. Langston Hughes, "My America," in Rayford W. Logan, ed., *What the Negro Wants* (New York: Agathon Press, Inc., 1969 [1944]), pp. 304–305.

77. *Ibid.*, pp. 304–305.

78. Bilbo, p. 77.

79. *Ibid.*, p. 208.

80. Sterling A. Brown, "Count Us In," pp. 308–344, in Logan, ed., p. 322.

HARLEM JIVE AND WHITE REPRESSION

Black jive developed out of the jazz and night life culture. The Harlem Renaissance cultural and intellectual leaders in the night-life and jazz world in the 1920s produced a highly sophisticated subculture with its own language and dress codes that filtered increasingly into the general population of whites and blacks. Black society usually was the first to accept the trends, and "hep" whites, usually those in the entertainment world, soon followed, bringing along white party-goers who also participated in the jive and jazz culture.

Jive and jazz were brought into the service of the Civil Rights movement and into the military during World War II to promote patriotism and participation. The Double V orientation—victory for racial democracy at home and victory for democracy abroad—of the leading jive and jazz cultural leaders during World War II led to black jive being repressed by whites opposed to social equality and cultural pluralism. Racial authoritarians feared Harlem's emergence as a social and cultural capital that increasingly threatened to overthrow racial segregation.

Black slang or jive talk became very popular in the late 1930s and early 1940s. Cab Calloway led the way with his "Harlemese" language or jive talk. He published *The Cab Calloway Hepster's Dictionary* and another book called *Professor Cab Calloway's Swingformation Bureau* from 1938 to 1944. Dan Burley, a black newspaper columnist and editor of the *New York Amsterdam News*, published a handbook of Harlem Jive—*Dan Burley's Original Handbook of Harlem Jive*, illustrated by Melvin Tapley. W. Thomas Watson wrote a jive language column for the *People's Voice*, a New York newspaper. Calloway for a full year in 1942 did a Sunday vaudeville radio show called "Quizzical," broadcast from the road on MBC's Blue Network. It was a parody of big-band leader Kay Kyser's "College of Musical Knowledge." Calloway and several band members answered questions about music and musicians. They "shucked and jived" by speaking the "slick" and highly developed Harlemese subculture street and entertainment language. Actually a dialect in its own right, it became the language of the jazz world. Dizzy Gillespie was a master of the jive language as was Mezz Mezzrow, a Jewish jazzman and hepster from Chicago, who lived and operated out of black Harlem. Calloway called the language "Negro slang, the super-hip language of the times."[1]

Malcolm X was thrilled by the nightlife of large urban black ghettos. Jive language greatly impressed him with words such as "chicks" (females), "cat" (male), "cool" (composed), "hip" (street wise), "stud" (male and often in terms of sexual prowess), and "rubber" (a car, wheels). This secret language was a mystery at first, but soon opened doors to a whole new world and way of life for Malcolm X. It contrasted sharply with the country dialect or black English to which he was more accustomed. Hip jive language was an urban dialect that separated the country hick from the city slicker. "Harlemites" spoke "Harlemese" this way: "Struttin' on the Avenoo" in my "glad rags (fancy clothes) doin' the streets up brown." They were "in there" with the "foldin' stuff that is the root of all evil" (money). "I capped an underground rattler to the land of nod" (I took the subway to Broadway). "Groovy." "Here, one can see Zoot Suits and drip drapes with reet pleats, that really come on in a big way." "Home-boy, a Zoot-Suiter." "Cats' and gators" (alligators, a cool animal, and reptile and alligator shoes and purses, etc., were admired as expensive and classy) rejected war-waste theory. They dressed and lived extravagantly. They danced and jived at the Savoy. "Dig this gate with the solid kicks and drape; he's solid tuitty" (Look at this man [alligator] with the good-looking and expensive shoes and jitterbug pants [wide pants with tight-fitting ankled hems called "pegged"] on; he's a real boss [tuitty is the colloquial Italian word for boss]).[2] Jive language, Zoot suits, and fancy "kicks" (shoes) bound hipsters into a world and style apart that often completely befuddled the uninitiated.

Jazz and blues singers sang jive called "scat singing." Calloway said, "Scat singing, all that hi-de-hoing, those Zoot Suits and wide-brimmed hats, they were all a way of communicating joy to people. They were a way of telling people, listen, I know it's rough out there, but drop that heavy load for a while. Laugh and enjoy yourself. Life is too short for anything else."[3] Other jazz singers scatted when they forgot the words to songs while on stage singing. It became, however, a studied high art form, and Ella Fitzgerald became famous as the high priestess of scat singing. Film star and all-round entertainer Scatman Crothers took on the name itself as his signature. Many black and white entertainers took a great deal of pride in their jive as the language of their profession.

The Zoot suit became the preeminent code of dress for the extreme hipster during the World War II. Malcolm X's friend and "homeboy," Shorty, recommended a clothing store which offered purchases of Zoot suits on credit. "I was measured, and the young salesman picked off a rack a Zoot Suit that was just wild: sky-blue pants thirty inches in the knee and angle-narrowed down to twelve inches at the bottom, and a long coat that pinched my waist and flared out below my knees." The salesman at the Roxbury, Michigan, store gave Malcolm X credit on the word of his friend Shorty. A long, gold-plated chain, four-inch-brim blue hat with a long feather, and thin leather belt with the emblem "L" (for Malcolm X's last name Little) on it were thrown in to complete the Zoot suit uniform. Malcolm X got a "conk" hair style (ingredients used to straighten coarse black hair). He took three pictures in a coin photography booth and "posed" the way "hipsters" did who wore Zoot suits to "cool it"—"hat dangled, knees drawn close together, feet wide apart, both index fingers jabbed toward the floor."[4] This was the Zoot suiter salute pose.

The black newspapers carried ads selling "jitterbug pants." These were Zoot suit pants without the coat. They were "for young men and girls. The pegs from the store that made Harlem peg-conscious," read one ad. The cost was $3.95 and up.[5] Another advertisement, "Jitterbug Specialists" to sell Zoot suits, was run by National Clothing Stores. "Topcoats, O'Coats, Drape, Model Pants, write 4606-08, South Ashland Avenue, Chicago, Illinois." "The Harlem Mail Order, 243 W. 125th St., New York, New York," advertised "New York Shoe Styles Direct to You." Moreover, "Pegged pants draw attention to your shoes. Don't wear ugly shoes. Get these smart shoe styles. At only $4.65. The New Yorker Style."[6] Zoot suits and their wearers were considered jitterbug dancers and advertisers used this attitude to encourage sales. Zoot suits, jitterbug pants, and New York-style shoes became popular in the black urban centers during the war. Jive, jazz, jitterbugging, Zoot suits, jitterbuggers and Zoot suiters became a symbol for the city slicker and the civilian model on which G.I. Jive was based.

The *Pittsburgh Courier* carried a drawing of a black military officer in an officers' club smoking a cigarette and looking smug while playing 78-rpm jazz records with two white women hovering over him, one wearing a short skirt sexily revealing her crossed legs and the other with voluptuous breasts, jutting out from a low cut blouse, both obviously entranced by the black officer, black jazz, jive, and jitterbugs. The caption read, "Ah, I don't believe in heredity. My mother was crazy about collecting phonographic records but it never, but never, but never, but never affected me!" The record labels read, "Eddie South," "Lionel Hampton" and "Cab Calloway."[7] The officer's pose and words indicated he did not really buy his own statement, but was basking in the popular notion that blacks naturally had rhythm. This rhythm and jive attracted some white women. Of course, white racists had made this same association previously and opposed jazz, jive, and jitterbugs as dangerous.

Another drawing with the caption "Quartermaster" revealed a black Zoot suiter in full garb trying on a military hat while looking in the mirror. His wide-brimmed Zooter hat with a long feather in it rested on the counter. The military hat was too big. The black Zooter told the black quartermaster, who had an angry scowl on his face, "Nope, Sarge, It Ain't Quite Me!"[8] The message was that the Zoot suit was a uniform that Zooters were passionately attached to, and the military uniform and code of conduct had no attraction for Zoot suiters, who were perceived by many whites and some blacks as "slackers" or draft dodgers.

Malcolm X and his Lansing, Michigan, associate Shorty avoided the draft by duplicity. Their circle of friends felt it was a white man's war and since he owned and controlled everything, "Let him fight." When Malcolm X got his classification papers, "I started noising around that I was frantic to join . . . the Japanese Army. When I sensed that I had the ears of the spies, I would talk and act high and crazy. A lot of Harlem hustlers actually had reached that state. . . . The day I went down there, I costumed like an actor. With my wild Zoot suit I wore the yellow knob-toed shoes, and I frizzled my hair up into a reddish bush of conk." Then "I went in skipping and tipping, and I thrust my tattered Greetings at that reception desk's white soldier—Crazy-O, daddy-o, get me moving. I can't wait to get in that brown." Some whites and blacks were "amused." Malcolm noticed "the stony-faced rest of them looked as if they were ready to sign up to go killing somebody—they would have liked to start with me." Malcolm was classified 4-F, as was Shorty and their circle of friends in Lansing, and they never heard from the draft again.[9]

Buck Clayton, a famous jazz trumpeter, was drafted in 1943 while a member of Count Basie's band. He lived in Harlem's famous Theresa Hotel. His friends regretted that he was drafted and "every day someone wanted to tell me some way to beat the draft. Some would tell me . . . to eat soap." Others told him "to break open a benzedrine nasal spray and put the chemicals used to make it in a bottle of Coca-Cola and drink it. I did that. Then I was told to be sure to act like I was gay and they wouldn't want me. I couldn't figure out how to do that but I did keep it in mind." Nevertheless, despite actually trying some of these suggestions, he was drafted.[10] Moreover, as a hep jazzman, "I had bought a special tailor-made soldier suit and beautiful cap that I wasn't supposed to wear" and hep shoes. "I didn't know that you were not supposed to wear these tailor-made things, only the officers" could do so.[11] Harlem dandies, Zoot suiters and hustlers, and their counterparts across the country, reenacted this scenario often enough to make a lasting impression and gain an unsavory reputation as being anti-war in a time of wild patriotism.

The *Pittsburgh Courier*'s characterization of some Zoot suiters as anti-war, because some among them, as well as some prominent black intellectuals, said it was a "white man's war, let him go fight," had some basis in fact. The *Pittsburgh Courier* carried another cartoon by Ted Shearer depicting a military officer, chest filled with medals, wearing black leather belt and shoulder strap, tall black boots and officer's cane, who stood in shock and wonderment at a black Zoot suiter with a wide-brimmed hat, asking for a cigarette light. The caption read "Next Door." The officer appeared confused as to what type of "uniform" the Zoot suiter had on and what branch of the military, if at all, could he possibly be from.[12] On the other hand, many other blacks joined the military or responded to the draft and strove to be

first-rate soldiers on the advice of such black leaders as Walter
White and William Hastie who promoted black patriotism and
participation in quest of the Double V.

Black soldiers were encouraged to challenge Jim Crow on
the spot to batter it down, or at least register a protest under
enforced compliance with Jim Crow rules. Black entertainers
fighting for racial democracy and cultural pluralism entertained
black troops to ease their pain and promote their morale under
severe provocation and humiliating circumstances.

Another more direct cartoon with the caption "Uncle Toms:
Young and Old" by Holloway depicted a Southern slavemaster
standing in the middle of two blacks held by slave chains. On
the left was a polka-dotted handkerchief-headed Zoot suiter with
a cigarette in a long holder, cane in the left hand, long pointed-
toe shoes with one foot at a high step to symbolize an arrogant
gait, and head erect and arrogantly viewing his white master
over his shoulder. The year 1943 written over the head of the
black indicated that he was a modern-day Uncle Tom. On the
other side was the year 1843 with a hunchbacked black slave
wearing the same white and black polka-dotted handkerchief on
head, ragged overalls, dirty tattered shirt, both hands resting on
a tree-carved stick on which he leaned, in a shamed and cowed
posture sheepishly peeping over his shoulder at the master fearing
a rebuke or displeasure. In the background behind the Zoot suiter
loomed the modern city and behind the rural slave a plantation.
Commentary below the depiction said, "they play the part of
clowns and sycophants" and "the young Uncle Tom, who blithely
befouls his nest for a price, is definitely a MENACE who deserves
no quarter and should receive none."[13]

The *Pittsburgh Courier* ran a more definitive article and
illustration against blacks who dressed extravagantly but lacked
dignity, manners, and morals. "Clothes Are Not Enough,"
illustrated by Holloway, a black artist, showed a stout man and
woman in fancy dress, the man with a derby, cane, cigarette,
evening clothes, and the woman in gown, pearls around her
neck, fur coat: both had the face of a hog. The long commentary
below read in part that "Clothes make the man" is only partly
true. Finely dressed blacks without manners or morals who were
uncouth "are the people who shame us in public places and
bring notoriety to our neighborhoods." What is more, "they are

the people who demand that they be treated like other human beings and yet who act like hogs." They are disgusting. "They push their way in where they are not wanted, make no effort to curb their emotions, are brash, selfish and vituperative. They have no standards except those of hogs and no goal except the satisfaction of animal desires." Finally, "the way to rid society of these human hogs, who think clothes are enough to hide the unpleasant creature underneath, is to stop encouraging them by attention and to simply boycott them from our association, our homes and our respectable circles. Show them that clothes are not enough."[14]

Malcolm X fit the description "clothes make the man." "I'd come to work, loud, and wild and half high on liquor, reefers, and I'd stay that way"—while working on the passenger train from New York to Washington, D.C. "I'd go through that Grand Central Station afternoon rush-hour crowd, and many white people simply stopped in their tracks to watch me pass" in my Zoot suit, "knob-toed orange-colored 'kick-up' shoes," with a "fire-red" conk (hair straightened with chemicals to make it look straight and slick to resemble European hair) hairstyle. "My conk and whole costume were so wild that I might have been taken as a man from Mars. I caused a minor automobile collision; one driver stopped to gape at me and the driver behind bumped into him."[15] Within the black community a social and cultural struggle developed between the jazz, jive, Zoot suiter culture of the black street and entertainment society and the more staid, conservative, genteel black church and bourgeois-oriented stratum.

The black conservatives attacked the manners and morals of the black "sportin' life" crowd or the common culture as being socially and culturally inferior and not fit to integrate into middle-class black and white society. P.L. Prattis, a columnist and editor for the *Pittsburgh Courier*, attacked Cab Calloway's MBC Blue network quizzical program: "Hi-De-Ho King Plays Villainous Role in Radio Quizzicale." He charged that the Sunday program was vulgar, while Calloway's scripts allowed for "some worse jokes, some stupid questions, and . . . to start shooting craps in the nation's parlors Sunday evenings."[16] Prattis believed that Calloway's show would ruin any chance for a worthwhile black radio program to get on the air. Joseph D. Bibb, a columnist, attacked, saying, "Vulgar Songs: Salacious Tunes Retard Progress and Contaminate Our Communities." In almost every black community jukeboxes blared with vulgar music. "There is frightful danger in these terrible, vulgar tunes. They stimulate bad acting on the part of colored people and leave them the hapless victims of prejudice and discrimination forced upon them by clever, scheming and cagy critics."[17] He thought blacks should demand censorship of vulgar music. Other blacks attacked black Zoot suiters as "The Revolt of Youth" or "'Bigger Thomas' Mentality Grips Zoot-Suiters; Sign of Mental Frustration" or worse: "This type of clothing is the property of the jitterbugs, the juvenile delinquent, muggers, and even murderers."[18]

Racist whites excluded blacks simply on grounds of race. The black Victorians, however, felt that if they could distinguish themselves from the black commoners, they could promote their class and status differentiation for integration with whites but excluding the poor and uncultured black elements. Class and status tensions were expressed in the *Pittsburgh Courier* series on Zoot suiter illustrations and commentaries. The *Pittsburgh Courier's* Double V program promoted racial social mobility and opportunities for blacks, but it also promoted black middle-class status, manners, morals, and dress codes that conformed to the those of whites. The demand for rigid black middle-class standards, in fact, reflected the black middle-class demand for special considerations over the black masses, while at the same time they protested and demanded equal treatment in the name of the whole race.

Walter White had charged early in the war that Southern whites had a disproportionate number of officers and men in the military because Northern whites pursued other professions. Timuel Black, a black soldier, observed, "Generally they made illiterate blacks from the South the noncommissioned officers to be over us, who had education. Here you have a somewhat resentful Southern black guy, glad to have a chance to kick this arrogant Northern city slicker around."[19] Southern whites encouraged conflicts between urban and rural blacks. Northern urban blacks often felt superior to rural blacks, who were considered backward and lacking the urban sophistication often associated with jive language, Zoot suits, and conk hairstyles— manners and dress in general—during the war. Urban blacks tended to be more militant and objected to Jim Crow laws and practices.

Buck Clayton recalled that when he was drafted in 1943 out of Count Basie's band and stationed at Camp Upton, New York, "Boy, did they give us hell. 'Jody! Jody! Jody!' [Jody was a derogatory word for urban recruits who were stereotyped as pimps and hustlers] they would yell at us as if we were the newcomers and they were the experienced soldiers, hard and tough." He was singled out: "Well, look who we got here. Count Basie!" They yelled when they saw Clayton, "Well, you're not with Count Basie now, Jody. You're in Uncle Sam's Army." Then Clayton and the new recruits from New York were ordered, "All you pimps fall in over here! Line up over here!" Clayton turned out to be a disciplined soldier because "I knew they were giving me the business but I didn't want to give them the satisfaction of saying that I was a jazz musician and couldn't take it."[20]

At Camp Shank, New Jersey, he met jazzmen Sy Oliver, Mercer Ellington (son of Duke Ellington, the famous black jazz band leader), Jo Jones, Lester Young, and others. Lester Young, a great saxophone player, could not take the discipline and the yelling at him by officers. His objections resulted in long terms in the stockade. He wrote the jazz score "D.B. (Detention Barracks) Blues." Clayton wrote "Khaki Tan" and "Blues on the Double" and other tunes as a form of lamentation and protest against military life and regimentation.[21]

Harlem had a long tradition of converting many black country folk into dandies. It resulted in racial and status tensions and major confrontations during World War II as blacks became more urban and adopted jazz and jive. In 1927 it was common for rural blacks to make radical conversions from country to urban culture. "He is a seedy, collarless, slouching fellow, wearing a battered old soft hat." Soon he changed his dress, speech, walk, and other social and cultural habits. Now, "as he strolls jauntily along the avenue, swinging a cane, with his head erect, his most intimate friends of the plantation would not recognize him." Moreover, it was said that "silk shirts, bright ties and gay spats and form-fitting garments of every make may be seen on a Sunday afternoon on Lenox and Seventh Avenues north of 125th Street. . . . When the many churches disgorge their large congregations, men and women appear in the latest and newest creations of the tailor's and dressmaker's art."[22]

Well-dressed black dandies and "sportin' life" women
outraged many whites, especially Southern whites, who associated
such behavior and dress codes with arrogant public rejection of
menial labor roles and cringing social inferiority to whites.
Stereotype images portrayed blacks as a subordinate racial caste.
Black writers such as James Weldon Johnson, Claude McKay,
Ralph Ellison, Walter White, Langston Hughes, Paul Lawrence
Dunbar, James Baldwin, and Richard Wright often wrote about
black dandies being lynched and burned by white mobs. Hughes
wrote in *The Ways of White Folks* (1933) about an accomplished
black musician who won fame and fortune, was well dressed,
educated, and sported a cane, returned home to the South from
Europe. A white redneck mob attacked and killed him for talking
with an elderly white woman. Roy Williams returned from Europe
and acquired a reputation as an "uppity nigger" because he was
perceived as a threat to white superiority in education and the
arts. As Trudier Harris analyzes it, "The men in the crowd respond
in the only way they deem appropriate; their ritualistic roles
have been decided by their culture." They lynched Roy Williams
because "Roy's superior education and clothing have made the
whites look ridiculous. . . ."[23] These stories reflected reality. Many
Northerners more often were amused by black dandies, but the
South felt threatened by them and their self-assertion. The South
also keenly resented Northern whites who criticized the rural
white Southern traditions because these people lacked urban
sophistication.

　　　H.L. Mencken, the famous American editor and critic,
blasted the South's vaunted white purity and supremacy with
devastating attacks in the 1920s. In the South, Anglo-Saxons ruled
"and in the whole South there are not as many first-rate men
as in many a single city of the mongrel North." In the South
were "fundamentalism, prohibition and Ku Kluxery," rules in
which Anglo-Saxons dominated.[24] Mencken attacked William
Jennings Bryan, the South's hero and defender of fundamentalism
in the famous Scopes trial in Tennessee in 1925, as a "charlatan,
a mountebank, a zany without shame or dignity." Moreover,
"what moved him, at bottom, was simply hatred of the city men
who had laughed at him so long, and brought him at last to so
tatterdemalion an estate. He lusted for revenge upon them." He
sought to incite and lead the "anthropoid rabble" against urban

civilization itself, Mencken charged.[25] Nevertheless, Tennessee, with the help of Bryan, convicted Scopes of violating state law by teaching Darwinian evolution over the Bible's version of Creation.

Mencken mocked the South as the land of "yokels of the hills, poor whites." He called the Scopes trial of 1925 in Dayton, Tennessee, "the Dayton buffoonery" of Bryan, who served as a prosecutor. Tennessee needed "civilizing" and was "ready for missionary work on a large scale." Inquiry and culture were held in suspicion and "blocked by the idiotic certainties of ignorant men." Poor whites in the South were biologically inferior, Mencken charged, and were unfertilized, unlike the black mulattoes, with the superior genes of the old white aristocracy in the South who preferred black mistresses. He added, "It is not by accident that the Negroes of the south are making faster progress, economically and culturally, than the masses of the whites. It is not by accident that the only visible aesthetic activity in the south is wholly in their hands. No Southern composer has ever written so good as that of half a dozen white-black composers who might be named. Even in politics, the Negro reveals a curious superiority." Surprisingly, in the matter of race that preoccupies whites, "they have contributed nothing to its discussion that has impressed the rest of the world so deeply and so favorably as three or four books by southern Negroes."[26] Certainly, Booker T. Washington's autobiography, *Up from Slavery*, was the most prominent.

Some prominent Southern white intellectuals were so outraged by Mencken's charges that they rejected modernism for the South, and in a book of essays in 1930, *I'll Take My Stand*, stood for Southern conservativism, fundamentalism, violence, and white supremacy. Donald Davison, one of the twelve who took this stand, referred to the "jeering accompaniment of large-scale mockery directed against Tennessee and the South [that] broke in upon our literary concern like a midnight alarm." The Scopes trial and Mencken's and other Northerners' attacks "started a boiling controversy, and started a reconsideration" of the Southern intellectuals' role in the South. Twelve Southerners decided to defend the South as it was, with its traditions.[27] They helped cultivate the Southern whites and their conservative culture that feared and violently resented the social and cultural pluralism of blacks, Jews, and modernist whites who made Hollywood, Harlem, Broadway, Nashville, and New Orleans the cutting edge of modern American urban social and cultural development. Artists from those cities as civilians and G.I.'s led the social and cultural Double V program to which the South, more than any other region, was dedicated to suppressing through official and mob violence.

At the turn of the century large numbers of blacks migrated from rural areas of the South to cities in the South, the North, and the West. This reached a peak during World War I. This pattern was repeated when hundreds of thousands of Southern blacks moved from the South to the North and West during World War II seeking better opportunities and jobs. They continued to shed their rural folk culture in favor of an urban one. The great migrations led to an explosion of black urbanites, who adopted some or all of the elements of jive, jazz, jitterbugging, conks, liquor, drugs, and Zoot suits as a form of social, cultural, and even racial rebellion. Eldridge Cleaver recalled that when his family moved from Arkansas to Los Angeles during the war:

> My school was right around the corner from the house. The first day I went there the other kids poked fun at me, allowing as how I was fresh out of the woods. They laughed at my country boy haircut: I wore bangs, a hairstyle popular among blacks in the South in those days. The hair in the front was allowed to grow as long as it would and the rest was cut as short as you could. Then the front was packed with grease and combed over one's peel head. The kids laughed at me because they had been laughed at in their turn, just as I would later laugh at the new country kids who came after me. The kids also laughed at my Southern accent. This reached its peak one day when I said something about "way over yonder." That's when the fighting began.[28]

Cleaver shed his country culture and became a black hipster. He was resocialized by the black hipsters he observed and emulated on Central Avenue, the black social and cultural hub of Los Angeles during the war.[29] He became a hustler, violent criminal, and revolutionary leader of the Black Panther Party in the ensuing years.

Malcolm X had a similar experience. His father had fled

the South to a small town, Mason, Michigan. Malcolm X as a youth went to live in Roxbury, a bigger city. He recalled: "I looked like Li'l Abner. Mason, Michigan, was written all over me. My kinky, reddish hair was cut hick style, and I didn't even use grease on it. My green suit's coat sleeves stopped above my wrists, the pants legs showed three inches of socks." One of his first black acquaintances, Shorty, said of Malcolm X then, "Man, that cat still smelled country. Cat's legs was so long and his pants so short his knees showed—an' his head looked like a briar patch!"[30]

Malcolm X had an immediate and vigorous response. He shed his country culture and fervently embraced the urban black hipster codes of language, dress, and behavior. "I'd also acquired all the other fashionable ghetto adornments—the Zoot Suits and conk that I described, liquor, cigarettes, then reefers—all to erase my embarrassing background. But I still harbored one secret humiliation: I couldn't dance."[31] The experiences and reactions of Cleaver and Malcolm X were typical of many rural blacks moving to Northern cities with their families seeking jobs and new opportunities during the war years. This social progress helped fuel the Zoot suit culture and the Double V social and cultural thrust for equality and pluralism from the bottom up.

In January 1943 the *Pittsburgh Courier*, the black newspaper that spearheaded the Double V campaign, warned blacks, "Glamour Clothes Out—Sport Things In." Blacks should dress for the occasion at USO clubs and not wear glamour clothes— a code word for Zoot suits and fancy urban female gowns. This was especially true in the South because the camps were located where there was plenty of dirt and rain that caused mud. Avoid wearing leather or suede shoes in this environment, advised the paper. Moreover, it warned blacks not to complain and open "a third front."[32] The *Pittsburgh Courier* had recently run a political-military cartoon critical of Zoot suiters as draft dodgers because they were unwilling to give up their Zoot suit culture and code of dress for the black military Double V campaign. As a result, the *Pittsburgh Courier* implied that Zooters were bringing opprobrium upon blacks as a race and endangering the political and military Double V campaign. The war crisis exacerbated race relations as well as the internal political, regional, social, linguistic, and cultural differences among blacks.

New York City and State Democratic Party politicians established a political relationship with the black community, especially with Harlem, as its black population increased dramatically over the years due to blacks migrating from the South, and black political power emerged as a significant force. Democratic politicians responded by supporting black causes and aspirations for greater recognition and opportunities. This also extended to the arts and jazz. Alfred Smith, in his 1928 campaign for the presidency, tried to hire Walter White of the NAACP to work for him. Smith told White, "I know Negroes distrust the Democratic Party, and I can't blame them. But I want to show them that the old Democratic Party ruled entirely by the South is on the way out, and that we Northern Democrats have a totally different approach to the Negro." He promised White that he would build on the New York legislative records of Franklin D. Roosevelt and Robert Wagner. Smith, however, had to make accommodations with Southern politicians to win the nomination and, as a result, he did not make a forthright statement on the race issue. This led White to refuse to work with the Smith campaign. W.E.B. Du Bois added his voice in opposition to Smith for the same reasons. Smith refused to hire any blacks to high positions in his administration. He failed to rebuke the national Democratic Party for sending out racist campaign literature. He rejected black Major Charles Young to head the New York 15th Regiment despite the fact, Du Bois said, that "the army would have been perfectly willing to lend him to the National Guard. Governor Smith was asked to appoint him. He peremptorily refused and placed a white man at the head of the colored 15th Regiment." Du Bois charged, "A vote for Al Smith is a vote for the Bourbon South, and that reactionary bloc will not let Smith take a single really liberal step."[33]

In January of 1940, Mayor Fiorello La Guardia of New York City told a black fraternity at the 128th Street YMCA in Harlem, "The Negro in the professions doesn't only have to be good; he must be better than others to break down the barriers of prejudice." Moreover, he advised, blacks "must have the best type of leadership that can be marshalled."[34] La Guardia worked closely with Walter White and other Harlem black leaders to undergird black leadership.

Frank Schiffman, manager and director of the famous

Apollo Theatre in Harlem, which showcased nationally known black entertainers, publicly announced in September 1940 that he wanted to use the Apollo stage to introduce Harlem black leaders to the people. "We are anxious to do something down here to be of civic value to Harlem, and we think we know nothing better than a series of forums, short and snappy of course, on our stage to acquaint the people with their own leaders who they only know by reading of them or occasionally seeing them." He wanted people such as A. Philip Randolph and Mary McLeod Bethune to speak there. He sought to establish a black "Information Please" forum to keep blacks abreast of events and programs in their interest.[35]

The Apollo attracted a large black crowd and even whites came, and it was an excellent forum to mobilize blacks and their allies in civil rights affairs. Schiffman gave away thirty-five tickets every day to soldiers, largely blacks, at the Harlem Defense Recreation Center so they could attend Apollo shows. Prominent black entertainers such as Cab Calloway, Earl "Fatha" Hines, Willie Bryant, Bill "Bojangles" Robinson, Lucky Millinder, Billie Holiday, Ella Fitzgerald, The Ink Spots, and Lena Horne performed and mixed with the servicemen. Tuesday at the U.S.O. Center was "Apollo Night."[36] The Apollo attracted soldiers and civilians and boosted their morale in the war effort. It promoted the social and cultural Double V program.

In late 1941 Mayor La Guardia held an outdoor mayoral campaign rally in Harlem with 25,000 onlookers cheering. "Harlem is enthusiastic" in their support for the Mayor, it was reported. The event opened with the "Colored Division of the Citizens Committee for the Re-election of La Guardia Campaign." Cab Calloway's band played. La Guardia arrived at 10 P.M. to the campaign song, "From the Halls of Montezuma." Calloway and band then broke into "several jitterbug numbers" and the crowd swayed and shouted: "Yeah Man!" "Hey Butch!" And "That's Our Mayor!" These refrains were repeated over and over to the beat of Calloway's band. People hung out of windows in nearby apartments enjoying the celebration. Calloway said La Guardia was "the best Mayor the city ever had." La Guardia was so impressed by the crowd that he said, "This is not a political meeting; it is just a party among friends." Cheers went out when it was announced that Bill "Bojangles" Robinson would attend.[37]

La Guardia told the crowd that before his mayorship blacks received only "several menial jobs" and a few "traffic lights on the avenue," but now under his administration, new schools, housing projects, libraries, and health centers had been built, all within eight years. The Mayor boasted that "my administration and myself have not treated Harlem any differently than any other section of the city, but we have insisted in giving Harlem what any other section gets." When Bill Robinson appeared, amid an uproar from the crowd, La Guardia said, "The Mayor of New York now welcomes the Mayor of Harlem, Bill Robinson." La Guardia soon left to wind up his campaign at his "Lucky Corner" at Colonial Park, Bradhurst Avenue and 148th Street, as he had done for 21 years. Vito Marcantonio was Representative of the Twentieth Congressional District, which the Mayor formerly represented. He "was home in Harlem." "The people in this city today are healthier, the children happier, our people have obtained new self-respect, so that no one is ashamed of being a New Yorker."[38]

Politics, jazz, and jive were part and parcel of New York politics because it was the cultural capital of the United States. Black Harlem played a key role as part of the cutting edge of cultural pluralism not only in New York City, but in the nation. The Mayor and many others recognized this fact of life. La Guardia promoted black social, political, and cultural equality and used it to boost his political career.

Harlem blacks had many social and economic problems, due largely to institutional racism under a fundamentally racial authoritarian society that excluded blacks from the mainstream of the nation's social and institutional life. Frank Schiffman said 125th Street, the main artery and business street of Harlem, was controlled exclusively by white merchants who refused to hire any black clerks or employees. Restaurants excluded blacks. Schiffman forced integration at a local restaurant, Frank's, after he took a black entertainer there and insisted on joint service at the same table.[39]

Two blacks and two whites had been refused service at Marianna Restaurant in Harlem in November 1940. The proprietor said he would serve the two races separately, but not together. The group sued. Judge Marks of the Municipal Court of Manhattan agreed with the proprietor that separate but equal service had been applied as provided for under the then prevailing national law, *Plessy v. Ferguson*, which upheld legal discrimination and separation of the races.[40] Increasingly, whites, including Jews, sought to host their black friends and clients in segregated restaurants and clubs. This often led to commitments for racial democracy.

New York's 52nd Street was vibrant during the war. Black musicians there and elsewhere drew a lot of attention from women, including white women at the jazz clubs. Many Southern white soldiers and civilians resented the easy race mixing observed in some New York clubs. Famous musicians such as Dizzy Gillespie, Billy Taylor, and other blacks had close encounters and difficulties in getting out of clubs because white women aggressively pursued them, often resulting in threats by angry white male patrons. Police closed the White Rose club on Sixth Avenue in the summer of 1944 because it was a late night hangout for musicians and drew an interracial crowd that mixed intimately.[41] Some musicians used drugs and a few sensationalized arrests played up in the newspapers tarnished the reputation of jazz, clubs, and some musicians. Some jazz journals warned that too much booze, drugs, prostitutes, pimps, and "tea peddlers" ("tea" meaning marijuana) injured the jazz profession. This activity became even more dangerous around jazz clubs that attracted soldiers followed by police and federal agents guarding their morals.[42]

Since the 1920s Harlem had gained a reputation for jazz, booze, and nightlife, along with illegal sex and other vices. Playing the numbers (illegal gambling) was a pastime for many Harlemites. Fortune tellers and herb peddlers abounded, as well as mystics. "Harlem is hooch-ridden. The wash of the booze-sea has not left Harlem out; that district may well claim a deeper inundation than any other." Most drugstores sold liquor and most were owned by whites.[43] Cab Calloway said Harlem had more jazz and booze in the 1920s and 1930s than any other section of New York City.[44] This tradition continued and reached a crisis during World War II. During the war, Malcolm X said Harlem hustlers, often Zoot suiters, and prostitutes plied their trade in significant numbers. Servicemen with money were eagerly sought. Muggings and robberies occurred with increasing frequency. Prostitutes accosted servicemen: "Baby, wanna have some fun?"

Pimps and hustlers approached servicemen: "All kinds of women, Jack—want a white woman?" Or they said, "Hundred dollar ring, man, diamond; ninety-dollar watch too—look at 'em. Take 'em both for twenty-five." The police started advising servicemen to avoid Harlem.[45] Small's Paradise was the one club still recommended by authorities as safe for whites.

Despite Harlem's crucial role as a cultural capital, its reputation suffered increasingly as it became more a ghetto of crime and poverty. Jack Schiffman charged that Bill Robinson's and then Willie Bryant's designation as "Mayor of Harlem . . . was a joke, a bone of condescending affection tossed to the community to appease its tattered pride."[46] An earlier critic of Harlem chastised radicals, especially Communists, for wasting their time trying to radicalize blacks because "Harlem is not a center of agitation of any kind. Its noisiest element comprises the jazz musicians who go out every night to play for white dancers." He estimated that they numbered 10,000. What is more, Chester Crowell said, in 1925, blacks such as Roland Hayes, the opera singer, and Paul Robeson achieved "wealth and applause," but "could not be sure of very much more." Blacks were loyal Americans and conservative. "A people who sang its way to happiness while in slavery offers about as poor material for an organizer of discontent as the human species affords." Moreover, "Harlem is tolerated, but not coddled."[47] The criticisms of Schiffman and Crowell were largely correct.

The South resented black dandies, especially from the North and Harlem. In 1939 Roland Hayes received the NAACP's Joel Spingarn Medal for his outstanding achievement in the arts. In 1942, while shopping in Rome, Georgia, with his wife and nine-year-old daughter, his wife was rudely insulted and ordered out of Higgin's Shoe Store, but not before she retorted to the clerk, "This sort thing is out of place at a time like this. You ought to go over there with Hitler." She left the store after being threatened with bodily harm and told her husband, a block away, what happened. They returned to the store, but soon left. Thirty minutes later as they passed the store again, a police car pulled up and two officers got out. One officer grabbed Hayes by the belt and pulled him over to the store manager. Hayes protested, to no avail. He was beaten on the sidewalk and thrown onto the police car floor, then beaten again. He and his wife were arrested. His nine-year-old daughter was left on the streets. At the police station one of the arresting officers told Hayes, "So, you are the great Roland Hayes, world famous concert artist! Well, you are going to be up for a long, long time." A national outrage developed over Hayes's treatment. President Roosevelt shot off a memo to his Attorney General, "Will you have someone go down and check up . . . and see if any law was violated. I suggest you send a Northerner." Governor Eugene Talmadge and local officials defended their handling of Hayes, and the "good citizens" of Georgia refused to speak out in his defense.[48]

Horace Wilkerson of Birmingham, Alabama, a leading lawyer of the Alabama bar, called for an organization to resist integration and to preserve "white supremacy." He said before the Bessemer Kiwanis Club: "If there is room in this country for a National Association for the Advancement of Colored People, then there is need for a league to maintain white supremacy. It is ridiculous for a 10 percent Negro population to undertake to shape the policy of the Southern states, and it is tragic for the white people of this country to sit idly by and allow these Negroes to misguidedly place their self-interests ahead of an all-out war effort." He objected to black protest over the treatment of Roland Hayes in Rome, Georgia, and the lynching of two blacks. "This Roland Hayes was indignant and kicked the policeman," charged Wilkerson. Moreover, "We are going to keep the Jim Crow laws and protect them and will not allow the whites and the blacks to be taught in the same schools and colleges of the state of Georgia."[49]

Southerners especially resented Northern blacks with fame and wealth such as Roland Hayes. Southern officials often warned whites and police to be on the lookout for uppity Northern blacks who flouted Southern white-supremacy customs and laws, and to suppress violators with vigor and violence.

White resentment and terror against black artists visiting or touring the South was not new. Cab Calloway, on his second Southern tour in the early 1930s, met intimidation and discrimination that threatened to get out of hand. In Memphis, Tennessee, white stagehands refused to set up the stage for his band. He asked them, "What's this crap I hear about you guys not setting up the bandstand for us?" He offered them a drink and talked to them about their sitdown strike. Impressed with

Calloway's personal diplomacy, one remarked, "Ah, hell, man, we didn't mean nothing. We figured you guys was some slick New York musicians and we said to hell with that. We ain't settin' up for no New York City niggers. But you are just regular guys. Shit, we'll set up for you."[50] This tactic did not always work. It did not work for Roland Hayes. Whites countered blacks' charges of racial harassment and crimes by highlighting black crimes. The black press, too, played up black crime to attack the lower class who they felt injured good race relations and caused whites to reject integration with all blacks because many whites stereotyped the group as lower class without refined manners or morals.

New York City, like many cities during the war, became increasingly concerned with crime as the war destabilized the social structure. Race riots, large and small, military and civilian, became commonplace. Fears of crime waves gripped the nation. In the early 1940s, New York police and the courts feared a crime wave and juvenile delinquency in Harlem were under way and worried as to its containment. Justice Stephen S. Jackson proposed a "Plan for Prevention of Juvenile Delinquency in the City of New York." It was partially implemented but budget restraints caused its collapse. Mayor La Guardia defended the black community against the periodic crime-wave scare stories in the press. He boasted that Harlem had received the finest government-sponsored facilities and support and had proud, law-abiding families. But the *New York Amsterdam News* in late September 1940 reported, "4 Murders in Week Rock Harlem, B'klyn—Cops Busy." A man had killed his wife, then himself, after a lovers' quarrel. Two women had fought in broad daylight, one was stabbed to death, another wounded in the fracas. Another woman had been slain by her fiancé after she had broken the engagement.[51]

Another headline screamed, "New Rochelle Crime Decried." It reported, "A spree of lawlessness of Negroes never before equalled in the history of this town." During the month of August 1940, thirty-six blacks and thirty-seven whites were arrested. Although blacks were only ten percent of the population, they accounted for fifty percent of those arrested. A black committed a murder in 1940 in New Rochelle, the first since 1932.[52] "3 Young Killers Seized," read the *New York Amsterdam*

News, October 5, 1940. "The all-time high in crime and violence rocked Harlem out of its usual calm last week when six persons were murdered." Police boasted they had things under control because all of the murderers except one were arrested. In late 1941 C.M. Hall complained that he had been robbed twice. In Harlem, he observed, "every street corner is full of blacks, either shooting crap or lounging around waiting for someone they can rob." Another white man's observation was that "Harlem is rapidly becoming a sort of jungle, much to the distress of the great majority of decent colored people."[53] The *Amsterdam News* reported Harlem's crime wave with alarm. Harlem had enjoyed relative peace in the preceding years since the 1920s and had a relatively low crime rate, with the exception of the disastrous Harlem riot of 1935.

By 1943, federal and local authorities started closing clubs and repressing musicians because it was feared that they were corrupting and exploiting soldiers and civilians by playing jazz and selling them booze, drugs, and sex that dissipated their health and morals. Clubs kept people out late at night and caused absenteeism and tardiness at war-plant jobs and military bases. It was alleged that some caught venereal diseases from women who frequented these clubs. As a result, the soldiers' fitness to fight was impaired, and war workers' efficiency was reduced. This harmed the war effort.

Westbrook Pegler attacked jazz as an "insult to American character": it was "vulgar" and "low" and "dirty." In New York, the Two o' Clock Club was raided repeatedly by police despite its having been declared illegal in February 1943. Drug arrests of famous jazzmen like Gene Krupa on the West Coast and drug raids on 52nd Street jazz clubs and jazzmen increased and were sensationalized by the press. Jazz magazine *Downbeat* editorialized against drugs with such items as "Tea Scandal Stirs Musicdom" and "Tea and Trumpets Are Bad Mixture."[54] Many jazz musicians and promoters had struggled for years to raise jazz to respectability and were keenly disturbed by drugs and crime associated with jazzmen and jazz clubs.

The *New York Times*, characteristic of the white press, covered the crime outbreaks in Harlem, which became another reason to suppress the jazz capital because more whites felt threatened by its possible spread. In November a headline read,

"Crime Outbreak in Harlem Spurs Drive by Police," and Mayor
La Guardia described it as a "bad situation." Two people were
killed. "Youth [were] seen [as] running wild" because young
thugs had attacked people in the parks. Three black youths
stabbed to death a fifteen-year-old white boy. A man was killed
in the park. A civic group protested to the Mayor. Police said
that charges of police brutality against blacks helped the criminals.
Many blacks distrusted the police and did not want to serve as
witnesses in trials. Merchants refused to stop people who
committed petty theft for fear of a riot or persistent harassment.
White teachers requested and received police escorts from Harlem
schools. Milk and insurance agents who operated in Harlem were
robbed, and some businesses as well. Prostitutes openly solicited
on Harlem's 125th Street, even motorists, and robbed them with
the help of crime partners. Many whites failed to press charges,
and arrested persons had to be released. "Veteran policemen in
Harlem warn white men against walking through the side streets
even during the early evening hours." A white woman was raped
in Central Park by a group of eighteen- and seventeen-year-old
black and Puerto Rican youths. Police assigned a fifty-man squad
to the park to prevent rapes and strong-arm robberies for watches
and money. Muggings occurred with greater frequency in the
parks and on the streets. Fourteen mothers from lower Harlem
marched on the mayor's office to make a formal protest against
the crime wave and demand police protection.[55] Harlem crime,
and the perception of it, became a persistent problem and concern.

La Guardia rejected the attacks on Harlem blacks in a report
on crime and slum conditions by the Kings County Grand Jury
in 1943. He also rejected the periodic crime-wave reports by the
press as slanderous and racist. He argued that Harlem received
the best government-sponsored facilities possible. He boasted
about Harlem's good families and traditions.[56]

In January of 1943, the editor of the newspaper *PM* said
that race prejudice was promoted by identifying the race of the
culprits in crime stories. *PM* banned the use of racial identities
in most crime stories unless it was necessary.[57] Blacks, merchants,
and others were concerned that Harlem was tarnished by the
crime-wave reports. More white patrons started to avoid Harlem
as too dangerous, even for its nightlife. *Philadelphia Daily News*
editor Lee Ellmaker said his paper treated blacks fairly but would

improve its coverage in response to a letter sent by attorney Raymond P. Alexander. Ellmaker said his newspaper used racial identifications in crime stories only where warranted. He felt that an "iron-clad rule" on racial identities was impossible to formulate.[58] Blacks and editors in major cities were concerned about the impact of constant references to race in crime. Blacks did not want to be stigmatized as criminals and allow racists to use such an identification to justify repression and segregation. Walter White of the NAACP was concerned with the press, crime, and racial identification as a justification for lynchings and mob law against blacks.[59]

The South reacted to black protest, the Double V program, and crime with a combination of truth, exaggeration, and false rumors. Some rumors were so powerful that they took on a reality all their own. In South Carolina and North Carolina there was widespread fear of the Double V program. "I've heard that the Negroes have a two-victory slogan, 'V' for victory abroad and another 'V' for victory at home. The colored race wants absolute equality, wants to be able to sit at the same table, go to the same dances, schools, etc." Another rumor was that "the Negro is going to win a 'double v'! Conditions will not be the same after the war." In Virginia it was said, "There was a rumor that cars had been seen with a Double V sign on the license plate, . . . for the victorious uprising of the Negroes."[60] More alarmingly, it was rumored that blacks were purchasing guns through the Sears, Roebuck catalogue. Whites felt justified in arming and committing violence, given perceived black aggression.[61]

There were more disturbing and dangerous rumors spread against blacks in the South. "Hitler will make white people slaves and the Negroes the leaders." It was reported that a black maid, reluctant to mop her employer's floor, told the white woman, "Well I'll go scrub it, but when Hitler comes you'll be scrubbing mine." Another rumor spread that people said, "You just wait until Mr. Hitler gets over here, then you'll be working for me."[62] In the South it was widely rumored and believed that black women were quietly organizing to "put the white woman back in the kitchen." Whites called this secret organization "Eleanor Clubs" because they thought Eleanor Roosevelt, the activist wife of the President, was behind it. Its slogan was reputed to be "A white woman in every kitchen by 1943."[63] Whites feared this would destroy black subordination and racial etiquette.

A prominent white businessman who traveled widely in the South charged that Eleanor Clubs and black Zoot suiters were in league to destroy Jim Crow. In Alabama it was rumored that "whenever you saw a Negro wearing a wide-brimmed hat with a feather in it, you knew he was wearing the sign of the Eleanor Club." A North Carolina rumor had it that the size of the feather in the hat of a black determined his rank in the Eleanor Clubs. The greater the number of feathers, the larger the feathers, and the brighter the color, the higher the rank. In Alabama blacks called Mrs. Roosevelt "Great White Angel" or "The Great White Mother." It was rumored that black impudence was a result of Eleanor Clubs, and that riots would result. Servants came in the front door and demanded to be called Mrs. or Mr.[64] These rumors were so widespread and caused such fear that the NAACP asked the Federal Bureau of Investigation (FBI) to look into the matter. The rumors about the clubs were "alleged to have very militant Negro domestic memberships." Attorney Francis Biddle, friendly to blacks and the Double V, released an FBI statement that it found no evidence of truth that Eleanor Clubs existed in the South or that they were inspired by Axis propaganda.[65]

Dangerous rumors spread across the South and the nation about the impact the war and draft would have on racial and sexual relations. In South Carolina it was rumored that "when white men go to the Army, the Negro men will have the white women." In Virginia it was said, "A Negro made the remark that he had his white girl 'picked out' just as soon as the Negroes take over." A Georgia Negro reportedly said, "Aren't we going to have a time with these white women when all these white men go off to war!" A black man said to a white couple, "You'd better be necking now because after the war we'll be doing the necking." A black in South Carolina reportedly told a white man, "When you come back from the Army, I'll be your brother-in-law."[66] These highly inflammatory rumors caused whites to fear that having too few blacks in the armed services would leave them at home to menace white women. Also too many, because returning black veterans might pose a serious security problem.[67] Southerners carried these fears with them all over the nation, into factories, farm communities, and the armed forces. These rumors affected the perceptions and behavior of other whites, leading to a more suspicious and violent reaction to black assertiveness. Rumors such as these were self-serving. White supremacists and the white masses needed to justify group suppression of blacks and steadfastly refused to recognize the morally untenable position of white racial authoritarianism amid an all-out campaign declaring that they were fighting a worldwide war for democracy for all people.

By 1943, as large numbers of blacks had joined the ranks of the military and entertainers performed on the USO circuit, the Double V program for social equality and cultural pluralism had clearly become evident. Rumors and reality merged to promote a power racist backlash. Official and mob action mounted to suppress the Double V program and strategy, especially at the source from which it had been cultivated and had achieved its highest state—Harlem, New York.

The Savoy Ballroom in Harlem was closed by Mayor La Guardia in June of 1943 because of charges of prostitution and the spread of VD. The Savoy Ballroom was called the "Home of the Happy Feet" because of its expert dancers. It had opened in 1926, and in 1927, after Charles Lindbergh's flight from New York to Paris, blacks started a dance called the "Lindy Hop" that was still popular during the war. Harlem believed the Savoy was closed because interracial dancing had become popular. Black Zoot suiters, dandies, and hustlers had high profiles at the Savoy, with their dancing and flamboyant styles of dress and behavior. The Savoy management, Walter White, and Allan Knight Chalmers of the NAACP charged in a telegram to the Mayor that the police closed the club because it refused to halt interracial dancing. Mayor La Guardia replied that the "revocation of the Savoy Ballroom license has been affirmed by the Appellate Division of the Supreme Court of New York. . . ." He pleaded that "I am helpless" and lacked authority to overturn a court ruling. The Savoy had been given a notice on April 22, 1943, by the court and police before it was closed two months later.[68]

Cornelius O'Leary, Fourth Deputy Commissioner, heard the Army agents and detectives who had visited the Savoy testify that it that had been a "jitterbugging haven" for the past seventeen years, that police had opposed interracial dancing, and had warned the Savoy against admitting whites and to stop advertising in the papers. The Savoy management said, "Over a year ago the management dropped and stopped all advertisement in papers and stopped booking white name bands" in response to police pressure. Moreover, three years earlier it was forced to fire all dance hostesses, but Broadway dance halls with segregation policies had not. It stopped selling liquor to keep its license from being revoked. Savoy manager Charles Buchanan said the Savoy had served nine million people in seventeen years. The Savoy's troubles started when its best employees and ballroom attendants were drafted and it hired inexperienced people. An incident in the restroom where an employee introduced an agent to a man who offered sell him a prostitute resulted in the Savoy's closing. This unfortunate incident was not a policy of the Savoy and the newly hired person had acted on his own. The Savoy attracted the cream of the crop in celebrities from the all over the world. "The Savoy is the shrine of syncopation addicts the country over." Buchanan rejected the court's charge that citizens and soldiers said they had caught VD from Savoy prostitutes. He and many Harlemites felt these were "trumped up" charges and resented the slander.[69]

The black press and civil rights leaders launched a crusade to reopen the Savoy. Joe Bostic of the newspaper *People's Voice* attacked "the cult of Southernism" and fear of "interracial socializing" as well as the four years of harassment of the Savoy and its management because it had "failed to make social jimcrow a prerequisite for their pattern of entertainment." Moreover, "no other similar recreation hall had been subjected to the exasperating surveillance and hounding that fell to the lot of the Savoy." What was even more shocking, it happened in the "most cosmopolitan city in the world—the New York of that arch 'liberal,' Fiorello La Guardia." New York Justice Cornelius O'Leary, who signed the closing order, questioned the validity of the two reasons for its closing but signed the order despite his misgivings. He said, "No evidence was offered of the police regulation, which the petitioner is claimed to have violated . . ." and ". . . no competent evidence was offered that the single incident complained of occurred with the permission, express or implied, of the licensee. . . ."[70] The Savoy and Harlem blacks had good grounds for questioning the Savoy's closing on such flimsy evidence. Actually, it amounted to closing the Savoy on the word of military and police agents alone—two institutions that enforced Jim Crow laws.

Bostic charged that the police had started over-policing Harlem in 1939 because of the World's Fair. White-owned and segregated downtown hotels, clubs, and restaurants warned visitors not to go to Harlem unless they had guides and protection. The Savoy employed 83 people with an annual salary of more than $150,000. Black bands were hired because white downtown hotels and clubs refused to hire them. The Savoy's closing caused a hardship for employees, artists, and patrons. Bostic asked, "Where do they go now? To the downtown hotels and dancehalls?"[71]

The *People's Voice* sent a special reporter with two witnesses to investigate the segregated white dance halls downtown. It reported: "Savoy Still Closed; PV Exposes Vice and Filth In Downtown Dance Halls." They had pictures of servicemen meeting dates procured by an "operator" for $2 to $25, and most dates involved sex. It was common to operate in this manner downtown. Eight of New York's best known taxi-dance halls were investigated. "Sex perversion and 'dignified' robbery are prevalent." It was reported that fifty to seventy-five percent of the clients were in uniform. It was common for big spenders to get offers from hostesses to exchange sex for money. These taxi-dance halls were hangouts for white prostitutes and pimps. Dance tickets and corners were sold for "an orgy of semi-fornication." Police outside did not interfere with obvious rendezvous for sex for money with soldiers. The *People's Voice* reporter said that by comparison "the Savoy is a Christian youth center."[72]

Harlem writer Ann Petry wrote "An Open Letter to Mayor La Guardia" regarding the closing of the Savoy. She charged the Mayor with inaction despite his willingness to intervene in other affairs. She and other blacks took pride in the celebrities who came to the Savoy. The closing had caused many to lose their jobs and income.[73] Blacks regarded the "incompetent evidence" presented for the closing as unjustifiable. The manager, Charles Buchanan, boasted that such well-known entertainers, film stars, tycoons, and writers as Orson Welles, Jimmy Cagney, Dolores Del Rio, Marlene Dietrich, Edward G. Robinson, Gene Tunney, Carl Van Vechten, Pearl Buck, the Rockefellers, and many state and local officials came to the Savoy.[74] The Savoy was a respectable place. It enjoyed a worldwide reputation for excellence and probity.

The Savoy had engaged in many wartime patriotic activities. It sold war bonds and stamps, and held rallies by A. Philip Randolph, who said its closing was an insult to many. Carroll Boyd, a pianist at Club Encore, said, "It is most unfair that police restrictions seem to apply to Harlem only." Mrs. Helen G. Peale, the home executive of the Brooklyn YWCA, said, "I recognize the closing of the Savoy as what it is—another one of the Army's segregation stunts. It is absurd that Harlem should be selected for this sort of stigma." Was sex and VD all right in other clubs?, she asked. *Newsweek* magazine had reported that "actually, the New York City Police and Army authorities had tried for at least a year and a half to shut the place, on the theory that this would remove a potential source of race trouble."[75] This confirmed blacks' fear that it had been closed for reasons other than those stated. The authorities had closed it as a preemptive move because they anticipated racial trouble or a riot that might injure the war effort. The trouble, it was believed, would arise from the social racial mixing and dancing that implied social equality and cultural pluralism. Worse, it might lead to interracial sex. The Savoy would remain closed for nine months before it was allowed to reopen.

Racists, especially Southern politicians, had waged a long war on New York's tendency toward granting social equality to blacks. New York liberalism inspired and influenced blacks and whites everywhere. State civil rights laws were extensive. In 1909 racial discrimination was outlawed in law practice, jury service, public school admissions, and some areas of public accommodations. Civil rights laws touched areas of employment, work relief, and public works projects during the Great Depression. The state legislature in 1937 created the Temporary Commission on the Condition of the Urban Colored Population to help formulate remedial legislation. In 1938 the equal protection of state laws was made a constitutional provision to prohibit discrimination "because of race, color, creed or religion."[76] New York liberalism outraged Southerners, especially politicians who never failed to attack it and the black and white citizens and politicians responsible for it.

In 1930 Senator J. Thomas Heflin of Alabama attacked New York Senator Royal Copeland on the Senate floor for allowing Phil Edwards, a black man and "captain of New York University" to marry "a pure Nordic woman [white woman]."

He charged that "such mixtures have always resulted in weakening, degrading, and dragging down the superior to the level of the inferior race." What is more, he charged, "in New York under alien influence, that line of demarcation between the great white race and the Negro race, the 'Great divide,' that once constituted the 'dead line' in America on questions of social equality and marriage between whites and Negroes, have been repudiated by those of the Roman/Tammany regime now in charge of New York City and New York State." New York whites must hold the line. "Scores of Negroes in Harlem, New York, members of the so-called Democratic Tammany organization, have been permitted to marry white wives with license granted by and with the hearty approval of the State and City government presided over by Governor [Alfred E.] Smith and [Mayor] Jimmy Walker and now by Governor Franklin Roosevelt and Jimmy Walker." Heflin added, "These things are shocking, disgusting, and sickening not only to the Democrats but to the true representatives of the great white race in all parties the country over." Catholic schools also were integrated. Heflin had opposed Catholics and Al Smith in 1928 for these reasons. He said dance halls allowed interracial dancing where black men and white women and white men and black women dance with each other. He repudiated it saying, "It could not exist a minute in my state"—Alabama. "This is certainly a fine field for protection of white women by the Knights of the Ku Klux Klan."[77] Heflin said "this place they call Harlem" is horrible and dangerous. "I believe that is the name of that Negro heaven up there." (This was a reference to Carl Van Vechten's novel *Nigger Heaven*, 1926, which promoted the reputation of Harlem and whites who came to patronize Harlem cabarets.) Harlem, with its white supporters and patrons and interracial relations, Heflin charged, instigated black rapists everywhere because "when Negroes in other States read about some Negro marrying a white girl up in New York under Tammany rule, it puts the devil in them in other States in the Union."[78]

Senator Allen J. Ellender of Louisiana in 1938 charged on the Senate floor that in Chicago, Harlem, Indianapolis, and Rochester, blacks had used their votes to force white politicians to support a civil rights program. He said Father Divine, a Harlem minister who claimed he was God, "practices voodooism" and "other forms of barbaric fanaticism." Divine, he said, delivered the black vote to white politicians for civil rights support. Senator Theodore Bilbo of Mississippi was outraged: "Note the recent marriage of the twenty-one-year-old white girl from Canada to the corpulent, fraudulent, pot-bellied, coal-black, seventy year old Negro who calls himself Father Divine." Ellender feared its consequences because race mixture "has developed a mongrel type, which is not able, which has not the capacity above the shoulders, to carry on civilization." What is more, "political equality leads to social equality" which results in sexual and racial amalgamation.[79] Decay was evident in Harlem, in his view, because of race mixture. "What in a small measure it is bringing to Harlem in New York, as I am going to show by the doings of Father Divine, a Negro" injured both whites and blacks. His political activities among blacks and whites was dangerous to white supremacy, charged Ellender. He said that a Southern black was "polite by instinct," but if he went North and associated with whites and returned to the South, "he becomes impudent" and "gets into trouble." He believed that Northern blacks were more criminal than whites and cited statistics he thought proved his point. "We in the South know how to handle the Negro problem," said Ellender.[80] He advocated lynch law by Klan mobs as well as official Jim Crow restrictions to suppress uppity blacks, especially Northern black dandies.

Senator Bilbo said in 1938 that "if one goes to New York and makes a visit to the famous Cotton Club, or drives down the street of Harlem, he'll see certain unmistakable evidence of the process of amalgamation betwixt the races. If he goes to Chicago and spends a while in the black belt, on every hand he sees evidence of the amalgamation that has taken place within the last century." Even more alarmingly, "it can be observed all over the United States. Such intermingling will drag down the civilization of the Caucasian race in America."[81]

Key Southern racists were disturbed by the racial accommodations in big Northern cities and politics. These racists were aware of the Harlem Renaissance and its goals. They opposed it for many years. During the war, Southern racists suppressed Northern blacks in military camps in the South by terroristic violence. Many black college youths were ambitious and experimented with new goals and sought equality.

Southerners feared Southern blacks might follow "Northern" leaders.[82] Northern blacks tended to be more militant than Southern blacks and often challenged Jim Crow practices in the South.

Racists used political protest, direct action in the South by officials, police, and mobs, propaganda in Congress, the press, and a combination of fact, distortion, and racial rumors to mobilize racists into action. They tapped the ever-present national Negrophobia to challenge and suppress the Double V program in any quarter in the United States. Harlem as a social and cultural capital came under vigilant scrutiny during the war years as it boomed and competed with white segregated downtown hotels, restaurants, clubs, and entertainment and pleasure centers for white patrons. These local forces were joined by Southern and national forces of reaction to suppress the incipient racial, social, and cultural democracy developing in New York, and especially in Harlem. As a result, Harlem failed to flourish as a center of commercial and cultural life after the war in the way that Chinatowns and Little Tokyos provided Asian Americans a base for entrepreneurial training and capital accumulation.

Malcolm X said police and federal agents infiltrated Harlem to guard the morals of the servicemen. Small's Paradise owners told him and other employees not to "hustle" soldiers but to leave them alone. Police told whites who wished to go to Harlem to go with guides or protection. Police recommended only Small's as a "safe" place for whites.[83] Certainly, race riots at home and abroad had caused widespread apprehension among officials. They feared that fights, violence, and riots most likely would develop at clubs and social functions with interracial patrons and dance policies. Many objected to social and intimate interracial contacts. It was also believed that drugs and vice abounded in or near clubs. Jazz and dance clubs and places of entertainment came under rigorous scrutiny in order to police and repress illegal activities.

Blacks demanded a new hearing for the Savoy Ballroom because they felt it had been set up by authorities who had been harassing its management for over a year. They charged the War Department had closed the Savoy because it objected to interracial dancing and feared interracial sex might result. A War Department official replied that the department and the Secretary of War, Henry L. Stimson, were in no way responsible for closing the Savoy.[84] Officials denied that the closing was a racist or political move to suppress blacks and interracial dancing. Blacks and the Savoy management had good reason not to believe them. Here, too, fact and racial rumors merged with an unstated policy on the separation of the races and white supremacy to suppress social equality, cultural pluralism, and intimate integration as harmful to the social peace and national security of a society based on white supremacy. The Savoy was allowed to reopen after it had been closed nine months. The damage and stigma of racial conflict had taken its toll, and things were never the same. The police as a matter of policy warned whites away from clubs where incidents had occurred.

The suppression of the Savoy was a blow against the growing racial and social equality and cultural pluralism of the Double V program. The Savoy symbolized black pride, jive, honored entertainers, and a tradition of musical culture in the service of civil rights. The Double V and its strategy and goals were no secret to whites. The chamber of commerce groups in downtown New York City saw the economic competition, danger, and challenge to white domination of the social, cultural, and entertainment life if Harlem continued to be hospitable and safe for whites. The combined pressures from local, Southern, and national reactionaries intensified and resulted in the suppression of Harlem. On a Sunday night, August 1, 1943, Harlem exploded in a riot following an altercation and shooting at the Braddock Hotel.

The Braddock Hotel in Harlem had a respectable reputation among blacks. Many black entertainers and dancers stayed there because white hotels rejected black patrons. Needless to say, many parties went on at the Braddock, which the authorities resented because they constantly feared interracial mixing. It had been raided recently for vice violations. Marjorie Polite had rented a room with guests for a drinking party and complained of unsatisfactory accommodations. She became loud and boisterous. She demanded a refund and the return of a $1 tip she allegedly gave the elevator operator. Patrolman James Collins tried to calm her, but was cursed. He told her to leave the premises. She refused and continued to curse him. Polite started shouting: "Protect me from this white man." Florine Roberts, visiting her son, Robert

Bandy, on leave from the Army's 703rd Military Police Battalion in Jersey City, stopped to witness the confrontation. Bandy asked Collins to release her. An altercation occurred after Collins brandished a blackjack and Bandy grabbed it and ran. Collins shot him in the shoulder.[85] Rumors of the incident quickly spread throughout Harlem and a riot erupted immediately.

Walter White said, "Like many riots, this one had been caused by a wholly false rumor: that a Negro soldier had been shot in the back and killed without cause by a white policeman."[86] Malcolm X vividly recalled the riot. "Finally rumor flashed that in the Braddock Hotel, white cops had shot a Negro soldier. I was walking down St. Nicholas Avenue; I saw all of these Negroes hollering and running north from 125th Street. Some of them were loaded down with armfuls of stuff." Moreover, "Negroes were smashing store windows, and taking everything they could grab and carry—furniture, food, jewelry, clothes, whisky. Within an hour, every New York City cop seemed to be in Harlem." A Chinese merchant quickly scribbled a sign which read, "Me Colored Too." People on the streets were amused and laughed at the gesture.[87] Harlemites nevertheless appreciated the gesture at racial solidarity expressed by the Chinese man because many blacks felt isolated and without allies.

Walter White first was called by an NAACP staff member who told him of the riot in Harlem. Then Mayor La Guardia called. They agreed to meet at the West 123rd Street police station with Police Commissioner Louis Valentine. Roy Wilkins of the NAACP joined them. "La Guardia had ordered all available police officers into the Harlem area and had telephoned Governor's Island for military police to get all soldiers and sailors out of Harlem." Only white MPs were sent. Walter White suggested that an equal number of black MPs be sent and be teamed up with white MPs to reduce black hostility. This helped reduce the tension.[88] White, Wilkins, and the Mayor drove into Harlem. La Guardia got out of the car and hollered at rioters to stop. He was ignored. They heard and watched blacks breaking plate glass windows and looting stores. White motorists were attacked as they drove into the riot area, unaware of what was happening. A black crowd had gathered at the 28th precinct police station, the Braddock Hotel, and the Sydenham Hospital angrily demanding to know what had happened.[89] They were told that the black soldier had not been killed and that false rumors were spreading.

Walter White and Mayor La Guardia used a sound truck to broadcast the facts of the Braddock incident. "The rumor is false that a Negro soldier was killed at the Braddock Hotel tonight. He is only slightly wounded and is in no danger. Go to your homes! Don't form mobs or break the law! Don't destroy in one night the reputation as good citizens you have taken a lifetime to build! Go home—now!"[90] Bitter and angry blacks at first ignored him, but the rioters had spent their energy, and slowly the message took hold. They had thrown missiles from rooftops at the police. Over and over on the radio the Mayor and Walter White told the facts of the case. Both talked about the injustices heaped on blacks, such as the repeated labor shortages at a Long Island aircraft plant that refused to hire blacks; the Camp Stewart oppression of blacks; the violent assaults, murders, and lynchings of black troops and civilians. The black press had widely reported these events which had angered many blacks.[91]

White and the Mayor had limited impact on the black rioters. They worried whether rioters would even recognize them and obey their orders. True to the Harlem Renaissance, Black G.I. Jive artists who were widely known and recognized led White and Mayor La Guardia in a search for as "many well-known citizens of Harlem as possible." "Roy [Wilkins] and I [White] got on the telephone, to learn to our disappointment that many of those we wanted, such as Duke Ellington, Adam Powell, Joe Louis, and Cab Calloway, were out of the city. But we got the Reverend John H. Johnson, Rector of St. Martin's Protestant Episcopal Church; Parole Commissioner Samuel Battle; and Ferdinand Smith, secretary of the National Maritime Union."[92] They revealed the facts and the anti-riot message. J. Henricks advised, "Have Bill Robinson talk to his people." Robinson was very popular in Harlem. He had annually given out food baskets and Christmas toys to Harlem's poor from the Cotton Club. He joined any kind of fund-raiser for such causes and certainly would cooperate. A black woman suggested that spirituals be broadcast over the radio.[93] Rumor control, police suppression, the ordered withdrawal of military personnel, black-white teams of MPs and the spent energy of the crowd finally brought the riot to a halt.

The riot damage was large: five million dollars in damage,

550 blacks arrested, 185 injured, and 5 killed.[94] White and the Mayor pleaded for understanding and forbearance. White said that "Bigger Thomases" (a reference to a character in Richard Wright's novel *Native Son*, 1941) had emerged in Harlem to riot. Whites and blacks blamed the riot on hoodlums. W.E.B. Du Bois charged, "The black folk in this land have developed a dangerous criminal class." A white man reacted by saying in a letter to La Guardia, "The nigger can afford to dress 'and strut' far better than a lot of whites."[95]

Many whites and blacks, of course, were aware of the high profile black entertainers and Zoot suiters had acquired. Many whites resented this intensely. They reacted to fact and fiction over the behavior and intentions of the black G.I. Jive movement, Zoot suiters, and entertainers. Racists bitterly resented the social and cultural Double V program and its strides toward greater recognition and success. The high profiles of black entertainers and Zoot suiters gave whites the impression that blacks were making more economic and social progress than was actually the case.

The Harlem riot was disastrous for Harlem. Malcolm X said that "after the riot, things got very tight in Harlem. It was terrible for the night-life people, and for those hustlers whose main income had been the white man's money. The 1935 [Harlem] riot had left only a trickle of the money which had poured into Harlem during the 1920s. And now this new riot ended even that trickle." He added, "Some hustlers had been forced to go to work. Even some prostitutes had gotten jobs as domestics and cleaning office buildings at night."[96] Black Harlemites unwittingly played into the hands of their adversaries, Southern racist politicians, the New York City Chamber of Commerce, downtown merchants, and national forces hostile to the emergence of a vibrant Harlem nightlife that attracted national and international celebrities who often broke the racial taboos against racial intimacy, social equality, and cultural pluralism.

On September 7, 1943, the National Urban League held its annual convention. Lester Granger, the director, urged President Roosevelt to come and speak, but he only received a letter from President Roosevelt to be read at the convention. Elmer Davis had drafted the letter, and President Roosevelt had toned down the final draft. Still, it was a direct statement for the times. It said in part, "We cannot stand before the world as a champion of oppressed peoples unless we practice as well as preach the principles of democracy for all men."[97] Roosevelt with this statement embraced the Double V program in theory, but his "win-the-war-first" strategy took priority. Nevertheless, the Double V program proved a compelling issue that no one could ignore—not even the president.

New York's black and white officials and allies organized the Emergency Conference for Interracial Unity in September to heal the wounds of the Harlem riot and to reduce white reaction. The group was chaired by Marian Anderson, the great black opera singer. Adam Clayton Powell Jr., Ruth Benedict, and Duke Ellington were among several hundred attending. It followed the Harlem Renaissance theory of artists with high visibility in the media and civil rights working for black freedom. More than 2,000 people met at Hunter College, and more than 350 organizations were represented.[98] Despite the success of the National Urban League in getting a supportive presidential response and the Emergency Conference for Interracial Unity, Harlem was finished as an entertainment capital. It had become a battlefield and a ghost town, and had taken on the character of a classic, black, poverty-stricken ghetto. It was a historic tragedy of immense consequences because all over the country other black communities had imitated to lesser degrees the Harlem night-life pattern with local white patrons. Harlem as a cultural and entertainment capital had lost the potential to serve as a setting for the economic development of a black entrepreneurial class and a black commercial district. Instead, it fell victim to Jim Crow jive.

More important, Harlem had weakened its well-known reputation of openness to integration because blacks were now perceived as violent anti-white race rioters, especially after the two Harlem riots of 1935 and 1943. Most whites viewed integration as distasteful and violently opposed it, while the added perception of an unsafe Harlem frightened other whites who had been willing to break racial taboos. Fewer and fewer whites would "Take the A Train" to Harlem. Before the riots the black community had shown a remarkable tolerance and pride worth supporting. True, most of the clubs and entertainment world were segregated. It was also true that race barriers were falling, and had been falling, under the assaults led by entertainers with a social and political conscience. The Harlem Renaissance theory had been updated when black G.I. Jive had given the Double V strategy a sharper cutting edge through the sponsorship of the USO, even despite its "separate but equal" policy. Some canteens patterned after the USO clubs added their support to the forces seeking racial and cultural democracy.

Race riots on Army bases, in neutral territory, or in white commercial and entertainment districts did not destroy blacks' fight for the Double V. Indeed, it sometimes led to a search for common ground, for racial dignity, and for peace. Black Zoot suiters, dandies, hustlers, and nightlifers became symbols of black progress and arrogance that whites deeply resented. They were cultural rebels who threatened white supremacy by violating racial taboos in music, social interaction, and entertainment. The Harlem riots were attributed to the black common class and to the social and cultural rebels who refused to abide by the white middle-class rules—especially the racial rules of subordination to and respect for white authority.

The Harlem riots of 1935 and 1943 proved to be disastrous for the black middle class—as well as for the black workers and under class, as Malcolm X pointed out. It put them on the defensive and prevented Harlem from becoming a permanent cultural capital with the potential to assert social and cultural authority, command political and economic respect, and lessen the difficulties of gaining equal opportunity for people regardless of race, creed, color, gender, and national origin.

Notes

1. Cab Calloway and Bryant Rollins, *Of Minnie the Moocher & Me* (New York: Thomas Y. Crowell Co., 1976), pp. 114, 178–182; Arnold Shaw, *Fifty-second Street: The Street of Jazz* (New York: Da Capo Press, 1977), pp. 240–241; Mezz Mezzrow and Bernard Wolfe, *Really the Blues* (Garden City: Anchor Books, 1972), p. 290; W. Thomas Watson, "Dig This Gate with Kicks and Drape; He's Solid Tuitty," *People's Voice*, 27 February 1943, p. 23, col. 1; Frank Driggs and Harris Lewine, *Black Beauty, White Heat: A Pictorial History of Classic Jazz, 1920–1950* (New York:

William Morrow and Company, Inc., 1982), p. 132; "Cab's Quiz Program Leaves MBC Network," *Pittsburgh Courier*, 4 October 1941, p. 21, col. 2; "Cab Airs Anthem over Quiz Program," *Pittsburgh Courier*, 4 October 1941, p. 21, col. 6.

2. Malcolm X (Little) and Alex Haley, *The Autobiography of Malcolm X* (New York: Grove Press, 1984 [pbk.]), p. 43.

3. Calloway, p. 5.

4. Malcolm X, pp. 51–52.

5. "Jitterbug Pants," *Pittsburgh Courier*, 2 January 1943, p. 12, col. 7.

6. "Jitterbug Specialist," *Pittsburgh Courier*, 2 January 1943, p. 17; "Mail Order, 243 W. 125th St. NY, NY," *Pittsburgh Courier*, 2 January 1943, p. 17, col. 2.

7. E. Simms Campbell, "Sketches—Officers Club," *Pittsburgh Courier*, 2 January 1943, p. 13, col. 4.

8. E. Simms Campbell, "Quartermaster," *Pittsburgh Courier*, 16 January 1943, p. 13, col. 4.

9. Malcolm X, pp. 71, 105, 100.

10. Buck Clayton assisted by Nancy Miller Elliot, *Buck Clayton's Jazz World* (Basingstake: The Macmillan Press, Ltd., 1986), p. 115.

11. *Ibid.*, pp. 115–116.

12. Ted Shearer, "Next Door," *Pittsburgh Courier*, 6 February 1943, p. 22, col. 5.

13. "Uncle Toms: Young and Old," illustrated by Holloway, *Pittsburgh Courier*, 27 February 1943, p. 6, col. 2.

14. "Clothes Not Enough!," illustrated by Holloway, *Pittsburgh Courier*, 20 March 1943, p. 6.

15. Malcolm X, pp. 78–79.

16. P.L. Prattis, "The Horizon: Hi-De-Ho King Plays Villainous Role in Radio Quizzicale," *Pittsburgh Courier*, 20 September 1941, p. 13, col. 1.

17. Joseph D. Bibb, "Vulgar Songs: Salacious Tunes Retard Progress and Contaminate Our Communities," *Pittsburgh Courier*, 27 February 1943, p. 13, col. 1.

18. J.A. Rogers, "Rogers Says: Zoot-Suit Craze, Originated by a Young Negro, Signifies the Revolt of Youth," *Pittsburgh Courier*, 26 June 1943, p. 7, col. 1; Horace R. Cayton, "Exhibitionism: 'Bigger Thomas' Mentality Grips Zoot-Suiters; Sign of Mental Frustration," *Pittsburgh Courier*, 26 June 1943, p. 13, col. 1; Charlotte Charity, "Billy Rowe Told Film Producers Willing to Help," *Pittsburgh Courier*, 3 April 1943, p. 25, col. 5.

19. Studs Terkel, *The Good War: An Oral History of World War Two* (New York: Pantheon Books, 1984), p. 278.

20. Clayton, pp. 117–118.

21. *Ibid.*, pp. 118–120.

22. Jervis Anderson, *This Was Harlem: A Cultural Portrait, 1900–1950* (New York: Farrar, Straus & Giroux, 1982), pp. 141–142.

23. Trudier Harris, *Exorcising Blackness: Historical and Literary Lynching and Burning Rituals* (Bloomington: Indiana University Press, 1984), pp. 83–84.

24. Alistair Cooke, ed., *Mencken* (New York: Vintage Books, 1955 [1917]), pp. 127–137.

25. H.L. Mencken, *Prejudices: Fifth Series* (New York: Alfred A. Knopf, 1926), pp. 68–69.

26. Fred C. Hobson Jr., *Serpent in Eden: H.L. Mencken and the South* (Chapel Hill: The University of North Carolina Press, 1974), pp. 151–152; H.L. Mencken, *Prejudices: Second Series* (New York: Alfred A. Knopf, 1924 [1920]), pp. 136, 153, 148–150; see Charles Scruggs, *The Sage in Harlem: H.L. Mencken and the Black Writers of the 1920's* (Baltimore: Johns Hopkins University Press, 1984).

27. Hobson, p. 150. For Southern reaction to Mencken and Northern criticism see William C. Harvard and Walter Sullivan, eds., *A Band of Prophets: The Vanderbilt Agrarians after Fifty Years* (Baton Rouge: Louisiana State University Press, 1978); Twelve Southerners, *I'll Take My Stand: The South and the Agrarian Tradition* (New York: Harper & Brothers Publishers, 1930); Donald Davison, *The Attack on Leviathan: Regionalism and Nationalism in the United States* (Gloucester: Peter Smith, 1962 [1938]); Daniel Joseph Singal, *The War Within: From Victorian to Modernist Thought in the South, 1919–1945* (Chapel Hill: University of North Carolina Press, 1982); Donald Davison, "The Artist as Southerner," *The Saturday Review of Literature*, II, No. 42 (15 May 1926), pp. 781–783.

28. Eldridge Cleaver, *Soul on Fire* (Waco: Word Books, 1978), pp. 51–52.

29. *Ibid.*, pp. 52–55.

30. Malcolm X, pp. 39, 43–44.

31. *Ibid.*, p. 56.

32. "Glamour Clothes Out—Sport Things In," *Pittsburgh Courier*, 2 January 1943, p. 10.

33. Walter White, *A Man Called White: The Autobiography of Walter White* (Bloomington: Indiana University Press, 1970 [1948]), pp. 99–101; W.E.B. Du Bois, "Is Al Smith Afraid of the South?" *The Nation*, 127, No. 3302 (October 1928), 392–394.

34. "La Guardia Addresses Fraternity," *New York Amsterdam News*, 6 January 1940, p. 11, col. 8.

35. "Schiffman Eyes Weekly Forums at the Apollo," *New York Amsterdam News*, 28 September 1940, p. 16, col. 5.

36. Ted Fox, *Showtime at the Apollo* (New York: Holt, Rinehart and Winston, 1983), pp. 135–136.

37. "Mayor Winds Up at 'Lucky Corner,'" *New York Times*, 4 November 1941, p. 19, col. 1.

38. *Ibid.*

39. Jack Schiffman, *Uptown: The Story of Harlem's Apollo Theatre* (New York: Cowles Book Co., Inc., 1971), p. 188.

40. "Judge Upholds Segregation in Harlem," in C.L.R. James, George Breitman, Edgar Keemer, et al., *Fighting Racism in World War II* (New York: Monad Press, 1980), p. 57.

41. Shaw, p. 255.

42. *Ibid.*, p. 256.

43. Winthrop D. Lane, "Ambushed in the City: The Grim Side of Harlem," *Survey*, 53, No. 11 (1 March 1925), 692–694, 713–714.

44. Calloway, pp. 10–11.

45. Malcolm X, pp. 74–75.

46. Schiffman, p. 188.

47. Chester T. Crowell, "The World's Largest Negro City," *Saturday Evening Post*, 198, No. 6 (8 August 1925), 8–9, 93–94, 97.

48. White, *A Man . . .*, p. 181; Charles S. Johnson, *To Stem This Tide* (Boston: Pilgrim Press, 1943), pp. 77–78; Philip Blake, "Racist Terror in the South" (orig. pub. in *The Militant*, 22 August 1942), in C.L.R. James, et al., *Fighting Racism in World War II*, pp. 194, 196; Richard M. Dalfiume, *Desegregation of the U.S. Armed Forces: Fighting on Two Fronts, 1939–1953* (Columbia: University of Missouri Press, 1969), p. 129.

49. "South's Leaders' Reject Pleas Asking Democracy," *Chicago Defender*, 1 August 1942, p. 17.

50. Calloway, p. 130.

51. "4 Murders in Week Rock Harlem, B'klyn—Cops Busy," *New York Amsterdam News*, 28 September 1940, p. 1, col. 4, p. 5, col. 5.

52. "New Rochelle Crime Decried," *New York Amsterdam News*, 5 October 1940, p. 17.

53. "3 Young Killers Seized," *New York Amsterdam News*, 5 October 1940, p. 1, col. 3; Dominic J. Capeci Jr., *The Harlem Riot of 1943* (Philadelphia: Temple University Press, 1977), p. 124.

54. Shaw, pp. 252–254.

55. "Crime Outbreak in Harlem Spurs Drive by Police," *New York Times*, 7 November 1941, p. 1, col. 3, p. 15, col. 1.

56. Capeci, pp. 9–10.

57. "PM Bans Race Identity in Most Crime Stories," *Pittsburgh Courier*, 30 January 1943, p. 12, col. 8.

58. "Broader Racial Policy Promised by Newspaper," *Pittsburgh Courier*, 13 February 1943, p. 12, col. 5.

59. White, *A Man . . .*, pp. 5–6, 42, 49, 126–129, 131.

60. Howard W. Odum, *Race and Rumors of Race: Challenge to American Crisis* (Chapel Hill: The University of North Carolina Press, 1943), p. 92.

61. *Ibid.*, pp. 99–101.

62. *Ibid.*, p. 133.

63. *Ibid.*, pp. 68, 73.

64. *Ibid.*, pp. 77–79.

65. "No 'Eleanor Clubs'—FBI," *Pittsburgh Courier*, 23 January 1943, p. 4, col. 6.

66. Odum, pp. 57–58.

67. *Ibid.*, pp. 105–106.

68. Malcolm X, pp. 82–83; "Mixed Dancing Closed Savoy Ballroom: La Guardia Denies Power to Remedy Court Act, He Says," *New York Amsterdam News*, 1 May 1943, p. 1, col. 1.

69. "Mixed Dancing," p. 1, col. 1.

70. Joe Bostic, "What's Behind Savoy Closing: Is It Police Move to Bar Whites from Harlem?" *People's Voice*, 1 May 1943, p. 1, col. 1, p. 3, col. 1.

71. *Ibid.*, p. 1, col. 1, p. 3, col. 1.

72. "Savoy Still Closed: PV Exposes Vice and Filth in Downtown Dance Halls," *People's Voice*, 8 May 1943, p. 1, col. 1, p. 3, col. 1.

73. Ann Petry, "An Open Letter to Mayor La Guardia," *People's Voice*, 22 May 1943, p. 4, col. 3.

74. "Indignation Grows over Savoy Case: Check on Other Spots Shows Ballroom Finest among the City's Lot," *New York Amsterdam News*, 15 May 1943, p. 1, col. 6, p. 3, col. 5.

75. *Ibid.*

76. Capeci, p. 31.

77. Senator J. Thomas Heflin, *Alabama, Congressional Record, 71st Congress, 2nd Sess.*, Vol. 72, Part 3, 7 January 1930 (Washington, D.C.: U.S. Government Printing Office, 1930), pp. 3234–3236, 3239.

78. *Ibid.*, p. 3239.

79. Senator Allen J. Ellender, Louisiana, *Congressional Record, 75th Congress, 1938*, Vol. 83, Part I, 17 January 1938, pp. 622, 817–818, 684, 758, 756; Theodore G. Bilbo, *Take Your Choice: Separation or Mongrelization* (Poplarville: Dream House Publishing Co., 1947), p. 56.

80. Senator Allen J. Ellender, *ibid.*, 14 January 1938, pp. 504, 166.

81. Senator Theodore G. Bilbo, Mississippi, *Congressional Record, Proceedings and Debate of the Third Session of The Seventy-Fifth Congress of the United States of America*, Vol. 83, Part 2, 1 February 1938, p. 1340.

82. Odum, p. 45.

83. Malcolm X, pp. 80, 90, 105.

84. "Army Didn't Close Savoy, War Dept. Official Says," *New York Amsterdam News*, 8 May 1943, p. 2, col. 3.

85. Capeci, pp. 99–100; White, *A Man . . .*, p. 234; Walter White, "Behind the Harlem Riot," *New Republic*, No. 109 (16 August 1943), 220–222.

86. White, *A Man . . .*, p. 234; Capeci, pp. 99–100.

87. Malcolm X, p. 113.

88. White, *A Man . . .*, pp. 233–234.

89. *Ibid.*, p. 233; Capeci, p. 101.

90. White, *A Man*, p. 237.

91. *Ibid.*, pp. 238–239, 235; White, "Behind . . .," pp. 220–222; Malcolm X, p. 113.

92. White, "Behind . . .," pp. 220–222; White, *A Man . . .*, p. 237; Capeci, p. 104.

93. Capeci, p. 131; James Haskins, *The Cotton Club* (New York: Random House, 1977), pp. 114–115.

94. Capeci, p. 102; White, "Behind . . .," pp. 220–222.

95. White, "Behind . . .," pp. 220–222; Capeci, pp. 121–122, 136.

96. Malcolm X, pp. 114–115.

97. Capeci, p. 155.

98. *Ibid.*, pp. 159–160.

CONCLUSION

The ideology of the Harlem Renaissance survived the decline of the literary writers of the 1920s. Charles S. Johnson visited Los Angeles in 1926 and organized the Ink Slingers, a group of blacks who apparently read rather than produced literature similar to that of the Harlem Renaissance writers. Many in this group became militant critics of Hollywood's negative film stereotypes of blacks. Members of the Ink Slingers organized groups to monitor and protest the images of blacks produced by Hollywood. These blacks continued the Harlem Renaissance debates begun in the 1920s over how blacks should be portrayed in the mass media. They wanted blacks portrayed as normal human beings.

Los Angeles's black critics in 1942 compelled the NAACP's executive secretary Walter White to intervene in Hollywood to alter its stereotype images of blacks on the silver screen. Time and again, militant blacks called for Walter White and the NAACP to sponsor a mass boycott of Hollywood for its abuse and negative portrayal of blacks. White preferred negotiations and gradualism.

Los Angeles blacks tried to gain employment in Hollywood as actors and actresses by duplicating Harlem culture in Los Angeles's Central Avenue black nightclubs and in the small black Hollywood colony of movie actors. Many blacks worked in Hollywood as domestics and chauffeurs for film industry employees. In film, these roles were more plentiful than normal roles and paid much higher salaries than could be earned in many other occupations. As a result, many blacks sought even those roles despite the protests of blacks who sought other roles and the eradication of film roles stereotyping blacks as menials or clowns. These roles in Hollywood accented the same issues that went unsolved in the Harlem Renaissance: How shall blacks be portrayed and should employment and principles of positive projections of the race in the mass media take precedence over employment? Walter White tried to solve the problem by negotiations and group pressure politics with some success.

Mayor La Guardia of New York, Walter White, and Wendell Willkie tried to persuade Hollywood to drop stereotypes and to return the film industry to New York. They intended to merge Hollywood and Broadway, using the well-developed cultural institutions and Harlem blacks to transform Hollywood's portrayals of blacks into acceptable images. Hollywood's financial investments were too entrenched and extensive to abandon and relocate. As a result, increasing numbers of Harlem blacks trekked to Hollywood to make films.

Some blacks and whites hoped this migration would transform Hollywood by bringing Harlem to Hollywood and when Harlem met Hollywood, a new perception of blacks would emerge, with old stereotypes replaced by the sophisticated and highly acclaimed Harlem entertainment culture and values. A powerful Harlem in Hollywood movement emerged, but it was protest-oriented and confrontational. Walter White took up this protest and adopted negotiations and persuasion instead of direct-action boycotts. Nevertheless, the Harlem Renaissance infused its culture into Hollywood films, into the black Hollywood colony, and on Central Avenue, in Los Angeles's black social and cultural district.

Harlem Renaissance culture spread into the general culture of whites, too. It had an impact on the USO and the various servicemen's canteens during World War II. G.I. Jive became a dominant pattern of entertainment. Jazz and swing bands emerged in the armed forces and competed with traditional martial music. Swing music and dances patterned after black styles made popular in Harlem became the norm during the war years. Blacks and whites defended and promoted this culture, winning a significant measure of respect and acceptance. Cultural and racial democracy gained a strong foothold and became entrenched in the national American culture. Blacks won a significant measure of cultural democracy years before political, economic, and educational democracy triumphed.

Many racist whites were alarmed at the emergence of a vibrant and increasingly modern black national culture. Racists resented whites who appreciated or patronized black entertainment and entertainers. Sections of the white business community feared the rise of Harlem as an important cultural capital patronized by whites at home and from abroad. These racists put pressure on Harlem, smeared its reputation, and provoked violence and riots in 1935 and 1943. Harlem gained a reputation for its increasing crime rate, violence, militant protests against racism, and isolation as a black ghetto.

In the 1960s, when the civil rights movement won its struggle for racial democracy in the political, economic, educational, and housing arenas, Harlem and its black counterparts across the nation had declined. Black entertainers increasingly performed outside the ghetto and for white or mixed audiences in entertainment districts controlled by whites. Blacks did not develop their entertainment culture into a self-owned ethnic business district (as Harold Cruse in his book, *The Crisis of the Negro Intellectual*, 1967, bitterly points out) like the Japanese, Chinese, or Jews with their Little Tokyos, Little Chinatowns, or Hollywoods. The demise of the Harlem Renaissance was a grand tragedy for true independent cultural democracy. Black entertainers pulled other people's wagons and often received the least financial rewards in exchange for their generally recognized first-rate talent.